D1591082

THE DOG CRISIS

IRIS NOWELL

THE DOG CRISIS

ST. MARTIN'S PRESS
NEW YORK

Library of Congress Cataloging in Publication Data

Nowell, Iris.
    The dog crisis.

    Bibliography: p.
    Includes index.
    1. Dogs.   2. Dogs—Social aspects.   I. Title.
SF426.N68   636.7   78-21402
ISBN 0-312-21613-0

For Nellie Clarke

Contents

Acknowledgements ix

Preface xi

Introduction by Dr. Alan M. Beck xiv

1 **The Man and Dog Partnership** 1
The Dog as a Working Animal 1
The Dog as an Object of Worship 8
The Dog as a Pet 15

2 **The Psychology of Pet Owning** 18
The Emotional Need for Pets 19
  A dog teaches a child responsibility 20
  A dog teaches a child the facts of life 21
  A dog's death acts as a preview
    for the human tragedy 22
  A dog teaches children kindness 23
  A dog is a companion for old folks 25
  A dog is kept only for the "proper" reasons 26
    Fighting dogs 27
    Party dogs 29

3 **The Pet Population Explosion** 34
The Numbers Game 35
The Root of the Problem: Strays, Uncontrolled
  and Abandoned Dogs 39

4 **The Commercial Dog Business** 47
Puppy Mills and Pet Shops 48

5 **The Pet Food Industry** 56
Size of the Industry 59
Development of the Industry 62
  Dry pet food 63
  Canned pet food 63
  Semi-moist pet food 64
  Luxury, gourmet, specialty foods 65
  Treats 65
  Humanized Pet Foods 66
  Products of the Future 67

	The Psychology of Feeding	68
	Formulation	72
	Research	76
	Advertising	78
	Feeding Scraps	84
	Unfit for Human Consumption?	86
	World Shortage of Protein	91
	Protein Alternatives	93
6	**The Actual Costs of Dog Owning**	98
	Veterinary Care	101
	How to find a good veterinarian	102
	Licensing	103
	Pet Supplies and Accessories	104
	Boarding and Kennelling	108
	Grooming Parlours	110
	Dog Shows and Trials	111
	Pet Burial	111
	Estate Planning for Pets	115
	Psychiatric Services for Dogs	116
	Training	118
	Acupuncture for Dogs	119
7	**The Social Costs of Pets**	121
	Public Costs	121
	Livestock and Wildlife Destruction by Dogs	124
	Car Accidents Caused by Dogs	127
	Threat to the Eco-system	127
	Dognapping	129
	Barking Dogs	131
8	**Diseases You Can Get From Your Pet**	134
	Toxoplasmosis	137
	Toxocara canis (roundworm)	143
	Cutaneous Larva Migrans (creeping eruption)	147
	Ancylostoma caninum (hookworm)	148
	Hydatid Disease (tapeworm)	149
	Dipylidium caninum (dog tapeworm)	149
	Leptospirosis	156
	Rabies	158
	Ringworm	162

Fleas 163
Rocky Mountain Spotted Fever (tick-borne typhus) 166
Scabies (sarcoptic mange) 167
Other Diseases Transmitted by Household Pets 168
Dog Bites and Attacks 169

9　**Planned Parenthood for Pets** 176
Mass Killing of Surplus Pets 176
Spaying and Neutering 179
Pet Contraceptives 187

10　**Dogs or People?** 191

11　**A Few Modest Proposals** 203
Education 203
Dog Owner Responsibility 205
Limiting Pet Ownership 206
Pet Industry Tax 206
Pet Food Alternatives 207
Small Dogs 208
Advertising 209
Packaging 211
Non-renewable Resources 211
Licensing 212
Identification 213
Breeding Controls 213
Obedience Training 214
Animal Welfare Organizations 216
The Veterinary Profession 218
Governments 218
The Individual 221

Appendix A 225

Appendix B 231

Appendix C 232

Appendix D 233

References 243

Selected Bibliography 263

Index 267

Acknowledgements

One of the dark undersides of the writing trade is having to ingratiate oneself to nice, decent people in order to coerce information out of them, and then subsequently performing a hatchet job. To those who feel somewhat cut up, although it doesn't help much, I apologize. I cannot overemphasize that it is not you personally but most frequently what you represent that falls victim to this book's point of view.

There are so many people to thank. I recognize how difficult it is for professionals to communicate scientific material to lay persons, and for their efforts several patient people must be singled out. Thank you Dr. Alan Beck for your wise and ongoing counsel; Dr. Frank Loew, Division of Comparative Medicine at Johns Hopkins University in Baltimore, for your support from the very beginning; Dr. Phil Lautenslager, Veterinary Parasitologist, Ontario Ministry of Agriculture and Food in Guelph, for your crash course in parasitology; Dr. Wally Stonehouse, Toronto veterinary practitioner, for being as helpful as you were gracious; Dr. William Carr at Beaver College, Glenside, Pennsylvania, for access to your annotated bibliography; Dr. James Sokolowski, animal health researcher in Kalamazoo, Michigan; Dr. Roger Mugford, animal behaviourist in Leicestershire, England and Dr. Jim Evans, President of the British Small Animal Veterinary Association, for your good humour and generosity; and Dr. Harry Rowsell, professor, Department of Pathology, University of Ottawa, for the time and counsel you gave to researcher Patricia Pattinson. I am also grateful to the First Canadian Symposium on "Pets and Society, An Emerging Principal Issue," held in Toronto, June 23-25, 1976, and organized by the Canadian Federation of Humane Societies and the Canadian Veterinary Medical Association, which helped set me on a reliable course of data gathering.

To the numerous medical officers of health and MDs of various disciplines in city, provincial, and state and federal health departments and hospitals all over Canada and the U.S., who provided reports and statistical data, my sincere thanks. Also thanks to all the persons in government, humane societies, and private animal welfare organizations, executives of pet food companies, marketing, advertising and public relations agencies and industry associations for your statistics and co-operation.

On my knees I thank my research assistants without whom this book would have taken twice as long to be published: Patricia Pattinson of Toronto, for insightful interviews and far-flung searches; Joan Coleman, also of Toronto, for diligent library ferreting and painstaking work on the bibliography; and Toni Burghardt, veterinary student at the University of Saskatchewan for special veterinary background and data.

To those who made comments and suggestions about the manuscript, notably Drs. Beck, Lautenslager, Loew, and Stonehouse, thank you very much. Scientifically you have been invaluable; however, the tone, the bias, and the outrage of this book are mine alone, as are any errors that may appear.

Thanks also to the Ontario Arts Council.

And most of all my thanks to the world's greatest man, who kept me together during all this.

Preface

During the writing of a cookbook about five years ago I became aware of an impending global shortage of protein, which struck me as odd, considering the trend towards junk food. Upon investigating I found that enormous quantities of protein were devoured day by day, year after year by dogs and cats. Not hundreds or even millions but *billions* of pounds of food fit for human consumption were being fed to pets while one-third of the world starved. Did people know about this, I wondered, and if they did why weren't they screaming in the streets?

In my search for answers I encountered even larger questions; and at this point my book was under way.

Since the early 1970s startling evidence has emerged which reveals that dogs are losing their reputation as wonderful and loyal pets and becoming a social nuisance that costs taxpayers millions of dollars annually. It is well-documented that dogs transmit a growing number of diseases to humans, many of them serious; more dogs are biting and attacking people, especially children; dogs are contaminating the environment with tons of feces, which they deposit on streets and sidewalks every day; they kill livestock; cause car accidents; and, due to changes in breeding patterns dogs' natures have altered, and they are becoming more aggressive and frightening to people. In addition to the colossal amounts of food they consume, dogs also use non-renewable energy and resources that are badly needed by humans the world over. In the past when there were fewer dogs in society the problems they created were tolerable, but since the onslaught of the canine population explosion, which started about fifteen years ago, dog problems have multiplied proportionately. Now there is no doubt that a crisis is at hand.

Identifying those who are responsible for the dog crisis was, to my great surprise, no problem. They fall into two equally culpable groups – irresponsible pet owners and the pet industry.

I discovered that people who own dogs are quite different from those who do not. Asking questions of dog owners frequently elicited a defensiveness about their dogs that bordered on hostility, an attitude which was maintained by professionals or executives in various fields, e.g., veterinary medicine, public health, the animal welfare movement, and the pet industry. By opening up discussions which were not always favourable to the dog I was often given short shrift, or information that was incomplete, and time and time again I found myself reaffirming my affection for dogs, quite as if I had been taking a loyalty oath.

People's concepts of dogs, I came to learn, stem from powerful roots that sink deep into history, religion, and psychology, and are kept flourishing by the media and advertising. When one has been conditioned since childhood to believe that dogs are exclusively good, especially one's own dog, an owner feels no obligation to restrict his or her dog and, as if it was a God-given right, allows the dog to run free. This, as we are now experiencing, is a major problem.

But people do not want to hear about problems dogs cause, I suspect because it makes them feel guilty to harbour negative emotions about an animal that has served man so faithfully for centuries. In spite of this, however, a growing number of people are beginning to break down the sentimental clichés about dogs as perfect creatures and assess the benefits versus the costs of keeping them as pets. Sides are now forming up and the result is a hot bed of emotion. There are the non-dog owners (inevitably dubbed the anti-dog lobby) who accuse irresponsible owners of causing all the problems by not keeping their dogs under control, and there are the dog owners who charge that their adversaries are simply crackpots who hate dogs. Both sides have attracted the lunatic fringe and all too frequently neither is taken very seriously. Worse yet, the warring factions may possibly be providing an ideal smoke-screen for the irresponsible pet owner's partner in the dog crisis – the pet industry – which expends millions of advertising dollars to sell their products and creates an ever-accelerating demand for dogs. And as long as the dog population continues to grow, so will the problems.

For approximately 40,000 years man's relationship with the dog has remained fairly stable. Now it is severely threatened. And until reason quells emotion, and the seriousness of the issue is publicized and addressed, neither man nor dog will survive the situation with dignity.

I.N.
June 14, 1978
Toronto, Canada

Introduction

Is the dog really man's best friend? This has become a very serious question in recent years. It is possible for dogs and all companion animals to be a sheer joy for their owners and to make no particular impact on the rest of the community; unfortunately, that is not the way things are now.

The facts in this book are not exaggerated. Dogs do bite – nearly 2 per cent of children five to nine years old are bitten each year by dogs. Each dog deposits an average of more than half a pound of feces on our streets each day. Our canine companions compete with us for food and food by-products. The pet food industry uses grains and various food by-products for pet food and the same grains and food by-products are needed for processed protein and pharmaceuticals for people. Dogs compete for tax money. What is spent for bite investigations, replanting of trees killed by dogs' urine, and municipal spay clinics, is often taken out of the same taxes that finance health care, police protection, and education.

Dogs alone cannot be blamed as the cause of the problem. It would be fair to say it was not their conscious intention to evolve into pampered pets, far from the habitats of their ancestors – often a far cry from their ancestors' original appearance and temperament.

Dogs are lovable and trainable creatures. However, their "culture" is different from ours. They use their teeth for play and to assert dominance; they use feces and urine to mark their territories and to communicate with other dogs. They have not evolved to the extent that they can fit into our culture without continuous supervision. It is reasonable to expect that dog owners be civilized themselves and exercise a degree of responsibility for their pets. Most of the problems associated with dogs and the effect they have on society are directly attributable to man, through not controlling his pet dogs, through his exploitation of them as merchandise used to amass profit, or his lack of concern for failing to demand legislation that would alleviate some of the problems.

In this well-researched book, among other things, Iris Nowell addresses the chief issues of dogs and dog owning and how both affect the general social welfare. Backed by reliable, authoritative, data she examines each of these trouble spots from many perspectives, and raises some important questions about the role of dogs in our society, as well as offering some intelligent and practical solutions which, if implemented, would benefit dog owners, dogs themselves, and the public.

One of the major problems that affects man most directly (and dogs as well, as we shall see) is something that could be eliminated by responsible behaviour on the part of dog owners; the problem of loose-running dogs. Few would disagree that dogs should not run free, especially in densely populated urban areas. As mentioned earlier, the dog is an alien in our culture, and we take a dim view of those who communicate assertiveness and play by biting, who promiscuously defecate and urinate on public property, who turn over trash cans, and run out in traffic. All the above practices are common to and typical of dogs and all of them, to say the least, inconvenience people. But regardless of how put out we may be, the dog is perhaps the most inconvenienced.

Dogs are often punished, or on occasion destroyed, for biting; they contract worms and leptospirosis due to excessive amounts of feces and urine on city streets and in parks; they find and consume non-nutritive edibles in garbage; and die under the wheels of cars. Considering the dangers free-running dogs face, I find it surprising that humane people do not demand that leash laws exist and that they be rigorously enforced. Dog lovers are curiously silent on this issue.

Owners who clean up after their dogs would be benefitting dogs as well as people. A de-wormed dog will not become reinfected if there are no infective fecal deposits for him to smell and eat. (Yes, dogs do things like that.) An owner should not be concerned about any health risk in cleaning up after his or her dog since freshly passed feces do not contain eggs that are capable of infection – they are infective after being on the ground for a few weeks. Stooping and scooping might be unappealing, but to do it would be in the best interest of the pet and the community.

Several diseases that are transmitted from animals to man (zoonoses) could be prevented by responsible ownership practices. I have already noted how cleaning up after dogs would reduce the embryonated egg load in the environment, which in turn would cause less visceral larva migrans in people. However, several other zoonoses are primarily diseases of wildlife that unsupervised dogs may pick up on their forays into the woods and fields and bring home with them. Rabies is one such disease. Well controlled in the dog population of the United States and Canada, rabies is more often observed in the fox and skunk populations of North America. People are rarely bitten by a fox or skunk but they are bitten by loose-running pet dogs, which may previously have met with a rabid fox or skunk. Rocky Mountain spotted fever is another example of a wildlife disease which may be transmitted by pet dogs that contract the American dog tick found on small, wild mammals. Similarly, the leptospirosis strain dogs can contract from the urine of infected wild animals (*Leptospira icterhae-morrhagiae*) causes more serious disease symptoms for dogs and people than does the dog-to-dog type, *L. canicola*. In other words, direct supervision of pet dogs is as appropriate and important in rural areas as in the city.

In addition to cleaning up after dogs, then, an effort toward more careful supervision, the enforcement of leash laws, or simply not letting dogs run loose in the city or in the country, would protect both pets and people from disease.

Another area of major concern is the overpopulation of dogs and the difficulty of finding effective and humane solutions. This book examines some of the factors contributing to the pet overpopulation, among them, unscrupulous breeders, the media, advertising, the pet food and accessories industries, and discusses some of the methods being practised to arrest the population growth – i.e. the killing of surplus dogs, development of spay clinics, and pet contraceptives. Of interest also are the attitudes of pet owners who are reluctant to confine dogs in heat, who do not want to interfere with their freedom to reproduce, and the numerous reasons, mostly unfounded, why people refuse to have their dogs sterilized.

There is one aspect of the dog problem that I believe is not in the best interest of pets or people, namely, low-cost spaying programs. Strictly speaking, low-cost spaying means using short-cut methods and cheap materials. Presumably, no one really means low-cost surgery. What is meant is municipally subsidized or defrayed cost surgery, that is, someone other than the dog owner paying for the procedure. To be sure, spaying and neutering are highly recommended. The sterilized animal is more tractable, lives longer, and appears more content with captivity. Sterilizing one's dog is part of responsible ownership, as is proper medical care and good nutrition. This elective surgery should not be, as it all too often is, the burden of the taxpayer. To make it so would divert funds from other animal programs, such as the collecting and housing of free-roaming dogs, adoption of animals, and rabies and other disease control programs. Spaying is beneficial for dogs but leashing and responsible supervision is all that is necessary to avoid an unwanted pregnancy. It has always seemed curious to me that so many people suggest all of society help the dog owner pay for an elective sterilizing operation, yet no one suggests helping the dog owner who is faced with the tragedy of not having the financial means to pay for a life-saving operation for a beloved pet.

Now I invite you to read *The Dog Crisis*. It is time such a book was written, for it is needed by both pet owners and non-pet owners. Iris Nowell discusses the history of dogs, the role they play in the lives of men, their exploitation, the pet industry, the social cost of dogs, disease and public health risks, the overpopulation of dogs and many other issues related to or caused by these household pets.

The statistics that come to light in this book are alarming. I would hope that the information provided will open people's eyes to a potentially threatening situation, one that places man and dogs in jeopardy. At the very least, one will be forced to examine priorities, re-evaluate choices. The author offers many worthwhile solutions to problems and I urge you to work actively toward their implementation.

It is not inconceivable to me that future books about dogs will be reminiscences about the good old days when people were allowed to own them.

Alan M. Beck, Sc.D.
Director, Bureau of Animal Affairs
Department of Health
City of New York

1

The Man and Dog Partnership

Although seemingly irreconcilable, there is a logical explanation for why one person bakes a birthday cake for a dog and invites other dogs to the party, while another person shoots a dog that defecates on his property. Dogs evoke the full range of human response quite simply because they have been associated with man for up to 40,000 years in such intimate roles as hunting partners, objects of worship, and as pets. It is useful to review these different relationships in order to come to grips with the emotionalism currently surrounding the issue of dogs, and to see where the once vital partnership has been distorted.

The Dog as a Working Animal

It is safe to say that generations of archaeologists have been more interested in studying exciting creatures like dinosaurs or unearthed objects that shed light on lost cultures than in probing the background of the common dog. Financed by institutions that expect excavations to yield monuments, written records or artifacts, in far too many cases archaeologists have assumed information about the dog without saving evidence. Take bones, for example. To save tens of thousands of bones for proper scientific study would require painstaking examining, cleaning, sorting, and classifying – the kind of job, like many tedious jobs, that invariably falls by the wayside. As a consequence, the history of the dog and its association with man has been the victim of an archaeological blind spot. Whenever the subject is reviewed scholars are compelled to use such phrases as "Although we are not certain," "It seems reasonable to suppose," or "On the basis of present information," and even fairly assertive statements need some qualification.

Zoologically speaking, the history of the dog is equally vague. No theory has received universal acceptance, but several have withstood time-tested arguments, probably because each is plausible; i.e., the dog has descended from the wolf, *Canis lupus*, from the jackal, *Canis aureus*, or from a third species which includes wild dogs such as the Australian dingo, the Indian dhole, certain wild dogs of Africa, the pi dog and two dogs from which only fossils remain, *Canis poutiatini* and the peat dog, *Canis palustris*. A viewpoint commonly held by naturalists is that *Canis familiaris* is a handy rather than an accurate zoological classification, that the dog is neither a species nor a descendant of any one particular species, but whose line of descent may be variously wolf, fox, jackal or hyena, depending on geographical location. This reasoning holds together when one considers the ease with which dogs will breed with wolves, foxes, jackals and hyenas, the great variance in canine types (it is difficult to believe that a Chihuahua, a Basset Hound and a St. Bernard all have a common ancestral sire), the similarity between dogs and wolves, foxes, jackals and hyenas in terms of temper, intelligence, and manageability, and how quickly dogs revert to the wild state. Perhaps this confusion led to the last theory, that God had a dog; it came with Him when He created heaven and earth.

Although the social and zoological history of the canine is imprecise there is little disputing its importance to early man. Archaeologists and zoologists agree that the dog has been domesticated for between 9,000 and 12,000 years and throughout this time has performed an astonishing repertoire of duties

2

in the service of man. One historian flatly states, "It would appear that man was able to fight his way up from a state of nature to civilization only with the aid of the dog."[1]

There is no doubt that primitive man, despite his limited intelligence and verbal skills, communicated with animals. Written history, being only 4,000 years old, provides no record of what early man "said" to the beasts around him, but if one accepts the commonly held zoological theory that several characteristics are as much animal as human in nature – responses to fear and pain, curiosity, sexual and courtship behaviour, the behaviour of mothers toward their young[2] – a basis for some form of communication certainly existed. It stands to reason. Animals were all that primitive man had.

By most accounts man and dog first came into contact with one another at least 40,000 years ago at the scene of man's kill, where a pack of wild dogs would be quick to arrive. If the kill was plentiful, man probably tossed some scraps to the dogs. Sooner or later man must have realized that, unlike himself, dogs could scent animals and using simple communication he capitalized on this characteristic by training them to help him round up the beasts required for his food and clothing. In return the dogs shared the spoils.

It has been suggested that pack dogs had no qualms about transferring their allegiance from a canine pack leader to man, a new leader who was smarter and perhaps stronger than their previous one. Historian and zoologist F.E. Zeuner, having stated that dogs are far superior to other carnivores in intelligence, theorizes, "The cunning of the dog and his concerted efforts on hunting expeditions are not unlike the hunting practices of early man. It is therefore not impossible that young wolves or jackals or other wild dogs, which grew up in or near the temporary camps of Mesolithic hunters, would quite naturally regard the men, who provided part of their food supply, as members of their packs, an association which the hunters would not have failed to turn to their advantage."[3]

The next advance in the relationship was quite likely prompted by man's desire for deep sleep, a risky activity in a cave without a door. After trusting the dog as a hunting partner, man probably realized that the dog would make a useful guard. When menfolk were away on a hunt, they surely felt secure leaving an older dog or nursing bitch behind to guard the camp. In exchange the dog received inside cave privileges. Compared to the dog's life in the wilderness, constantly threatened by larger predators, the arrangement must have been mutually comforting. Hence the bond of mutual dependence and friendship was struck.

Once the dog became proficient on hunting expeditions and at guard duty, man began training it for more specific tasks. Recognizing that if too much game was killed the meat would only spoil, man then trained the dog to corral and protect animals from larger predators. Thus he could have his meat on the hoof, and kill what he needed when he needed it. The plan worked splendidly, and to this day the dog is still a master herder. In Scotland, Australia, Turkey, Russia, and Lapland, the sheep dog is the king of dogs. With as many as two hundred sheep in its charge the average sheepdog, without any trouble at all, will channel sheep from barn to pasture and across roads and streams, round up drifters and stragglers and ward off predators – all more efficiently than a human, many shepherds believe.

In time, with additional domestic animals under his control, the acquisition of possessions, and the onset of a more diversified life, man began selecting through breeding the characteristics in dogs he required to meet his changing lifestyle. Certain dogs that were skilled herders would be bred for that purpose. Some dogs might swim better than others to retrieve feathered prey; others performed well on open plains or in forests; and the more powerful animals best protected the growing herds and encampments. In each case, as the dog's skills were refined through selective breeding and training, their physical characteristics stood more clearly apart. To this day, the objectives of selective breeding remain the same even though they began in the Paleolithic and Mesolithic Ages, from ten to twenty thousand years ago.

It is known that in the Bronze Age dogs commonly protected herds and the dwellings of agrarian peoples on the Nile, the Euphrates and in some European countries, as depicted on pottery from the Amratian period (3,000 B.C.). Early Scythians

4

kept large dogs to protect their cattle. In Rome dogs guarded the homes of the well-to-do and in the country Roman aristocrats kept massive, fierce dogs to maintain control over the slaves. Romans also organized extravagant hunts where thousands of birds and various game were cornered and killed by dogs, a pastime which subsequently led to the animal vs. human contests in the arena.

Dogs have marched along with armies since the first stone was hurled. Roman legions, having successfully bred dogs to an enormous size, took vast armies of them on their conquests and the Greeks and Persians trained them to fight in squadrons. When the Persian Xerxes invaded Greece, so numerous were the trained dogs that went along with him that Herodotus reported, "...certainly no one could tell their number." And when Alexander the Great stormed into Persia in 327 B.C., he was flanked by a large contingent of fighting dogs. Ancient woodcuts and engravings portray these warrior dogs, their chests covered with protective armour, and around their necks enormous collars – large spikes for gouging and blades for slashing. When unleashed on an unsuspecting enemy the dogs were capable of tearing men right off their horses.[45]

Since the beginning of their domestication dogs have served man in practical, exploitative and sometimes touching ways. Tibetan monks inscribed prayers on pieces of parchment which they then placed in a prayer wheel. Dogs were employed to run on a treadmill to spin the wheel, keeping the prayers, so the monks believed, in a constant state of being said. Similarly, in Europe, dogs ran in treadmill cages to turn roasting spits. Other household duties were churning butter and raising buckets of water from wells.

Hitched to a cart, the dog was one of the first door-to-door delivery services for bread, milk, and vegetables, in Europe and America. One of the earliest types of working dog in the United States was the railway dog, trained to keep the right-of-way clear of sheep and, not so widely publicized, of hobos trying to clamber aboard.

War dogs have served man for as long as sheepdogs and both are used to this day. At the time of the First World War Armistice it was estimated that ten thousand dogs had served at the front as sentries, carriers of medical supplies, rat killers in trenches and message dispatchers. As espionage agents they were unique. Russian spies cunningly distracted attention from message couriers by sending a peasant on delivery with a dog. The peasant might attract suspicion and be thoroughly searched, while the accompanying dog, with a message inserted in its rectum, was ignored.[6] Untold lives were saved during the attacks on London by dogs who scented humans under tons of debris in bomb-shattered buildings and alerted rescuers to their whereabouts.

At the height of the Vietnam War the U.S. military canine force was estimated to be one million strong. Dogs were used by both the United States and South Vietnamese at the beginning of the war but it wasn't until the Communists began to sabotage major U.S. bases in 1963 that the number of dogs was increased, which reduced sabotage significantly. The trainers and handlers of these dogs claim that they can hear twenty times, see ten times, and smell forty times better than humans. As the lone guard of an ammunition dump, a dog barking alerts the human guards; or if a patrol dog accompanied by a handler detects the enemy the dog freezes, signalling silently by wagging its tail. Patrol dogs evolved into a highly successful war "weapon," and it is claimed they reduced casualties on night patrols by as much as 65 per cent in Vietnam.[7]

The civilian counterpart of war dogs, city police dogs, perform a number of criminal assignments, such as night patrol in high density crime areas, subway patrol, riot control, and drug and bomb detection. Psychologically, the police dog acts as a potent crime deterrent. Hardened criminals commonly freeze in terror at the sight of a snarling, teeth-bared German Shepherd. A typical reaction to police dogs took place in Maryland during a Labour Day outing of teenagers which erupted into a block-long fight on the beach. When the K-9 (canine) corps arrived from nearby Baltimore the captain is quoted as having said, "In ten minutes the beach was cleared. We didn't do a thing – just walked along with the dogs."[8]

In rigorous training programs the dog is developed to peak physical condition and its extraordinary sense of smell is put to work in combating a variety of contemporary problems. Dogs in the U.S. customs department were trained so thoroughly in sniffing out drugs along the country's 96,000 miles of land and sea borders between Canada and Mexico that the thirty-seven-dog corps mustered in 1970 was expanded to 127 by 1977. One of the most sensational customs coups involved an eighty-nine-pound German Shepherd named Baron who, in 1972, discovered 851 pounds of hashish worth 3.5 million dollars on the street, stashed in a pickup truck arriving aboard a freighter from Belgium. In 1976 alone the "pot hounds" of the customs department contributed directly to the seizure of "24,020 kilos of marijuana, 1,933 kilos of hashish, 42 kilos of cocaine, 33 kilos of heroin, and 3,000,000 units of dangerous drugs." A dog with a handler can nose out five hundred parcels in a customs shed in half an hour, a job that would take any person several days. The average car search at a border crossing, which normally takes twenty minutes, is done by a dog in two minutes flat.[9]

Biosensor dogs, as they are called, are becoming so specialized that even rapists have cause to fear them, as in the case of a Detroit teenager who was apprehended in a school yard full of kids, after the dog traced his semen scent. And this was the dog's third such detection.[10]

Dogs have literally given a new life to the blind and deaf. Blind veterans of the First World War were first trained with dog guides in Europe. Since 1929 when the original seeing-eye school was incorporated in New Jersey, nine similar schools have been established in the United States, which train blind persons to be safely guided by dogs through city streets and traffic. Following on the success of the dog guide is a program called the Listening-Ear Dog, wherein dogs are trained to alert deaf persons to three common situations: a crying baby; a ringing doorbell or clock. Countless heretofore dependent persons have become sufficiently independent to seek employment, educate themselves, and more effectively rear children due to the help of dogs.

Throughout medical history, dogs in laboratory research have provided knowledge that has alleviated human suffering in ways that can never be properly assessed. One of the newest of these has been the use of dogs in the treatment of psychiatric disturbances.

"Pet-oriented psychotherapy" has shown certain good results

7

for a small number of clinicians treating children with mental problems. One of its pioneers, Boris Levinson, claims that the dog is a great facilitator, helping him to arrive at an early diagnosis. The dog also "breaks the ice." Instead of asking the child what worries him or what he dreams about, the psychiatrist asks him what he imagines the dog would think of his dreams, his parents, his bed-wetting, or the bullies on the street. For many children it has proved easier to relay their most confidential thoughts to or via a dog, rather than eyeball it out with the stranger behind the desk.[11]

In one study undertaken at Ohio State University a nineteen-year-old psychotic, who had remained unreachable throughout individual therapy, was given a dog. To everyone's amazement the boy immediately smiled and spoke more words than he had ever spoken up to that time, asking, "Where can I keep him?" The psychiatrist judged the dog to be "the turning point in the course of his recovery."[12]

The Dog as an Object of Worship

Intimately sharing his life with animals, man naturally attached magical meanings to what he could not understand. Because man was unable to fathom the nature of the sun and the moon, the winds and the rain, and knew he did not control them, it is worth postulating that he presumed animals did. Watching birds in flight or a fleet-footed stag in motion conceivably suggested an affinity with the wind. Beetles that laid eggs and pushed them along in the sand might well have been associated with the forces that moved the sun across the sky. The sight of a snake shedding its skin, the complex markings on a tortoise shell, the plumage of birds, must have filled man with wonderment and awe. Living in such close proximity to them, men were almost indistinguishable from animals. Primitives wore heads of animals when hunting to scare off predators, women suckled puppies and apes[13], and in early fables and myths man was human one minute, beast the next. An angry god or jealous goddess might turn enemies into snakes or fishes or, on a whim, a god might become a bird or beast. As they were fascinating, mystical creatures, it is no surprise to learn that man ranked animals with the gods.[14]

Although much of the social organization of pre-historic man is open to conjecture, solid evidence attests to the animal cults of the Egyptians, dating from 3,000 to 5,000 B.C. The Egyptians believed animals were true possessors of divine powers and deserved special care and attention while on earth. Since both animals and humans were believed to have souls that would be reincarnated in another life, burial rites were crucial to Egyptian life.

To the great credit of embalmers' skills, countless numbers of animals have been found in Egyptian tombs excavated in the nineteenth century. In the mid-1800s an entire cemetery was unearthed which contained 300,000 mummified cats* and one of Britain's foremost Egyptologists, Walter Bryan Emery, in his search for the tomb of Imhotep in 1964, presented hard evidence of the extent and seriousness of the animal cult with his discovery of a cache of mummified animals in mastabas (rectangular underground burial chambers) stacked from floor to ceiling like bottles of wine in a gigantic cellar. A rough count put the number at an incredible 1,250,000.[16]

The cult of the cat in Egypt is legendary. Bastet, the goddess with a cat's head, was the symbol of beauty for Egyptian women who sought to emulate her enigmatic gaze, serenity and noble pose. Herodotus, who travelled extensively in Egypt in the fifth century B.C., claimed that if an Egyptian's house caught fire he would allow his possessions to burn without much concern, but would risk his life to save his cat. When a person's cat died of natural causes all members of the family shaved off their eyebrows. However, if a person killed a cat he or she had to mount a convincing display of grief to prove it was an accident, or face execution.

As glamorous an idol as the cat was, what is not so well known is that the dog was even more universally worshipped in Egypt. Every town had a dog cemetery. When a dog died it was wrapped in linens and ceremoniously embalmed, and for

---

*Archaeologists ignored the find and as a result the twenty tons of mummies were sold to English farmers as fertilizer for £4 a ton.[15]

the entombment people would gather round, beating their chests in an expression of grief and uttering lamentations.[17] A person whose own dog died shaved off all the hair on his or her body as a sign of mourning.

It is said that worship of the dog originated with the annual overflooding of the Nile. Every year prior to this occurrence the star Sirius appeared on the horizon, as a signal for the river people to quickly move their flocks to higher ground. So dependable was the star's appearance that it became known as the "dog star," possessing, it was believed, characteristics of a watchful and loyal sheep dog. Respect and dependability led to veneration, it may be speculated, and the object of the people's veneration eventually evolved into a creature with a man's body and dog's head (probably more that of a jackal), named Anubis, god of the dead and one of the great figures in Egyptian mythology.

To honour Anubis a city, Cynopolis, became the scene of lavish festivals presided over by priests who sacrificed dogs to their god. Each inhabitant was required to provide a specific amount of food for the city's dogs. As a measure of their faith, rulers were known to declare war on a neighbouring city if one of its citizens captured and ate a Cynopolis dog.[18] Egyptians would eat one another rather than violate the taboo of eating the sacred dog.

Civilizations that did not outrightly worship animals observed close approximations. In totemism, members of a tribe regarded themselves supernaturally related to a particular animal, bird, or in some cases, plant. Since they believed that every living thing was descended one from the other, no one dared kill or harm his totem and to this day many Indian, Moslem, Hindu, African, and Oriental, sects will not kill animals, even the lowliest, believing that they could embody the soul of someone's devoted grandmother or uncle.

Certain early civilizations anthropomorphized animals, that is, gave them human qualities, to such an extent that the animals were held responsible for their own actions. In many cases animals were regarded as equals. The Zend-Vesta, an ancient Persian book devoted entirely to laws governing the behaviour of dogs, specified that if the dog bit a man or sheep, and the act was deemed premeditated, the dog was punished by having one of its ears cut off. For subsequent offences the other ear was cut off, then a foot and after that its tail – one mutilation for each crime committed.[19] One hundred and ninety-one cases of animals tried and condemned have been recorded in modern history from the year 824 to 1906[20], including the famous Salem, New England witch trials in 1692 when two dogs were accused of witchcraft along with twenty people, and all were executed.[21] Ecclesiastical courts tried lesser wild creatures, such as rats and locusts, and if found guilty they were excommunicated.

A vintner in St. Julien formally "laid charges" in 1545 against insects plaguing his vineyard – and the insects were even represented by counsel. The outcome was that public prayers had to be said and a mass celebrated while the Host was born in procession through the vineyard. And sure enough, the insects disappeared. Forty-one years later they reappeared and were retried. This time the debate centred on whether the Church had the right to kill the insects or whether insects had the legal right to live. Although the arguments were inconclusive, the evidence filled twenty-nine folios and still remains in the town archives.[22]

Five thousand years ago the Romans didn't think much of the burgeoning Egyptian animal cults and publicly ridiculed them. It wasn't long, however, before the Romans themselves adopted animals as divinities and soon the temples of Roman emperors were filled with animals. De-clawed lions followed rulers around like trained dogs. Numbers of animals roamed the streets freely and the chicken, a favourite venerated animal was consulted on the outcome of battles. Operating like a feathered ouija board, the bird was placed in the centre of a circle with grains of wheat representing letters of the alphabet. The grains the chicken approached were spelled out and read as omens. It is said that during the first Punic War a Roman admiral took along holy chickens to portend naval engagements but the chickens became seasick and were unable to perform at the wheat circle, whereupon the angry admiral wailed, "If they won't eat, let them drink," and pitched them overboard. Perhaps the chickens were onto something for the admiral was defeated in his next battle.[23]

In spite of their reputation for cruelty to animals the Romans were great dog lovers. They had up to 180 names for dogs, many of which expressed their high regard for them. "Catellus," for example, was a favourite pet name for both dogs and friends or lovers.

Ancient Persians granted dogs the same respect as begging friars, and it was Herodotus who told of the Persian governor, a celebrated dog lover, who kept them, "in such great quantity that four large villages in the plain were freed from other taxes in order that they might supply food for the dogs."[24]

In China the imperial dogs of the Han Dynasty (206 B.C.-200 A.D.) were titled, the emperors were vested with the highest literary rank[25]; and before Confucius, rulers and great men were commonly buried with a few of their favourite things – concubines, servants, and animals. One venerable gentleman went to his tomb with sixty-six people and 190 animals, among them a horse, several leopards, and tigers.[26]

The Ethiopians periodically elected a dog head of the government to preside over cabinet meetings, and ministers would set policy based on the dog's responses. Dressed in royal robes and wearing a crown for the special occasion, if the dog snapped at the foreign secretary the treaty he had prepared was torn up, and if the dog wagged his tail and licked the minister of defence, all was well in the war department. Subjects paid homage to the dog, and if it responded by licking a person's hand, an honour was conferred; if the dog growled or barked, this was just cause for a prison sentence and even death for the unfortunate individual.

Nowhere is animal veneration carried to such extremes as by the Jainist monks in India. In order to do as little injury as possible to animal life, they practise non-violence (ahimsa, the origin of vegetarianism) with inviolable discipline. A Jain monk never walks without carrying a feather duster to sweep away the insects in his path to avoid accidentally stepping on them, and for the same reason he would not take a stroll in the dark. His mouth is covered with a veil to prevent him from inadvertently inhaling small flying insects. Bathing is

12

forbidden, harming, it is believed, "both the water used for washing and the vermin on the holy man's body." Lamps are not lit after dark in monasteries, both out of respect for the "fire beings in the flames" and to prevent moths from flying into them.[27]

By the sixth century B.C. animal worship reached its zenith in both the East and West, but Christianity was directly responsible for its decline. The fundamental Christian belief in monotheism, as opposed to polytheism, and in a life hereafter, as opposed to reincarnation, left no room for pagan gods, and animals were rendered obsolete as the repositories of human souls. But, and this is crucial to today's attitudes toward pets, animal worship did not disappear with Christianity; it evolved into a different form of veneration. Dominating early Christian dogma was the precept that animals have no hope of a future life and therefore merit special consideration while they are alive. The saintly Cardinal Robert Bellarmino, for instance, permitted fleas to live in his beard, claiming, "We shall have Heaven to reward us for our sufferings, but these poor creatures have nothing but the enjoyment of this present life."[28] St. Francis of Assisi regarded his body parasites as the "pearls of poverty."[29] Such Biblical tales formed the anecdotal platforms from which Christian kindness to animals was taught. And still is.

Just as early myths and legends communicated the belief that animals were sacred, today's beliefs are communicated through the mass media, which many would argue have created the contemporary version of animal worship, now developed into a full-fledged cult. Fairy tales, books, movies, and television, have perpetuated the Christian belief that all creatures great and small deserve unconditional love. Indeed, dogs and cats, given humanized names, emotions, and thoughts, are frequently endowed with qualities more admirable than those of humans. Anthropomorphized animals, dominating children's literature since the sixth century B.C., when Aesop's fables set the style of using talking animals to depict man's foibles, vices, and virtues, to this day remain an effective teaching device. Hardly a school child has eluded the message that Lassie, Spot, and Rin Tin Tin are the epitome of perfection. Walt Disney, probably today's single most influential

13

force in forming children's attitudes toward animals, throughout his career presented animal heroes as exclusively cute and perfect.

Children have been conditioned by the media to believe that it is good to love animals and from the age of toddlers they have come to regard them as extra special. This attitude pervades adult literature as well. It is now a fictional cliché for the cold-blooded killer to dissolve at the prospect of harm befalling his dog.

Day after day, newspapers play a key part in perpetuating the animal cult. Conservative dailies commonly publish firehose-dog-boy photographs to illustrate a heat wave, or they run pictures of a dog wearing a funny hat or riding a skateboard. This not only offers relief from the bitter news but it keeps dogs and cats in an endearing light. Tabloids sensationalize and give as much coverage to the mistreatment of animals as they do to a domestic knifing, and in so doing precipitate a flood of letters to the editor. In 1966 *Life* magazine ran a story on animal laboratory experiments that generated more mail than any other article in the magazine's history. Whether the editorial policy is conservative or sensational in its coverage of animals, both approaches satisfy an audience, and both glorify animals.

It is in advertising that one begins to appreciate the staggering number of messages the average person receives every day about animals. Not an evening of television goes by without commercials for pet food. One writer reported, in 1971, that on an average day in New York more than 125 pet food commercials were broadcast on that city's television channels.[30] Commercials employ a number of tricks to sell more than just pet food. Elegant film sequences of dogs bounding over fences, cute cats and dogs that talk and attractive product names and packages are some of the devices used to sell a particular brand, while simultaneously a subliminal pitch is being made for pet owning. Feeding a beautiful, adoring pet is so rewarding that it becomes a product benefit. Just as better kissing is promised for using Brand X mouthwash, commercials promise a better life-style through owning a dog or a cat. In effect, advertising for cat food or flea collars or sterling silver dog dishes is thinly disguised advertising for dogs and cats themselves. Through tricky gimmicks in commercials one is seduced into acquiring a dog or cat in order to enjoy the rewards of pet owning, one of which is buying a particular brand of pet food. The veneration of animals has become grist to the mill of supply and demand.

The combined strength of religious teachings, the pet industry, and the media in shaping today's attitudes toward pets is further augmented by humane societies and animal welfare organizations. In their campaigns to encourage the adoption of homeless pets, animal organizations seek public sympathy by producing posters and pamphlets which feature a puppy or kitten, looking distinctly woebegone over the headline "Give him a home," a direct steal from campaigns designed to recruit foster parents for orphans in Third World countries. These organizations would have us believe the plight of the homeless dog is comparable to that of the homeless child.

But before one can equate dogs with humans it is necessary to elevate them from animal level; in short, a form of veneration is at work, kept alive by those who are involved in the humane movement. Typically these are people who have left business because the profit motive is not very satisfying; others have forsaken jobs in hospitals, prisons, and in various institutions where the rehabilitation of troubled humans is slow and job rewards small. From the first day of work at the animal shelter it is evident that job satisfaction is a reality through animals. When in the past a simple "thank you" was hard to come by from humans, now a pat on a dog's head and a "Good boy!" results in a flurry of affectionate handlicking and tail wagging. Because animals represent the professional salvation of many workers, both staff and volunteers repay animals by working zealously on their behalf. Under the circumstances, workers in the humane movement naturally worship animals. And they demand the same of everyone else.

The Dog as a Pet

There are a number of theories on the origin of pet keeping. The most popular is that as the dog spent more time with man as a hunting partner the bond grew stronger and as man evolved from hunter to harvester the dog remained with him out of loyalty and became a pet. But a more convincing theory might be that of F.E. Zeuner, who claims that a child likely caught a puppy from a litter, fed it, played with it and the puppy became socialized with man and was regularly fed, kept warm, and protected from its former hostile world.[31]

As early man migrated from encampment to encampment, dogs were undoubtedly his most valuable possession, marking their owner as a superior man and successful hunter. It was with the transition from agrarian to industrial societies that the dog evolved from working animal to pet.

Thorstein Veblen, in his 1904 classic work, *The Theory of the Leisure Class*, traced industrial development to the institution of ownership, which was first evidenced in the ownership of persons, primarily women and slaves, then property. Of lasting impact has been Veblen's term "conspicuous consumption," which he coined to describe ostentatious displays of wealth. Since these displays are often exemplified by a master-slave relationship and conspicuous waste, defined as devoting effort to that which is of no intrinsic value and is obviously expensive, the dog fits all these criteria perfectly. In Veblen's words, "He is the filthiest of the domestic animals in his person and the nastiest in his habits. For this he makes up in a servile, fawning attitude toward his master... With the dog, man's desire to master can be well satisfied." The most fashionable dog breeds are expensive to acquire and maintain; pet dogs take up time and serve no useful purpose and, as a consequence, Veblen claims, "their value to their owners lies chiefly in their utility as items of conspicuous consumption."[32]

Many civilizations valued dogs more highly than they did precious jewels. For the Assyrians and Persians awarding a brace of Greyhounds to a visitor carried higher honours than a royal decoration, and the sign posted on Roman houses, which translates to "Beware of the Dog," was a visible symbol of a person's wealth and position.

Today, large breeds in particular connote status for they exude expense and rarity. In advertising expensive automobiles and designer clothes, a sleek well-bred dog is a complementary accessory, just as an ad for crystal stemware graces fine table linen. Quentin Bell in *Of Human Finery* claims that the dog, above all other animals, is sumptuous due to its connection with socially reputable sports, such as fox hunting. As a fashion accessory the dog, following compliantly and elegantly behind its master, becomes an essential part of the overall costume, or "look." Bell goes on to say, "Dogs are the fashion because we can fashion them to our will."[33] Bred to look and perform almost exactly as we choose, it is difficult to imagine any other creature, certainly not children, serving us with such malleability.

An obvious link exists between the popularity of dogs as pets and the emergence of the middle class and its values. The poor, always tending to emulate the rich, were able to afford pets as soon as they ceased being chattels of the rich and emerged as the working class. However, this was slow in coming. Veterinary historian Charles Phineas claims that there is no mention of pets in English women's magazines of the nineteenth century and suggests that mass popularity of pet keeping began after the First World War, coinciding with the change in the family. When the family unit began to disperse – children off to seek their fortunes in cities, grandparents off to nursing homes – pets became a substitute for missing family members. Also, with the decline of servants in middle-class households, a need arose for another form of subordinance and pets were the ideal replacement. As family size decreases, pets often serve as surrogate children, and since many children are difficult to handle, pets are welcome as docile, undemanding, obedient creatures.[34]

It wasn't until people began keeping dogs strictly as pets that they discovered the huge psychological benefits. As already mentioned, dogs satisfied the desire to master and dominate, they gave owners unconditional love, they became surrogate friends, and to many people keeping a dog as a pet was an easy means of satisfying some basic psychological need. Only within the past few decades has the psychology of pet keeping and the enormity of its implications begun to be realized.

2

The Psychology of Pet Owning

Recent studies undertaken in England, the United States, and Canada on the psychology of pet keeping are defining people's attitudes toward pets more incisively than ever before and although the old reasons of mastery, domination, and companionship still apply a new interpretation has come to light. Pets serve as ready-made human substitutes. When describing their dog people commonly say, "He's just like a member of the family"; "I couldn't live without her"; "He's the child I never had"; or "She's good company." For those couples making the choice not to have children and for increasingly more men and women choosing to live alone or establish lifelong relationships with the same sex, they adopt a cat or dog as a substitute child. And for widows, widowers and the swelling ranks of divorced persons, a pet acts as a surrogate for the lost mate. The pet fits neatly and is perhaps needed more than ever for many people trying to cope with today's changing life-styles. If your wife divorces you, get a dog; when the kids leave home, get a cat.

Before any measures can be undertaken to resolve the dog crisis it is necessary to know something of the ties that bind people to pets and to examine the psychological reasons behind pet keeping. These are powerful forces to confront.

The Emotional Need for Pets

For countless persons, emotional needs are satisfied only by pets. Pets offer companionship and give love unconditionally. British psychologist Richard Ryder defines the popularly-held opinion that the fact dogs make people feel loved is probably their greatest function. "Dogs, of course, are tremendous flatterers. They hero-worship even the most appalling owners." To have a dog totally servile, even grovelling now and then, is an "almost indecent" ego trip. "Every dog owner can get some idea of what it felt like to be a Roman warrior returning triumphantly to Rome after conquering new lands simply by going down to the pub for a couple of hours and then stumbling home again. Whatever welcome is received from the wife, the dog greets you as a long-lost friend and hero."[1]

The increasing alienation of urban life demands palliatives, and a very handy one to take the edge off loneliness is a household pet. A pet is a balm, smoothing the way to social encounters on an evening's walk. To children, the pet is dependable. With more wives in the work force and more single parents bringing up children, the dog acts as a stable figure, always at home after school. It doesn't get mad, doesn't come home drunk, doesn't divorce, and day in, day out, it remains a child's ally against parental authority. The child and dog as a team are able to brave it out under the toughest dinner-banishing, television-curtailing circumstances. For parents, frustrated with hard-to-manage children, the pet is a welcome, docile respite.

A dog satisfies the human need for power, particularly in those individuals with little opportunity of exercising any. As sociologist James Bossard exclaimed, in reference to people who have been the victim of directives, shouts and orders all day long, "How soul-satisfying now to take the dog for a walk and order him about!"[2]

Dogs fill vacant spaces in people's lives. They provide

never-ending occasions for saying, "Come in," "Get out," "Lie down," "Stay here," "Be quiet," "Come here," "Roll over," "Say please," should conversation lag; and to relieve family tensions a discussion of the dog is a safe, neutral subject. When a couple is not on speaking terms, one may test the troubled waters with a non-emotional, "Have you seen Sparky?"

Queen Elizabeth likes to be photographed with her famous Corgi dogs because, being a shy person, she finds they genuinely relax her and the smile that results is warm and friendly, never stilted or formal.[3] Thoreau, it is said, kept a dog to stir up the dead air in a room.

Regardless of the numerous instances of pets fulfilling human emotional needs there is another side to the story — that the emotion lavished on pets is perhaps displaced from where it more appropriately belongs. A dog may be a boy's most loyal friend, but at the same time it can be argued that the dog diminishes the boy's need to develop good relationships with his peers. If people confided in, cared for, worried about, and fussed over other people as much as they do pets, the prospects for world harmony would be dizzying.

Pet adoration will continue unabated as long as human relationships have deficiencies and offer no guarantees. No amount of slipper-fetching or mink-giving will ever change that. One life in touch with another can be hurtful, and when the bruises of interaction turn into permanent scars a person retreats, unwilling to take any more chances with unreliable humans. All too frequently these people settle for a safer outlet for their emotions — a dog, a cat, or a bird in a cage.

Until the last decade or so, no one dared challenge the notion that a dog provides a great learning experience for a youngster or that a cat is good company for a senior citizen. Like it or not, serious opposition is being raised against these attitudes and many observers now consider them outmoded, sentimental clichés. Some of the notions and arguments against them are as follows:

A dog teaches a child responsibility

When a puppy, kitten, dog, or cat first comes into a household the children or one child is assigned the task of feeding it, taking it for walks, bathing, brushing, and so on, and the new regimen is fun. Ideally, this arrangement continues for as long as the pet remains in the household but more often than not the attraction soon palls, the duties become a bore, and the mother inevitably ends up assuming total responsibility for the pet. By doing so she, in effect, is encouraging the child's irresponsible development. Permitting the youngster to slough off caring for the dog carries the implication that the mother is similarly lax in other situations and hence the child is off to an early start in the lifelong expectation that there will always be someone around to do the dirty work for him. What kind of a learning experience is this?

A dog teaches a child the facts of life

Teaching a child the facts of life is recited as one of the chief reasons for pet owning. The family may eagerly await a dog's giving birth, but at the last moment the mother may suddenly decide the experience will be traumatic for her children. And she might be right. Watching kittens or puppies emerge from their pet's "belly" can be more frightening to young children than educational. There is no question that a child is thrilled to wake up in the morning and find four little pups when the day before there was only one fat dog. But where is the "lesson" in this, particularly when the parents are preoccupied with getting rid of the puppies? Parents, when acquiring a first dog, will state a preference for unaltered bitches in order that their children may experience "the miracle of birth." Animal shelter workers, however, sick of people bringing their unwanted litters to be killed, are beginning to counter with, "let them come here and see the miracle of death."

It is questionable whether the sight of fornicating dogs teaches children anything about sex. Titters or fear are more typical responses.

Boris Levinson, a New York psychiatrist who has written extensively on his use of pets as psychotherapeutic aids for children (see page 7), observes that when youngsters notice the dog licking its genitals or simulating sexual activity against the sofa, and sees that it is still loved and accepted may

21

assuage the child's own guilty and confused feelings about masturbation. Levinson states, "If the dog does not feel guilty, the child wonders why he should and if the dog is permitted to enjoy his body, the child wonders why he cannot." To use such animal behaviour to open up conversation about the differences between humans and animals can be worthwhile and educative, Levinson claims.[4] But if parents snatch their children away from dogs engaged in sexual activity or avoid discussion of the subject, not only are there no educational possibilities but the parents' action reinforces any negative or "dirty" thoughts young people may harbour about sex.

A dog's death acts as a preview for the human tragedy

Death of a pet is often regarded as "good for" children, a dress rehearsal, the preview performance of the human tragedy. This proposition might be acceptable in an ideal world, where dogs are animals, not anthropomorphic hybrids, and everyone relates in unity to all living things. But that is not how it works.

Children have been known to suffer deep depression when their pets die, and a natural reaction of concerned parents is to immediately get another pet. This attitude is a spinoff from today's replacement syndrome. When the dishwasher goes on the fritz get a new one immediately, when the car is two years old get a new one, when the husband no longer pleases get a new one. Replacing the cat or dog is an extension of the lessening of human values, and when the child can be made to appreciate that every worm, tree, dog and human must eventually die, then perhaps death of the pet can be turned into a learning experience.

Dr. Quentin Rae-Grant, psychiatrist-in-chief at the Hospital for Sick Children in Toronto, related a reverse situation of how a pet was acquired to alleviate the grief caused by human death. The idea backfired lamentably. Two young children were tragically killed in an accident and to ease the shock for the surviving child the parents bought him a dog. Dr. Rae-

Grant claimed that the dog not only postponed the child's feelings of loss but denied him the freedom of even talking about them. Said the psychiatrist, "The pet also conveyed a false message to the child, that there is no necessity for hurting, that the world will provide a replacement."[5]

A dog teaches children kindness

For as many acts of kindness as pets teach children there are far too many acts of cruelty practised against animals. In fact, extreme cases are coming to light in high crime areas of American and Canadian cities. The Humane Society of the United States claims it is receiving increasing reports of delinquent teenagers mistreating pets, and in its newsletter the Ontario Humane Society regularly decries the growing incidents of cruelty; inspectors have tripled their investigations from 1965-1975.[6] In 1975 the Framington SPCA in Massachusetts reported that beatings, starvings and other cruel treatment of animals doubled over those of the previous year.[7] Even inflation, that dumping ground for failed dreams, has been blamed as a perpetrator of cruelty to animals. One American humane worker said, "Even people who have a job and make reasonably good money are getting hurt by taxation and inflation. And often they're taking out their frustrations on their animals."[8]

When a child is abused or deprived of love, it is a "normal" pattern of behaviour for the youngster to lash out at the next one in the pecking order, the younger brother or sister, the dog or cat. One psychiatrist said, "It is very hard for a child to respect the needs of an animal if the child feels that nobody considers or cares about his own well being."[9]

In an *Esquire* magazine story about the dog problem in New York, the author, Clark Whelton, related his encounter with a couple of kids in the Bronx:

"If you had come here this morning you could have seen them throw two dogs off the roof," the kid said. "Right up the block from here."

"On One Hundred Forty-ninth Street?"

"No, man, on Fox Street. They got a lot of stray dogs on Fox Street."

"Did you ever throw a dog off the roof?" I asked the kid.

"No, I never did nothing like that."

"Yes, you did, you liar," the second kid said. "You took that dog with the double foot and threw him off the Willis Avenue Bridge. I was there when you did it."

"That's not a roof," the first kid said, smiling.

"That dog went down like a rock," the second kid said. "He tied a big piece of iron around its neck."

"So, that's nothing man," the first kid said. "You know what he does? He takes kite string and ties it around a cat's neck and whirls it around his head like a cowboy's rope. He walks up to you with this cat going around his head in a big circle and the cat begins to piss. It sprays all over you."

"I do not," the second kid said, blushing and smiling...

"Some kids on Walnut Avenue told me that they tie dogs up on the mud flats and let the tide come in and drown them. Is that true?"

"They're all faggots on Walnut Avenue," the first kid said.

A social worker in the area drew attention to the larger issue:

"Of course they didn't tell you why they torture animals," the social worker said. "They don't *know* why they torture animals. But I'll tell you one thing. The people of this city are goddamn lucky that those kids have animals to kill, otherwise they'd be killing more people than they do already."[10]

Although psychiatrists claim there is no consistent profile of the antisocial person, case histories of adult deviants frequently reveal a childhood pattern of cruelty to animals. One study reported in the *American Journal of Psychiatry* (1966) concluded that the childhood triad of enuresis (bed-wetting), fire-setting, and cruelty to animals, was common to three-quarters of the prisoners in the study who had been convicted of violent crimes. One twenty-year-old, charged with beating a man to death, used to catch pigeons and wring their necks or rub turpentine in wounds he inflicted on cats. Another, convicted of assault and armed robbery as a boyhood recreation, poured gasoline on dogs and set them afire.[11]

In the late nineteenth century visitors to the menagerie of the Tower of London could save the price of admission by tossing a live dog, cat or other pet through the bars to lions or tigers.[12] But we civilized folk have instituted laws to punish people for being cruel to animals. After the founding of cruelty to animal societies it took an additional two years in England, nineteen in Canada and forty-three years in the United States to enact laws prohibiting cruelty toward children.* While cases of child abuse are beginning to arouse growing public sympathy publicized cases of cruelty to animals send a shock wave through the community that sets off a deluge of letters, protests, and petitions. If children are not treated with love and respect, what chance do animals have? And if patient parents do not teach children that pets are not objects for abuse, nor are they toys, then the harsh treatment of animals can hardly be surprising.

A dog is a companion for old folks

It is heartening for us to see old folks happy with a dog, cat or canary, except, it is a façade. In the United States, England, and Canada, treatment of the aged is disgraceful. At sixty-five people who have contributed to their countries throughout their lives are discarded with miserable pensions and tucked away in tacky little rooms with no one to really care for them and nothing to fill the long days. Being warmed by the sight of an old person enjoying a dog is a convenient obliteration of

---

*Animal welfare societies often provided the impetus for formation of similar societies for the protection of children. However, there is quite a difference between a society with limited powers and the law of the land. Take, for example, New York, where the SPCA was founded in 1866 and the Society for the Prevention of Cruelty to Children was formed in 1874, yet legislation dealing with cruelty to children was not introduced until 1909 at the White House Conference on the Care of Dependent Children.

the tragedy of how we neglect our senior citizens. Sad to say, their pets are better treated than they are.

Veterinary surgeon Jim Evans, past president of the British Small Animal Veterinary Association, recently said, "I used to think pets were good for old people, now I'm not so sure." He explained that the responsibility, time, and energy spent on pets, in addition to the expense of upkeep, detract from an old person's well-being. It is a known fact that old folks commonly go without in order to feed their pets, and since many have difficulty getting around, a pet adds to their problem. "But I can see the value of budgerigars," he said.[13]

Research undertaken in Lancashire, England, by Dr. Roger Mugford and J.G. M'Comisky, was undertaken to determine what effects either budgies or house plants had on the social attitudes, mental health, and happiness of old people. The authors concluded: "Our overwhelming impression from the study is that the old people in our budgerigar groups had formed a surprisingly intimate (and presumably rewarding) attachment to these unsolicited pet birds. We found on our visits that they had become such a powerful topic for conversation that they could even displace the monotonous awareness and discussions of past and pending medical ailments."[14] [15] A bird in a cage is easy for old people to manage and its upkeep is not a drain on their meagre pensions. A cat or dog, which demands more care, may turn older people into social drop-outs. Stories commonly appear about recluses living in their houses or apartments with dozens of cats, dogs and not a sign of another human. By devoting themselves to pets they have lost touch with people.

A dog is kept only for the "proper" reasons

One of the commonest distortions about pet owning is that the relationship between man and dog is exclusively beneficial, that people keep pets for the "right" or "proper" reasons. Most do, and although some arguments have been presented against pet owning in general, there are those who keep animals for underground uses which the average person finds abhorrent. Into this category fall the dogs kept and trained to fight in the ring and those taught to perform sexual acts with humans.

Fighting dogs

It is estimated by the American Society for the Prevention of Cruelty to Animals that as many as 1,000 organized dogfights are conducted annually in the United States, with the big action taking place in the South. An article in the *New York Times* describes Texas as the dogfight capital and reports, "On any given weekend, up to a dozen fights might be held in and around Dallas, Austin, San Antonio or at other well guarded locations elsewhere in the State."[16] In Canada, Quebec residents have long been known to fight dog against dog, and recently Ontario has been implicated. With a concentration of activities in New England, this makes for a convenient hands-across-the-border exchange program.

Staffordshire Bull Terriers, also called Pit Bulls or Bull Terriers, are the breed of choice for this blood sport. However, "staffs" crossed with Bull Mastifs are bred especially for the ring. As puppies, contenders learn their trade by tearing the heads off kittens. Possessing abundant stamina, and a love of gore, a pit dog may kill as many as 100 kittens or captured stray dogs in the course of its training; nevertheless, there are purists in the business who reject the practice of using live animals and employ only mechanical agitation techniques to develop ferocity. Dogs spend long hours running on a treadmill, developing stamina, and hanging on to suspended grappling bars to toughen jaws and neck. After basic training, one dog is pitted against another so that owners may assess their potentials. These dry runs are halted before either dog is seriously wounded.

At a "convention," as the big, organized dogfights are euphemistically called, the first item of business for promoters is to ensure that the event remains safely under cover. Fights generally take place in barns, stables, back rooms of saloons, cellars, even bedrooms, and the dogs fight to the death.

A fight card may comprise six to ten matched pairs of dogs, with bouts lasting anywhere from twenty minutes to two and a half hours, and ending only when there is a kill, or a dog

27

"curs out." This is a disgraceful situation; a proud owner would prefer his dog to be killed by its opponent. *Harper's* magazine, in an article on dogfighting, reports, "If a dog 'curs out,' that is, if he turns tail and refuses to continue the match, his disappointed master will pull out a .45 and blast the dog in the head."[17] Fight fans paying from $3 to $10 admission consider it natural for dogs to fight and "die gloriously." A dog owner described in a *Times* article the average bet in the big Texas fights as being about $500 and the contests that generate only $5 or $10 bets as "just friendly hometown stuff."[18]

Such friendly hometown entertainment is not new. Romans trained dogs as they did lions to fight in the arena against other animals as well as with out-of-favour humans. At an emperor's accession to the throne, or whenever a conquering army returned, the citizens held a celebration in the amphitheatre where animal fights were a popular part of the fun. One memorable occasion was the return of Trajan from his final victory over the Dacians, an important conquest; he rewarded the cheering throng by holding a festival that lasted over 123 days and it is reported that more than 5,000 animals were killed, many of them dogs.[19]

Bull and bear baiting remained popular spectacles in England from the Middle Ages up until the nineteenth century. In 1822 it was declared illegal as a result of pressure from a group of activists who thereafter founded the Society for the Prevention of Cruelty to Animals. In bull baiting the dog grabbed the bull's nose and tenaciously held on until the victim roared, "which a courageous bull scorns to do," a seventeenth-century writer observed. Specially bred and trained for bull baiting, the Bull dog thus received its name and developed the no-snout face that allows it to breathe while settling in on a bull's nose.

Dogfights were not the exclusive entertainment of the masses. James I was known to be very fond of watching combats between lions and dogs, and long after bull and bear baiting were banned, dogfighting and "ratting" became familiar amusements. Although the engagement between Terriers and rats fighting it out together in pits will never touch the statistical importance of other sports, it must be noted that a top New York ratter in the nineteenth century could dispose of 100 rats in about half an hour, and one gifted contender, "Jack Underhill," polished off 100 in 11.5 minutes in New Jersey.[20] The record holder still appears to be Jacko, who in 1862, took care of 1,000 rats in less than one hour and forty minutes.[21]

To this day you will find in the southern states many grown men and idle boys playing coon-in-the-hole, an action-filled event which involves tying a racoon in a hole and sending three or four dogs after it. The winner is the dog who pulls the racoon out of the hole, by which time the dogs are badly cut up either by the terrorized racoon or by each other.[22]

Dogfighting has been illegal in New York State since 1856 – thirty-three years after England's ban – but as in all clandestine activities insiders keep abreast of events through a cautiously contrived word-of-mouth pyramid system. Previously a good source of dogfighting news in the American underground, newsletters such as *Pit Dog Reports* and *Pit Dogs*, originating in Texas and Florida, were put out of business by congressional investigations held in 1975. This may account for a cooling off of dogfighting in Texas. Also a factor might be the 1975 slaying of two noted dogfight promoters, which has since prompted keener police surveillance of suspected breeders of pit dogs and of places where dog fights are conducted. An Austin, Texas man, active in dogfighting until his dog was mysteriously shot, was quoted as saying that quarrels at fights were common and that he had personally been present when a shooting occurred. An editorial in one of the last issues of *Pit Dogs* denounced the recent shootings and the suspected use of drugs at fights, complaining that such things "were giving dogfighting a bad name."[23]

Party dogs

As students of Kraft-Ebing know, man has had sexual relations with everything from a barnyard hen to a circus giraffe. Ancient Greco-Roman mythologies are replete with human-animal relationships, such as the story of Leda, who cohabited with Zeus in the form of a swan, and the wife of the King of

Crete who loved a bull and produced Minotaurs. Human-animal affairs are not forgotten in world literature. One of the Arabian tales in *A Thousand and One Nights* concerns a girl who falls in love with an ape who kidnaps her. Balzac wrote about a soldier stranded in the desert who had an affair with a panther. And psychiatrist Karl Menninger notes, "Tarzan's love affair and marriage with Jane also must be viewed as a toned-down version of the common ape-woman fantasy."[24]

The extent to which human-animal sexual relations are practised in the twentieth century can only be guessed at. Menninger states, "With so much evidence of positive attachment between human beings and animals, it is perhaps surprising that overt sexual relationships are not more frequent than they are in everyday life. Perhaps they are more frequent than we know."[25] Kinsey reported that the occurrence of bestiality averaged 8 per cent in males, going as high as 17 to 50 per cent for farm boys, and commenting on these figures Menninger suggests that in the life of a farm boy such activity is the rule rather than the exception. Occasionally morality departments of city police forces lay charges of bestiality against stockyard employees, and the odd stag party will be raided and a girl charged with performing indecent acts with a dog, but whether such activities are diminishing, as sexual attitudes of males and females are more relaxed, or whether they go unreported, is unknown.

Dogs offer release for sexual emotions without "going all the way," to use the old high school phrase, through petting and caressing. Rubbing the fur of a dog or cat is sexually gratifying to many persons, some of whom reciprocate by masturbating their dog with about the same nonchalance as picking burrs out of his hair. On the cover of a prurient book entitled, *A Dog in My Bed*, sexual intercourse with dogs is described as the "latest sex fad to sweep the country," and "proof" is offered in a survey which claims that one in every seven adults has tried or will try a sexual act with a dog. A set of statistics, dubiously gathered, records those who first heard of the dog sex act, first tried it, first began marital participation, and first began group participation. It was noted: "Generally speaking, the forty- to fifty-year-olds led the field clear across the board, a clean sweep through the old dog house, you might say."

According to this book, a "party dog" will cost up to $1,500, depending upon the number of sex tricks it is able to perform, and even a low of $500 is a lot since the breeder has to keep and look after the dog for about a year, until it reaches sexual maturity. Training a dog to have sexual intercourse with a woman takes about a month and is conducted with a man and woman, frequently the trainer and his wife, engaging in the sex act while the dog watches, is stimulated, and then encouraged to take over from the husband. In another method, a trained sex dog will perform with a woman – again, the wife or sometimes a prostitute – while the trainee dog watches, until he gets the message. The dog graduates when at the sight of a naked woman in a sexual position, and on command, the dog performs his duties. A training program for fellatio involves a prosthetic penis which, if bitten, ejects a foul-tasting liquid. The book contains some handy hints: putting golf-club covers over the dog's paws to prevent scratching "in moments of extreme canine passion"; how to attract new friends with similar tastes by running an ad in an underground paper or in a daily personal column: "Broad-minded couple enjoys weekends in country with dog, seeks like-minded friends," or "Attractive girl, 27, enjoys men, martinis and dogs"; what to feed the dog to keep his sexual powers revved up; how to select the perfect canine sex partners; and the list goes on.[26]

In her book *The Happy Hooker*, Xaviera Hollander, probably the contemporary world's most famous prostitute, tells of sex with a dog:

> One day as I was lying by the pool thinking I would go ape out of horniness, I became aware of the big German Shepherd lying restless by my side. The dog had embarrassed me the first five days after my arrival by following me everywhere and sniffing at my legs. He apparently had a nose for sex so at this point, where I could no longer be choosy, I decided that—bizarre or not—my first South African lover would have to be him.[27]

A page and a half of explicit detail follows.

The public definition of what perverted is and what is socially acceptable is under constant revision. Only thirty years ago Jane Russell's décolletage in *The Outlaw* was breathtaking; today bare breasts are common on beaches the world over. If Canada is any example, as evidenced in Prime Minister Trudeau's famous remark preceding the changes in the law concerning sexual offences that "the government has no business in the nation's bedrooms," the state may indeed be averting its maidenly eyes from sex acts of one form and another. As history unfolds, what was shocking yesterday is all too often boring today. In seventeenth-century Salem, a man who was discovered "in buggery with a cow, upon the Lord's day," was executed along with the beast.[28] By contrast, news today that a woman is seduced by her Beagle or that a man's dog performs skilful fellatio on him is greeted in some circles with a shrug and a "*chacun à son gout.*" Regardless, the contemporary question of bestiality has many interpreters of the law in a quandary. In December 1977, a New York man was acquitted of the charge of wholesaling two obscene films depicting men in sexual activity with a German Shepherd dog because the jury found the films "too disgusting and repulsive" to fit the legal definition of obscene, which is, in part, to arouse lustful or lascivious desires or thoughts.[29] The laws of justice or morality notwithstanding, it must be remembered that the real victim is the innocent animal, and that of all the simple or complicated reasons for keeping animals as pets, those who keep dogs for the purposes of fighting with other dogs or performing sexual acts with humans are by ordinary community standards the worst exploiters of the dog.

The overwhelming message to come out of the 40,000-year history of the dog as a working partner with man, as an object of worship, and as a pet, is that dogs have served man loyally; at the very least they are harmless creatures and at best they are psychologically important to man. To ask people to think less of dogs, to acknowledge that dogs cause problems, is asking them to denigrate the dog's 40,000 years of loyal service to man. But the fact is, dogs are causing severe social problems, primarily because of the population explosion that has occurred in the canine species. Yet the overpopulation problem fails to arouse the attention it warrants because it is in direct opposition to the established sentiment of the dog as a nearly perfect creature. However, if the dog's status as a pet is to remain intact, the seriousness of the overpopulation problem can no longer be ignored.

3

The Pet Population Explosion

When word leaked out in 1973 that the United States Air Force was testing poisonous gases on 200 Beagles in Nevada, members of Congress received more protest mail than they had over the bombing of North Vietnam.[1] In 1974, the prestigious American Museum of Natural History in New York was caught with its test tubes down, conducting sexually-oriented experiments on seventy-four cats and on unknown numbers in 1975 and 1976, and an animal welfare group launched a mass citizen protest.[2]* Noble protests, one might say, but 13 to 15 million healthy dogs are put to death annually in American

* A concerned New Yorker, Henry Spira, obtained the incriminating information by invoking the newly passed Federal Freedom of Information Act. He then turned over his file to the Society for Animal Rights. In June 1976 they sponsored a series of protest marches against the federally funded experiments – one placard, featuring Felix the Cat, read, "Let my people go" – which continued until the experiments came to their planned conclusion in August 1977.

animal shelters[3] because no one wants them – and who is raising a voice? Compared to the furore over the museum and Air Force tests, barely a whisper is heard from animal crusaders. Do the isolated small cases, the one's and two's, consume the individual's store of expendable conscience, and in so doing defuse the larger issue? Or is it simply that 200 Beagles and seventy-four cats are a comprehensible amount, conjuring up actual images of dewy eyes and soft paws, whereas 15 million dogs is too vast a quantity to have any real meaning? Just as it was difficult to believe that six million Jews were routinely murdered during the Second World War, while eleven athletes slain at the Olympic Games in Munich was hideously perceptible, the public reacts to 200 Beagles but is unstirred over the slaughter of 15 million.

As can be seen on page 45 animal shelters (and veterinarians) spend a very high proportion of their time killing household pets. And for as long as dogs are allowed to proliferate with no controls, and breeders continue to fill pet shops with more puppies, about half of whom will be put to death before their first birthday, the serious overpopulation of dogs can only be dealt with by mass extermination. This fact alone disqualifies us as a society of animal lovers and will continue to do so until the dog population problem is given the priority it now demands.

The Numbers Game

The truism that any set of figures can be woven into either a trifling or horrendous tale depending on the weaver is exemplified by the social worker, who, in applying for a grant to treat 10,000 alcoholics, presents the figure as scandalously high. On the other hand, the politician boasting of his party's achievements in social reform, refers to the same 10,000 figure as a negligible number. Pet population numbers are similarly stretched or minimized to accommodate intent.

On behalf of the pet food industry, market research companies in 1975, using the nuclear family as the base in their surveys, reported from 38 to 42 million American households with a dog, cat, or both, making a total of about 65 million animals, 42 million of which were dogs. With this figure in mind, the Humane Society of the United States estimated the number at 80 to 100 million to include unowned animals. Some public health officials, along with miscellaneous observers, accepted the HSUS figure, then doubled it on the basis of an assumed greater number of stray and feral (domestic animals reverted to a wild state) dogs. Here we have three segments of the community assessing the same situation and arriving at three different sets of figures, 65 million, 80 to 100 million and finally, 200 million, from half to two-thirds of which would be dogs.

For the purposes of the pet food companies it does not matter what the absolute population is, 38 to 42 million are the number who buy commercial pet food for 65 million pets. But what about those dog and cat owners who do not buy commercial food at the local supermarket, owners of farm dogs, the significant number of people who don't trust the purity or nutritional content of commercial food enough for their pets and cook specially for them every day, or the military dogs, dogs in research, and the large number of stray dogs in society? Clearly, the pet food companies' figures cannot be construed as reliable population figures; they denote only the number of pet food purchasers.

The HSUS arrived at its 80 to 100 million figure through breed registration and, ironically, by how many pets were killed in animal shelters (13 to 15 million in the United States in 1975). The ASPCA in New York claims that every year Americans kill 16 per cent of their total pet population, but more commonly it is estimated to be 12 per cent. At 12 per cent of 13 million killed each year, the population would amount to just over 100 million.

To double figures in order to count strays is an admittedly handy though unreliable method of calculation. For example, in Georgia it is estimated there are 300,000 feral dogs and since the Georgia Fulton County SPCA reports the total number of dogs at 720,000,[4] it is easy to see how a double-it rule of thumb might be appropriate there, but wouldn't be reliable in London, where there are few strays, or in Tokyo, where there are many more strays than owned dogs. Taking all this into account, the most convincing pet population figure for the United States is slightly over 100 million, or 50 to 65 million dogs.

In England, however, because there are fewer strays, more licenced dogs, and possibly a more reliable reporting system, the population figures tallied by pet food companies, veterinary associations, the RSPCA, and local authorities, are not at variance with one another. A survey in June 1976 by Audits of Great Britain revealed there were 4.8 million dogs, and it is emphasized that these are owned dogs. Strays undoubtedly make up the difference in the Department of the Environment's Report of the Working Party on Dogs in 1976, which places the number at over 6 million.

The number of dogs in Canada is estimated at about 2.5 to 4 million, as corroborated by humane societies, the Department of Agriculture (through its Health of Animals Branch), and veterinary associations.

One researcher has established that a fairly accurate estimate of the dog population can be obtained by multiplying the number of licenced dogs by 4.5. Using this method of calculation the New York dog population is almost 1.5 million, slightly above the generally accepted figure. Another calculation shows that there is one dog for every seven persons in North America and in Europe. This may be a valid estimation for owned urban dogs, again using New York as an example, with a million dogs and about eight million people.

Regardless of who does the estimating and how much conflict exists in numbers, there is widespread agreement that dogs and cats are breeding at an explosive rate, far beyond that of the human population. In California, the state with the largest canine population, two counties predominantly suburban in character showed a human population increase of 23.5 per cent from 1960 to 1970, while the dog population increased 85.4 per cent. It is as if each new resident brought in 3.5 dogs or, looked at another way, there were seven people to every three dogs,[5] a much higher rate than the estimated seven to one. There is evidence that every year increasingly more families across the United States and Canada own dogs, more dogs are abandoned, more are straying, and still larger numbers are destroyed. To what extent can society tolerate such increases? As the following random facts demonstrate, the pet population has reached a critical point of growth:

- Over half the households in the United States, England and Canada own a dog, cat, or both (59 per cent in Canada, 55 per cent in the U.S. and 50 per cent in the U.K.).[6]
- Dog ownership has increased 39 per cent in the U.K. from 1962 to 1973, 36 per cent in the U.S. from 1964 to 1971, 30 per cent in the Netherlands from 1968 to 1973 and, 23 per cent in France from 1965 to 1973.[7]
- Dogs are fifteen times and cats thirty to forty-five times more prolific than humans.[8]
- In the U.S. 2,000 to 3,500 dogs and cats are born each hour, compared to 415 humans.[9] (This is a conservative estimate; some say it would be up to 10,000 if births of stray, abandoned, and feral dogs were included.)
- In Britain 220,000 dogs are born each month, compared to the human rate of 70,000.[10]

Some English observers claim their dog population is declining. Similar talk can be heard sporadically in the United States and Canada; however, the alleged decreases may be deceptive. For example, in 1973 and 1974, times of galloping inflation, people likely bought less prepared food and supplemented the dog's diet with plate scrapings, which would register a slight decline in the number of pet food sales – although due to increased prices the overall dollar volume rose. Market analysts might interpret this sales decrease as a decline in the dog population. Also, population may be confused with ownership. A British pet food company survey indicated ownership was down 4 per cent from 1973 to 1975, but over a longer period of time, from 1963 to 1975, the number of households owning a pet declined from 50 per cent to 49.5 per cent, a negligible change.[11] It must be born in mind, however, that if great numbers of dogs are abandoned and continue to produce litters, the population may rise even though ownership declines. New York City showed a 10 per cent drop in dog licences purchased in 1974 compared to 1973. This may have been a reflection of the economy, that people felt they could not afford a pet or the licence. The point is, every claim of a decrease in the number of owned dogs seems to be counteracted by reports of increased numbers of stray and feral dogs.

As can be seen, there is a full kit of mathematical tools for tinkering around with pet population figures; but no one knows for certain how many dogs and cats there are because no one has actually counted them. Several American associations, among them the American Veterinary Medical Association and the American Humane Association, lobbied vigorously for the inclusion of pets in the national census for 1970, but were rejected on the basis that adding a new question would mean eliminating an existing one. Nor will they be included in the 1980 census, claims a spokesman from the U.S. Bureau of the Census, on the grounds that pet questions do not qualify as ones that require mandatory answers.[12] Thus, opinion as to how many dogs there are in any given community remains polarized between those, primarily, dog owners and the entire pet industry, who claim all is well within the status quo, and those who see the increasing surplus of pets creating a serious social problem.

The Root of the Problem: Strays, Uncontrolled and Abandoned Dogs

Those on both sides of the pet fence, animal lovers and anti-dog activists, are equally aggravated by stray dogs, yet, it is strays that bring the two sides together in meetings, conferences, and panel discussions, where with exquisite clarity the problems are defined, solutions are put forward, lobbies are organized, everyone is in agreement, intentions are consolidated and that is just where it ends. The stray dog population remains a problem.

In 1975 the English Joint Advisory Committee on Pets in Society (JACOPIS) reported that one in ten people claimed their dogs strayed. (The commonly accepted definition of a stray dog is one who roams freely and has no owner in evidence.) This meant that the dog strayed only once and returned home, or it strayed repeatedly. JACOPIS categorizes loose and lost dogs into temporary or permanent strays and they are a result of:

- Dogs allowed to roam at will and only expected by their owners to return for food and shelter
- Inadequate restraint of bitches in season and dogs with mating instincts
- Failure of owners to ensure that their dogs wear collars with identification at all times

The uncontrolled dog, the most frequent cause of problems, is the most difficult for society to blame because as far as the family who owns him is concerned he is a wonderful, loyal pet. They will admit he has been out all day, but when he returns it is as a loving and loved companion. What the owner does not know, or will not acknowledge, is how much garbage the pet has strewn around, how many kids he has threatened or bitten, how many females in heat he has fertilized, how many droppings he has left on other people's lawns, the stress his barking has imposed on shut-ins, or the near car accidents he has caused. But, as is common knowledge, one of the prerequisites of being a dog owner is to have the unflagging conviction that other dogs create the problems, never one's own.

A permanent stray is defined by the JACOPIS report as an abandoned dog. The report points out that lack of genuine desire by the whole family to own a dog is the reason dogs are abandoned, and this is due to:

- Parents who are indifferent to pets acquiring a puppy as a present for a child
- Puppies given as prizes in, say, competitions
- Pressure by friends and neighbours to take one of their bitch's litter
- Over-zealous re-housing of strays[13]

The number of stray, abandoned or feral dogs can only be estimated.

- The Humane Society of the United States (HSUS) estimates the stray population to be one-quarter to one-half the number of owned pets.[14]
- A Friends of Animals survey of how forty-one cities deal with strays reports there are 25 million stray dogs and cats in American cities.[15]
- A veterinary consultant to the American Humane Association figures that any community of 50,000 people might have from 100 to 300 stray female dogs within its boundaries at any time.[16]
- The ASPCA estimates there are 150,000 strays in New York city alone.[17]
- Local police in England, who are responsible for stray dogs, take in 200,000 annually, but some estimate it as high as one million.[18]
- The *Christian Science Monitor* states that 40 per cent of the total pet population either roam free, are unowned, or are committed to shelters.[19]

The stray dog population is like a thermometer that takes the cultural and moral temperature of a country. Fifty million homeless American dogs registers a low, not-to-worry reading due to the nation's affluence, its easy come, easy go personality, the disposable plastic society that can replace a stereo as casually as it can a dog.

North Americans, wanting to disown a pet, will commonly drive out of town and shoo the dog out of the car on a country road, comforted by the fairy tale that it will get along fine foraging for groundhogs. One of three things happens: the dog starves, it is killed by other predators, or it toughens up and joins in with a pack of feral dogs who roam the countryside killing livestock. Countless large-breed dogs, such as German Shepherds, Doberman Pinschers, Huskies and Collies, purchased by nervous urban dwellers as protection against rising crime, can be detected running at large in almost every large American city, abandoned by people who have lost interest in them or who cannot afford the high cost of maintaining a large dog.

The English, on the other hand, are close to panic-stricken over the prospect of rabies crossing the Channel and this may account for the fact that in Britain a dog on the loose is a call to immediate action. Anthony Carding, a noted British observer of the world's dog problems, reports a very low stray or feral dog population in England and claims there are no strays in Korea, quite possibly because Koreans, like the Chinese and many other Asians, eat dog meat. Carding asserts there are more strays in Japan than anywhere else in the world. In his opinion the Japanese are not emotionally attached to pets, reserving their emotion for families. Hence when a dog strays there is no comradely search, unlike in Britain where friends and neighbours rally round with pluck and determination to find lost pets. The Japanese conclude a lost pet will never return. Carding makes special mention of Kobe, a city surrounded by beautiful hills which are popular picnic grounds where many people abandon pets, expecting they will have enough to eat from picnic remnants. But once the season tapers off and the food supply dwindles dogs seek their way down the hills into the city. Life as a city stray in Japan is short, however, for they are quickly snatched off the streets and shipped to medical research laboratories.

The Society for the Protection of Animals in Paris claims that the French abandon 300,000 pets in August before going on vacation.[20] The situation is worse in Italy. The SPA in Rome estimates that Italians abandon one million pets at vacation time. With the 1974 pet population being about 7.5 million, this represents a staggering one-seventh of the population abandoned in the month of August. Society president Bruno Ghibaudi states, "This is a grave problem in Italy today. Italians tend to take their pets for granted. Often they are acquired only for the children, like a new toy, to keep them happy. The parents have no feeling for the pets. Thus, when vacation season comes, it is a good time to get rid of unwelcome guests because the children's minds are on the holiday." What happens to the one million abandoned pets? "Most of these pets will die," Ghibaudi says. "Many cats and dogs cannot fend for themselves in Italian cities. They are unable to differentiate the city's danger signals and sounds and are run over by cars. Or they can't find food, especially now that most Italians wrap their garbage in plastic bags. Or they are stoned by the *portieri* [doorman], whose job includes keeping hungry animals away from houses, or clubbed by the gardeners who want to protect their gardens from intruders. Those that wander into the countryside run the risk of being shot or poisoned or caught in traps set for beasts of prey. Or they even have been tortured and set on fire by sadists and vandals."[21]

The first American study that perceived stray dogs in ecological terms was conducted by Dr. Alan Beck in Baltimore, the seventh largest city in the United States, in 1971 and 1972. Beck notes that stray dogs have a busy career just being strays. Seeking food is their number one activity and garbage their primary source. They grub about in bags, overturn cans and scatter refuse all over, which attracts flies and rats, and thereupon the garbage becomes a public health hazard. Beck notes that the civic budget squeeze in many U.S. cities may result in a decreasing level of sanitation, which in turn will increase the risk of infection along the disease transmission chain from flies to rats to dogs and cats to humans.

Strays travelling in packs – dogs instinctively associate in packs – generally are a menacing sight, with their hungry, wild-eyed look, scruffy coats, often revealing skin diseases, and their sickly-looking frames. In Pittsburgh, in 1977, an animal welfare society survey reported that in certain parts of the city people were as afraid of being bitten by packs of dogs as they were of being mugged.[22] Jersey City, on launching five dog wardens and vans to pick up the city's estimated 7,000 strays, was urged into action by increased dog bites, garbage litter and health problems caused by dogs, and by complaints that large dogs were harassing elderly people carrying groceries and young children with lunch bags.[23]

A popular activity of male strays is copulating with females in heat, thus ensuring rapid multiplication of their numbers. And whether stray or owned, every dog every day excretes feces and urine on city streets, lawns and parks, which is not only aesthetically insulting to citizens, but a burden on the sanitation system and a source of potential disease.

Dr. Beck discovered that in Baltimore the highest density of the stray population occurs in parts of the city with a rising crime rate, in places where open garbage is commonly located, in vacant fields and rundown parts of the city where derelict buildings provide shelter. It was also determined that people in Baltimore commonly leave pets behind when they move, and a great number of pets are stolen that consequently become strays if they escape or are released. Having a high tolerance for the nuisance caused by dogs, people in poorer areas are disinclined to call authorities to complain and, being unfamiliar with their civil rights, would not know whom to call even if the notion struck them. Presumably the poor relate to homeless animals and sympathize with their hand-to-mouth existence, for in several Baltimore neighbourhoods Beck reports that people regularly feed table scraps to stray dogs – the reason, of course, why strays keep coming round.[24]

A major concern with stray dogs in rural areas is their destruction, or "worrying," as it is sometimes called, of live-stock – particularly sheep. United States farmers are paid $10,000,000 a year in compensation for the damage inflicted by attacking dogs, and it is said that destruction by feral dogs has severely discouraged sheep farming in Scotland.* In Brit-ain a major problem relating to dogs is the number of car accidents they cause, for motorists will prang another car or run into a pedestrian rather than hit a dog on the street.

Having looked at what some stray dogs do, the next ques-tion is, What happens to them? Sooner or later those that survive wind up in animal shelters whereupon they are:

	DOE Report** (6 month period 1974) United Kingdom[25]	1976 New York ASPCA[26]	1976 Toronto Humane Society[27]
Returned to owners	30%	27%	10%
Destroyed	55%	83%	73%
Sold	15%		
Placed in hospital		5%	
Adopted		4%	17%

*See more about the destruction of livestock by dogs on page 124.

**Department of the Environment, Working Committee Report on Dogs, July 1976.

The figures within the "destroyed" column are a shameful indictment against nations who claim to love animals. Even a low of 55 per cent of dogs killed in Britain's shelters is shocking, but what about the 83 per cent in New York and the 73 per cent in Toronto? The Humane Society of the United States estimates that of all animals handled in American animal shelters 75 per cent are destroyed. Contrary to their original intentions private and public animal shelters, along with veterinarians, spend more time killing animals than they do protecting them. They have become dealers in death. And the local municipalities which support public shelters are the subsidizers of this massive extermination of pets. One vet, condemning the amount of killing forced on his profession, said, "The type of people attracted to this work are by nature humane and animal loving, yet they must spend 60 per cent of their time killing what they love."[28]

The horror of the killing of animals by the millions is compounded by the carcasses that remain and become environmental pollutants. What happens to them? People close their eyes to the fact that puppies and kittens are being rendered into soap. No one is quite sure to what extent – there are no trade associations issuing annual reports – but it is one of those known-but-whispered facts that carcasses are sent to rendering plants where they are turned into a number of products, including cattle feed. At the very hint of this recycling, animal welfare groups close in. When Saks in New York offered rugs and spreads for sale, which an animal crusader contended were made of natural dog skin, the company repudiated the charge, insisting they were of wild Chinese coyote purchased from a London company. However, Saks withdrew these rugs as a result of the protest.[29]

A small number of stray dogs received by animal shelters are used in certain types of research and go to veterinary schools for anatomy study. Usually categorized under the heading "Sold" (for approximately $6.00 to $10.00 each), the amount could be anywhere from 10 per cent to 18 per cent of the total animal population in shelters. A director of the Montreal SPCA stated that if they sold animals to research rather than kill them, this would generate an annual revenue of $250,000. However, he emphasized that they refrained from such a venture knowing it would greatly reduce their donations from animal lovers.[30] In pharmaceutical and clinical research studies strays are unsuitable because good results depend on the animals' good health, progeny, and normal behaviour. Also, in the case of strays, scientists have no way of determining whether the condition of the animal is due to breeding or environment. Without knowledge of the dog's history, assessing the results of various tests or surgical procedures is unreliable; thus many animals used for research are purebreds, raised specifically for this purpose.

Regardless of the disposition of stray and abandoned dogs, nice words cannot disguise the disquieting fact that animal shelters are forced to kill vast numbers of animals.

Technicians at the Toronto Humane Society expressed some thoughts about their jobs:

Dot: I don't think I'll ever lose awareness of what I'm doing. I don't think I'll ever reach a point where I don't have feelings for the animals. I'll always know a life was there, and now it's gone under my hands.

Vicki: It's especially hard if it's an animal you especially like. There are so many beautiful animals which must be put to sleep. Sometimes I say to myself, "How can you put so many animals down when you're supposed to love animals?" But, I know it's really for the best. It's better for the animals. But after it's over and I look at the pile, oh, wow, it's disgusting, it's sickening.

Margaret: Sometimes at the euthanasia door, it can really get
(shelter to me. Some days there are just too many. I get to
manager) the point where I've got to save one or two. I'll look for something special – an excuse so I can send them back to the stray room. It might happen twice on a heavy day. Sometimes I have nightmares. I look at them in the piles when it's over. It haunts me. If there is a God in Heaven and I have to justify . . . what then?[31]

4

The Commercial Dog Business

Accepting the fact that millions of dogs in society are put to death annually because they are unwanted animals, the really disturbing question is, How do these millions of animals continue to come into existence? One of the answers is that an ongoing demand is created by breeders and pet shops, which are multi-million dollar industries, and the way they operate is in large part responsible for the dog crisis today. But like any large-scale societal problem, the overpopulation of dogs is a manifestation of a complex series of events. Nevertheless, a solid case *has* been prepared against dog breeders and pet shops. Motivated by profit alone they merchandise puppies by the millions, like living squeeze toys, unaware of or unaffected by the fact that while they are doing so, about half of them are being destroyed annually in American animal shelters because the supply outweighs the demand.

Breeders and pet shops ensure that someone will always ask, "How much is that doggie in the window?" by filling the window with cute little balls of fluff scampering around on young, shaky legs. Caught by the irresistible attraction, and the impressions of a lifetime of fables, stories, books, movies, songs, newspaper photos and television shows depicting animals as exclusively wonderful, the window-shopper brings one of them home. What happens then is predictable. The puppy grows quickly; perhaps it isn't so cute anymore; in fact, it has grown into a nonstop eater, a barker, a furniture chewer, a runaway and the neighbourhood tough. Wanting a puppy not a dog, the family is unable to cope and the creature has a 50 per cent chance of ending up in a pound before its first birthday. Public concern now demands that the tactics of merchandising puppies and kittens be closely examined. Last year in the United States, the sales of pets and accessories in pet shops netted $804,000,000.[1] This represents pet shop sales only. A more realistic estimate of what people spent is nearly $4 billion, and that does not include the cost of pets themselves.* The average price for a puppy with registration papers is $300 in a pet shop, but prices of up to $500 are not uncommon, with as much as $800 being paid for blood that is true blue. Top show dogs may sell for thousands. Although there is big business in show dogs the difference between dog fanciers and dog merchandisers must be emphasized: the former breeds dogs for status, honour, personal recognition, pride, and achievement, while the latter breeds dogs strictly for money.

Puppy Mills and Pet Shops

Puppy millers are defined as breeders who put dogs, purported to be purebreds, on the market, either singly or by the thousands, solely as a means of making a fast buck. In 1976, these breeders made $310 million. Knowing that over half the animals will be put to death, because the supply is greater than the demand, these unconscionable people continue to glut the market with their product. According to the estimate of the Humane Society of the United States, they produced almost two-thirds of the 35 to 50 million puppies born in 1975. Raising dogs for profit is their business, but the puppy mills are starting to raise hackles on an increasing number of

*See Chapter 6 for more details.

citizens. Filth, disease, overcrowding, lack of food and water, and dubious veterinary care, incestuous breeding, and disregard for the animals are words commonly used by outraged animal lovers to describe puppy mills. Most are small operations, breeding from half a dozen to perhaps fifty dogs, although breeders of 150 dogs and more are known, and according to Lee Edwards Benning, author of *The Pet Profiteers*, "... the vast majority aren't even kennels. Instead, they're businesses run by farmwives who have five or more bitches where they used to house a flock of chickens. Instead of gathering the eggs daily, they breed their bitches twice yearly and sell the pups to get the modern-day version of egg money."[2] "Backyard breeders" are described as persons with one or two dogs they breed to supplement their incomes and the *Humane Information Services News* reports countless cases of an individual (inevitably referred to as a housewife) with one bitch, who breeds it every heat season and sells the litters, often at ridiculously inflated prices, until the dog drops dead after five, six, or seven years of this. One woman called her dog, "my little gold mine," and another, reported Benning, reckoned the products of her two English Springer Spaniels helped put her two sons through college.

Out of 5,000 registered breeders in the United States at least ten times that number are unregistered. An article in 1975 in the *National Inquirer* estimated there were 5,000 puppy mills in the country; however, some claim there are 100,000 amateur breeders in active operation.[3] The reason they do not bother obtaining licences is that as hobbyists they may claim breeding expenses on their income tax return. In California the annual loss in licence revenue is $15,000,000; this is based on a survey done by the Humane Information Services which discovered that of the 1,000 breeders advertising in the Los Angeles *Times* over a six-month period, only 100 were licensed. From ads placed over a one-year period, the Humane Information Service calculated that 400,000 puppies had been produced for market in that one state alone – making it easy to believe the estimate that 35 million puppies are born annually in the country.

Puppy mills have destroyed the credibility of breeding in

America by mating dogs every season with brothers and sisters, cousins and nephews, sons and daughters, frequently producing offspring that are deformed, bad-tempered, stupid, ugly, unsocialized, or sick. This lack of concern for genetics is directly responsible for the degeneration of many breeds. In the case of German Shepherds it was indiscriminate dog fanciers who wanted to alter the breed by producing narrow haunches that look good in the show ring. As a result, most German Shepherds bred in North America suffer from hip dysplasia, an arthritic-like condition which starts to impair the dog's movement and becomes very painful by the time the animal reaches five or six years of age. Concerned owners of German Shepherds, and of many other large breed dogs, invest great sums in vets' fees to ease their pet's suffering.

For the most part show dog breeders know how to select dams and sires that produce specific traits and will spend a lifetime improving the breed they are interested in. But puppy mills aren't interested in quality. When good stock is bred with inferior stock, over the generations fine characteristics are bred out and eventually only inferior stock remains. The results may resemble a breed, but the quality is so poor that these dogs cannot even get as far as the parking lot of a show ring.

A pet shop buys puppies with registration papers for an average of $40 to $50, as opposed to one without, which would cost only $9 or $10. (As with any other livestock on the market, these are wholesale prices.) With the fast buck always up front, the first objective of puppy mills is to secure pure-bred registrations, and they have no compunction about manipulating registry rules, breeding ethics, and, in some cases, wittingly or not, even the law, to get their hands on these valuable papers. There are several ways of doing this. One way, probably the most popular, is simply to lie when applying for American Kennel Club (AKC) registrations, by saying the litter is six when it is four. There is seemingly no practical way of checking this.

Another popular deceit in general practice among puppy millers is to acquire an inexpensive but good-looking mongrel pup from here or there and include it among the puppy mill's own stock and apply for AKC registration. Or, a registered female may die and a puppy miller will borrow, usually from a sympathetic relative or neighbour, a bitch of the same breed – regardless of whether or not it has papers – and continue right on breeding.

The age of a puppy is crucial to sales. At four weeks the puppy is barely weaned and much too young to be away from its mother. Nevertheless, breeders and pet shops know the powerful emotional appeal of these little fluff balls, and continue to sell them at this early age. Leaving it longer, a more humane eight to twelve weeks, raises the breeders' costs for keeping them and, more to the point, breeding discrepancies, if they exist, may begin to show up – an obvious impediment to sales. At sixteen weeks, the end of puppyhood, a pet shop is forced to reduce the price by as much as half because the animal is just past the optimum time for training and may suffer from "kennel syndrome," which, due to a lengthy kennel environment, precludes the dog being easily socialized with people.

Unscrupulous breeders who ship puppies at four weeks of age have, reports Benning, their special gimmick. They apply for AKC registration the day the pups are born and since it takes three weeks for processing, time for mail delivery, and allowing possibly a day or two for delay, the papers arrive when the puppies are four weeks old. On the average, 10 per cent of the litter will die, thus the puppy mill is left with a surplus of purebred papers. These are simply attached to other puppies of that breed, regardless of whether they are good or poor stock. Whenever the amount builds up the papers are sold at auctions for a few dollars to other puppy mills or to pet shops.[4]

Any other business that lied about its inventory, cheated in its manufacturing process, misled purchasers about the quality of the product, would soon hear from a regulating government agency. With animals, the jurisdiction is split, in Canada, America, and Britain, among at least three government departments – agriculture, health, and consumer affairs – and as a result one department just moves the ball to another. No one ever scores or defaults, which is the perfect political game as far as pet legislation is concerned.

One ethical breeder estimates that half the papers accompanying puppies sold to pet shops from puppy mills are fraudulent.[5] Litter registrations are the largest source of revenue for the AKC. In 1970, registrations topped a million, and have remained over a million annually since then.[6] In 1975, the AKC derived over $7,000,000 from puppy registrations (one million at $7 each; 84 per cent of their revenue). One wonders whether this income is more urgently needed in their posh Fifth Avenue headquarters in New York – dog fanciers have never been known to shun elegance – as opposed to funding field inspection, which might help curtail breeding abuses.

The Air Transport Association of America informed me in April 1977 that "more than 800,000 dogs and cats and non-human primates,"* are shipped annually by air, "the greater part of which by far are dogs and cats."[7] No standard shipping cartons being available, puppy mills knock together containers less sturdy than lettuce crates (to keep freight rates down) and pack the puppies in, sometimes four or more to a crate. If there is a shortage of cargo space, shipments are frequently detained at the airport, perhaps for a day or two, during which time no provision is made for puppies to be fed or watered. For the flight they may be loaded, unprotected, in the hold, where the temperature can drop to below freezing, they may be crammed together without proper ventilation, or, in cases of small cargoes, may in rough weather, bounce and slide all over the place. Under these conditions puppies often get sick and must endure the journey in their own urine, feces, and vomit. Also, once at the destination there is no guarantee the consignee will pick up his shipment on time, whereupon puppies may swelter in the heat or freeze in the cold, again, without water or food.**

Not everyone has the wherewithal of Lady Beaverbook who guaranteed, by the only sure method, that her Chihuahua and Terrier would not travel in the risky hold; she chartered a plane. For $17,000 an Air Canada DC-8 flew her, her sister,

---

* A parenthetical distinction was made: "(Non-human primates include gorillas, apes, baboons and monkeys.)"

**Since early 1978 numerous rulings are in effect or being processed by various carriers to curtail these abuses.

and the two dogs in family comfort from London across the Atlantic to Halifax; then a smaller jet took the distinguished party directly to Lady Beaverbrook's home in St. Stephen, New Brunswick.[8]

Travelling is a hazard even for healthy puppies, especially young ones. That half the puppies arrive sick, diseased, or dead, is not a surprise. One cannot imagine any other industry sitting still for 50 per cent damaged goods with each shipment; but everyone in the dog business is protected. The breeder doesn't care, he is guaranteed payment by the pet shop whether the puppies arrive dead or alive. In turn, for the pet shop, insurance pays.

On occasion, veterinarians add another link to the chain of abuses: a shop owner and an unscrupulous veterinarian might operate on the arrangement that the veterinarian accepts a phone call from the dealer who says his shipment is healthy, whether it is or not, and the veterinarian signs a health certificate attesting to the fact that the puppies have had their shots and have been wormed. Even if puppies are given the three-way injection against leptospirosis/distemper/hepatitis it is common for the shot not to "take."

For up to sixteen weeks of age puppies are gradually running out of the immunological system transferred from the mother before they are able to develop their own in response to vaccination. During this period there may be a few critical days when the puppy has no maternal immunity and none of its own, and is hence highly susceptible to disease: not only is the shot ineffective at this time but should a hot virus threaten, the puppy dies. One lady bought a Yorkshire Terrier from a pet shop for $350 and it died within twenty-four hours of her bringing it home. A husband and wife who paid $200 for a Terrier had to have it killed after one month due to a severe case of coccidiosis, an intestinal infection that, too, might have been prevented.* Frequently puppies have kennel cough, a respiratory infection that takes two to eight weeks to clear up once the puppy is brought home. Even in meticulous

* Negligence, however, is not always the cause of death; a puppy could be incubating a disease prior to receiving the injection.

kennels up to 100 per cent of newborn puppies may have worms (see tables on pages 151-155), which not only jeopardizes a puppy's health, but that of children as well, especially crawling, thumb-sucking toddlers who may touch a dog's feces and ingest infective larvae, a common route of transmission for *Toxocara canis*.*

Some pet shops seek the customer's confidence by offering a warranty on their merchandise which is intended to protect against inherited sickness or genetic deformities. However, what the purchaser does not realize is that the warranty is worthless; more often than not it expires before breeding abnormalities would have a chance to show up. Furthermore, just as a pediatrician cannot issue a certificate stating a child will not get arthritis or cancer, a veterinarian cannot guarantee a puppy will not contract a disease or grow into a deformed dog.

There is one final act in the breeder/pet-shop travesty. Should a prospective buyer waver, unable to decide on an expensive puppy, the pet-shop dealer saves a powerful sales clincher for the end. He assures the person that by breeding the puppy he or she will recoup the original investment with the first litter, if not make a bundle on successive litters.

Of all the underhanded transactions in the puppy business, this is the most destructive to the species. The backyard breeder creates so many genetic disasters through mismatched and mismated encounters that the puppies are not saleable as purebreds and have to be given away or, if deformed, destroyed. One breeder brought twenty-two freakish puppies to an animal shelter to be put down – all because of careless breeding.[9]

Without question, there are honest people who own pet shops; they give total customer satisfaction and are reputable in every way. Also, that there are marvellous dogs to be had from pet shops is indisputable. A man in the western United States completed American Kennel Club championships with ten dogs purchased from a pet shop. One of America's top Dalmations was bought as a puppy in a pet shop for only

*See more about *Toxocara canis* on page 143.

54

$75.00, and a highly respected Maltese kennel operation began with a puppy right out of a pet shop window.[10] Countless adored pets have a similar origin. However, the case against pet shops and breeders, especially puppy millers, is that they create the demand for pets which they themselves oversupply, and as a consequence contribute in a major way to the over-population of pets. And as long as people succumb to merchandising tactics the industry will continue to glut the market; that is, until concerned citizens and animal welfare organizations demand legislation which will purge the pet industry of some of its disagreeable practices.

5

The Pet Food Industry

It is only a few miles outside of St. Louis, Missouri. A total of
820 green acres of lush, manicured lawns, groves of shade
trees, running streams and immaculate white buildings – the
air of a millionaire's country retreat. To complete the pastoral
scene, a dog occasionally barks. Actually, it is only one of 700
dogs and 700 cats who live in verdant splendour at Gray
Summit, Ralston Purina's research facility for cats and dogs.

As the world's largest manufacturer of pet foods, Ralston
Purina is worth looking into, beyond the green lawns, past the
checkerboard packages, through the feed lots and into the
boardroom.

According to *Advertising Age*, the company's sales in 1976
were $3,393,800,000, an increase of 8 per cent over the pre-
vious year. At the fiscal year ended September 1976 earnings
rose 27 per cent to $125,900,000, the highest in the company's
history.[1] Ralston Purina originated in the 1890s as a health
club with over a million members. Partly as a means of
disseminating founder William H. Danforth's prodigious out-
put of books, poems and plays about good health, and in an
effort to provide a food worthy of the nutrition he preached,
the breakfast cereal Ralston was launched in 1898. In a company biography of Danforth it is suggested the name is

derived from the founder's devotion to *R*egimen, *A*ctivity, *L*ight, *S*trength, *T*emperance, *O*xygen, and *N*ature. Purina was added to indicate the purity of animal feeds and the company was re-named Ralston Purina in 1902.

Spreading its corporate tentacles first and logically to Canada in 1927 the company inaugurated its foreign manufacturing operation in Woodstock, Ontario. Since that time, expansion has reached more than twenty countries, with full manufacturing of pet food under way in Germany, Holland and Japan (as well as Canada).

An R-P employee told me – and probably shouldn't have – that the Pet Food Division accounts for 48 per cent of the company's profit. This does not include the Chow Division, that key aspect of the company which manufactures feed for livestock. The Professional Development Division, through which breeders, veterinarians, kennel operators, and various other professional dog fanciers buy dog and puppy food in twenty-five-, forty-, and fifty-pound bags, is a well-honed organizational machine which offers incentives for those buying bulk lots of five Purina dog food products. To qualify one has to own a minimum of three dogs or breed two dogs at least once a year. The buyer clips coupons at 1,200 points each and redeems them for about $24. The application form addressed, "Dear Professional Dog Influential," details the incentives and notes that over "200,000 dog owners have taken advantage of this money-saving plan."

Research is a special pride for Ralston Purina; through it comes expertise and leadership. At Gray Summit, several hundred persons conduct tests on a dog and cat colony of 1,400. Research on every product considered for production is undertaken for smaller companies contracted through R-P's Research 900 Division. Additionally, as their contribution to agri-business, the company has research farms in Missouri, Oklahoma, and Arkansas.

Ralston Purina consumer products are packaged under the labels Chex breakfast cereals, Chicken of the Sea tuna and Ry-Crisp biscuits. Embracing the corporate philosophy of growth and multiplication, R-P established a chain operation called Jack in the Box, now ranked as one of the ten fast-food chains, recently joined by other restaurant chains – Boar's Head, Hungry Hunter, and Stag and Hound. The company also grows and markets fresh mushrooms. Covered by the heading New Directions, R-P manufactures a full line of raw soy protein products, "some containing up to 95 per cent protein, which can be used for everything from extending meat to stabilizing puddings." Through this division it produces "a wide range of industrial proteins which have extensive applications in the adhesive and coating industries." Recognizing that the worldwide demand for protein is at an all-time high, and will only increase, R-P's Venture Management Division seeks to find more and better forms of protein through restructuring.

Company-employee relations appear to be skilfully managed. In 1970 R-P began Keystone Mountain Resort in Dillon, Colorado, where employees are given 20 per cent off lodging rates at certain times of the year (not in the ski season). Each issue of *Ralston Purina News*, one of a number of in-house publications, carries a human interest story of an employee or of employee clubs, covering how well they are doing at R-P, who won the bowling championship, the softball tournament, results of photographic contests, colour spreads of Checker Day, held every September 30, when employees in R-P offices all over the world dress up with the red and white checkerboard logo emblazoned on shirts, hats, and garters, to play music and dance and generally engage in official company highjinks. House organs keep employees up to date on corporate benevolence, as in the case of R-P's $200,000 grant in 1975 for an inner-city program involving 200 youngsters in St. Louis. R. Hal Dean, chairman of the board and chief executive officer of Ralston Purina, in a 1974 report on the company's contribution to the underprivileged said: "It is not only a matter of assisting others. It is also good business. A policy of corporate social responsibility recognizes the fact that our own business cannot continue to grow to the fullest possible extent if there are large numbers unable to afford to buy our products."[2]

The pet food industry in the United States in 1976 reached almost 3 billion dollars in annual sales. Just another giant, one might say, but when that industry processes six billion pounds of food annually to feed cats and dogs, while one-third of the world starves, one is forced to ask whether our social priorities are in order. A number of questions demand answers: Are pet food companies the real exploiters of pets and pet owners? Are cats truly finicky or is this an ad agency ploy to sell products? Do dogs need variety in their diets or are pet owners manipulated by guilt to try every new brand on the market? For that matter, what actually goes into pet food? Millions of dollars are spent by the leaders of the industry on research; they probably know all there is to know about the nutritional requirements of an eighty-pound German Shepherd, but those same manufacturers also make breakfast foods for humans and demonstrate their lack of concern about human nutrition by making cereals whose chief ingredient is sugar, an empty food that creates lifelong addictions in children and may contribute to health problems in later life, such as obesity, tooth decay, hypoglycemia, and heart disease.

The ethics of advertising must be examined. It is time to assess whether advertising provides pet owners with the knowledge to make brand choices, as its originators maintain, or whether in fact it primarily promotes the desire to own pets in order to keep the industry flourishing. If that is the case, the pet industry is then directly involved in creating an overpopulation of pets. One thing is certain: television commercials contribute directly to the anthropomorphizing of pets by portraying them in human situations, giving dogs and cats humanized names and voices, and by attaching such importance to them that they are elevated beyond the stature of man.

Producing increasing tons of food for pets poses a serious threat to human food supply. One can't help wonder, as do some low-income families at the present time, by 1984, will we all be eating Alpo?

Size of the Industry

A friend of my family always gets a laugh when he tells the story of the time he came home from work and found a hastily scribbled note from his wife, which read: "Darling, I probably won't make it home for dinner. Please fix something for yourself. I've fed the dog." It might be funny to his friends and anyone else who owns a dog, but feeding the dog is definitely no laughing matter for some 500 pet food manufacturers in the United States who, in 1976, rang up $2,900,000,000 in sales. Almost three *billion* dollars. That is as much as the gross national product of Ethiopia.[3] Looking at the industry in tonnage for the fiscal year ending July 1976, 6.2 billion pounds of pet food were produced, or enough to fill 56,000 freight cars.[4]

In actual fact, production is much larger. The figures quoted represent retail sales only, omitting "professional" sales, that enormous volume purchased at feed lots by dog breeders, kennel operators, vets, and for that matter, anyone with three or more dogs. How much this segment of the business would add to the 2.9 billion dollar figure is not known. In addition, no one knows how much is spent by people who buy ordinary meat and fish and eggs for their dogs. Hence, it must be borne in mind that hereafter sales figures denote retail sales of commercial pet food only.

Words used to describe the rate of growth of the pet food industry in recent years suggest the Hollywood movie industry – *colossal! shocking! stupendous! amazing!* In that these words are as fantastic as the billions of dollars and billions of pounds that also define the industry, some perspective may be enlightening:

- People spend 50 per cent more for pet food than for breakfast food.[5]
- In the United States, from 1963 to 1973 pet food sales increased three times as much as food sales.[6]
- From 1972 to 1975, space alloted to pet foods in American supermarkets increased by 20 to 30 per cent.[7]
- In England, people spend six times as much on pet food (in the United States it is seven times the amount) as they do on baby food.[8]
- The dollar volume of the pet food industry is sixteen times as much as is spent on cancer research in the United Kingdom.[9]

- The pet food industry is growing faster than either the computer, electronics or telecommunications industries.[10]

The following table shows the rate of growth, in billions of pounds, from 1963 to 1974 in the United States.[11]

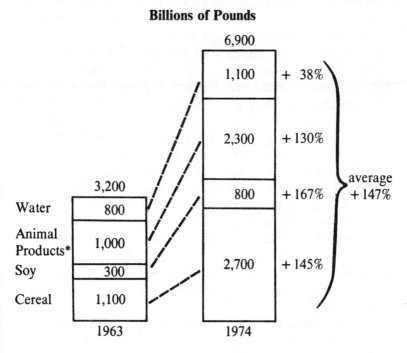

Fig. 1 Pet food industry ingredient usage

*Animal products are defined as meat, poultry, seafood, and their by-products.

What noble service does this giant industry bestow upon mankind? To what extent is it improving society and enriching lives? A growing response is "precious little," followed by a vociferous protest that it is socially unacceptable for billions of dollars to be spent and billions of pounds of food to be consumed by household pets when humans the world over are in competition for that food. Pet food manufacturers have slipped over to join cigarette and liquor companies in the "sensitive product" category and their self-consciousness is beginning to show. When I visited Ralston Purina's head office in St. Louis, the marketing manager asked if I would sign a statement allowing the company the right to approve my text in respect to Ralston Purina references. When I demurred, the marketing man declared that under those circumstances he was unable to discuss marketing with me; the interview terminated forthwith. It is only fair to say that if the situation were reversed I might have been of the same mind. The incident is related only to provide an example of the wariness encountered within the pet food industry of the United States, Canada and England. General Foods in Canada refused to see me, and in England one company neglected to send information it had promised in an interview; another demanded anonymity. As for Ralston Purina, which enjoys the largest share of the market in the United States, a whopping 31.6 per cent in 1977, with Carnation its nearest rival at a distant 11.5 per cent, and General Foods and Quaker Oats at about 10 per cent each, it is quite understandable that the company seals its corporate lips against prying interlopers. They are not number one by chance. Consequently, only some figures quoted in this chapter are supplied by manufacturers themselves. Most of the statistics are from trade publications, advertising agencies and associations, market research companies, the Pet Food Institute in the United States, and the Pet Food Manufacturers' Association in both England and Canada which represent about 95 per cent of the pet food manufacturing companies in those countries.

Development of the Industry

In the 1930s and forties, the manufacture of food for dogs and cats was just another business. At that time pet food was either packaged meal – kibbles, as it was called – made largely from grain combined with meat or fish, or it was canned food made from meat.

After the Second World War advertising tweaked the sleeping giant awake and in the early 1960s, with the introduction of no-muss, no-fuss convenience dog and cat foods, the new-born industry's whimper fast became a thundering roar. Luxury or gourmet foods, as they are called, were added and neither economic recession nor trebled prices muffled their clamour one decibel. In fact, at the height of the American recession in 1975, pet food sales increased 8 per cent with a 15 per cent increase the previous year, while orange juice dropped one percentage point. That the American people will drop orange juice one per cent and increase pet food 8 per cent is an interesting revelation of priorities.

Dry pet food

The first milestone in the industry occurred just after the Second World War, with the improved processing of soy products. A new extraction method, which separated the oil from soy meal, heightening the palatability of both products, marked the beginning of the industry's phenomenal upward spiral. Sales of dry pet food zoomed. It was inexpensive, easy to store and serve, and consumers had been promised it was nutritious. Made into meal, chunks or biscuits, in short order Purina Dog Chow, Chuck Wagon, Gravy Train, and Friskies became household words.

Canned pet food

The all-meat binge was started by a man named Robert F. Hunsicker, who during the Depression shopped around for a business in order "to make a buck." Dog food was his choice. He made another decision right then and there, which ultimately generated millions of dollars for him, to manufacture an all-meat product. The product? Alpo.[12]

In the early fifties ingredients for meat products began to change. Previously, horsemeat was used, but around this time the wild horse population started showing signs of depletion and with an ecological awakening and a rising repugnance against the consumption of horsemeat by either man or animal, manufacturers were compelled to switch to beef, sheep, pig, and lamb meat. Simultaneously, additional markets opened up that provided protein for pet food from whale meat,* tuna, herring, and poultry.

In 1964 Liggett and Myers, a multi-million-dollar company, bought out Alpo, and with the same expertise that made them product leaders in cigarettes, L & M pounded away with Alpo in a hard-sell campaign. It worked. Today Alpo is the largest-selling canned dog food in the U.S., with total sales in 1976 at $145,000,000, well ahead of its nearest competitor, Ken-L Ration (made by Quaker Oats), at $90,000,000.

Another pivotal point in the pet food business occurred in 1962 when a set of guidelines established by a Nutrient Requirement Subcommittee of the National Research Council specified formulation requirements and the type of product claims that could be made. It is difficult to say if the pet food manufacturers grasped the significance of this legislation at the time, but they were very much aware of the ramifications. It shifted the advertising pitch to nutrition. In a frantic attempt to out-nutrition each other, manufacturers besieged consumers to buy products of "complete nutrition," those which were "completely balanced," all of them touting "high protein." "My-stuff-is-better-than-your-stuff," the game no one can beat the Americans at, was under way with a vengeance.

Semi-moist pet food

According to industry spokesmen, introduction of semi-moist food, also called "soft moist," in the early 1970s turned the pet food business around. With the habit of convenience foods firmly ingrained in the North American psyche, it is not surprising that people grabbed at convenience foods for dogs. The quick acceptance of semi-moist pet food products is reflected in the astonishing sales figures: semi-moist food in the United States doubled in volume from 1972 to 1975. And

*Due to the public outcry in the early seventies against killing whales, the pet food industry has discontinued its use of whale meat.

small wonder. The pet owner simply snips open a packet and dumps the crumbly stuff into the cat's or dog's dish without it even touching the hands. No can to open, nothing to add, you don't even need a spoon.

Luxury, gourmet, specialty foods

Just as humans want to exchange hamburger for filet mignon now and then, pet food companies have convinced dog and cat owners that their pets want – correction, *deserve* – gastronomical favours as well; hence the development of what the industry calls its "luxury" or "gourmet" division. Upgrading the basic beef and liver flavours in pet foods relates directly to a growing familiarity with exotic foods and wines. Gourmet foods are no longer monopolized by the upper class, whether for humans or for dogs and cats. Any old alley cat can savour the twenty-two flavours of cat food offered in Variety Menu, a luxury canned cat food made by Quaker Oats.

Treats

Most pet food manufacturers make a line of "treats." If a kid comes home from school and tucks into a peanut butter sandwich, why can't the dog have a treat too? Gaines Biscuit and Bits, which has enjoyed the lion's share of the market up until 1976, has been challenged by the Liggett Group, previously a solo entry along with Alpo, and at present introducing doggie cookies, Liv-A-Snaps, Beef-Snaps, Char-O-Snaps and Chik-N-Snaps. Offering "good fun" for the dog, it took R.T. French's, the mustard people, to come up with a dog biscuit called People Crackers, shaped like postmen and dog catchers. The package copy suggests: "Give your pet a little somebody between meals! Mailmen, milkmen, policemen, dog catchers, burglars . . . the people dogs go for."

The following table shows the changing trends in types of products used in the pet food industry from 1963 to 1974 in the United States.

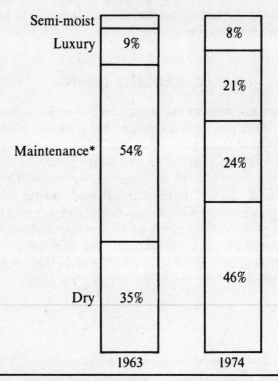

% Pound Sales

	1963	1974
Semi-moist		8%
Luxury	9%	21%
Maintenance*	54%	24%
Dry	35%	46%

Fig. 2 Pet food industry composition

Humanized Pet Foods

Remember those commercials in the 1960s that had the lady pouring water into the dog dish and gushing, "Makes its own gravy!" Obviously this product had little to do with the dog's preference; it was directed at the owner who probably felt a glow every time he or she served Gravy Train, quite like feeding the family a robust stew on a cold day. The association was straightforward – husbands and kids love stewy things, why shouldn't the dog?

*Canned pet food

And what average middle American family doesn't regard the hamburger as a fixed dinner-time feature? Precisely the thinking behind General Food's introducing Gaines Burgers for dogs. But G.F. went a step further with Top Choice Burgers by claiming they were even better than hamburgers. The commercial promised, "It also has all the vitamins, minerals and protein for the one-hundred-per-cent nutrition hamburger doesn't have." The company presumed people want their dogs to enjoy better quality hamburger than they themselves do.

Products of the Future

In the November 1976 issue of *The New Yorker* magazine an article examined the pet food industry's marketing and advertising tactics, quoting a motivational research study done for Liggett and Myers-Perk Foods Ltd. (the Alpo folks), which speculates on products of the future: "As people love their dogs more, placate and coddle them more and more, spend more money on them, vest their egos in their dogs, there is no reason why additional new product factors cannot be introduced to dog food buyers." Among suggested new product factors were "casseroles, meat loaf, chicken and dumplings, hot dogs, hash and snacks." The researchers even discussed such possibilities as "canned meat balls *au jus* or canned burgers with bouillon sauce."[14]

Among the major pet food manufacturers there is unanimous agreement that the market is heading toward the further specialization and humanization of foods. Already there are specialty products for obese dogs,* and in the near future there will be products for pregnant dogs, working dogs, lazy dogs, for even more finicky cats, and specialty foods containing contraceptives (see more about this on page 187) and since most owners do not know how to give a dog a pill, foods will also contain certain types of drugs. More research will be devoted to developing the most palatable foods for dogs and cats; and packaging of these new products will be another area for continued spending. In the case of semi-moist prod-

*Fit & Trim by Ralston Purina and Cycle 3 by General Foods.

ucts, packaging is important to shelf life. The pet food industry, forced to recognize the public hostility to city streets covered with dog droppings, is now researching the feasibility of low-residue foods, devised to produce fewer feces.

It must be stressed, none of these new product developments makes nice guys out of the manufacturers; their major concern is to sell goods.

The Psychology of Feeding

For the past 40,000 years dogs have been tossed man's scraps and now that pet food manufacturers have discovered the emotionalism connected to feeding pets, these animals have a three-billion-dollar industry cooking dinner for them.

Psychologists have plenty of things to say about why people feed animals in the manner they do and, not surprisingly, pet food manufacturers listen. It is essential for manufacturers to understand people's attitudes toward their pets, otherwise how would they devise products and convey messages to manipulate the consumer's thoughts and emotions? This is precisely why the top companies spend millions of dollars on market research studies and fiercely guard their findings. One study undertaken for the Pet Food Institute was issued to its members in a numbered, limited edition and bore on the cover a printed warning that no one was to have access without permission.*

Guilt plays a major role in the consumer's vulnerability to sales pitches. A pet owner might feel guilty about leaving the dog at home all day, not coming home on time and letting the dog go hungry, chasing him off the sofa, sending him out in the rain to urinate, even having a dog in the city where there is not enough room to run. Unlimited circumstances exist for producing guilt. Never losing sight of this possibility pet food manufacturers incessantly urge owners to indulge their dogs and cats, in other words, giving them a chance to ease their guilt. A Dr. Ballard's commercial ends with, "Feed your dog

---

* I obtained the required permission to see this study.

Dr. Ballard's Beef Stew. Isn't he worth it?" What dog owner is going to snort, "No!"

According to one executive in the pet food industry, a woman will buy moist dog food because it satisfies her need to treat the dog and, at the same time, to indulge herself; it is easier than opening a can. The advertising never suggests that she is serving a convenience food. "What you have to say in your advertising, in effect," the ad man reports, "is that even though it's convenient your dog will never know it. In a perfect world you could tell that woman about the advantages of the soft, moist product, how simple it is to open up out of the cellophane pouch, how simple it is to throw the pouch away without her hands ever touching the pet food. But you don't. It's absurd, I admit – does the dog know whether it's convenient or not? Yet there's that little feeling of guilt to reckon with – that the woman feels she isn't doing the very best thing."[15]*

Because owners feel inadequate serving the same thing day after day they are compelled to try new brands, just as they try new products for their families. But the fact is, regardless of the brand, the dog will eat it day after day, year after year, often times even if it has gone bad. A dog is one of the most indiscriminate eaters in the animal kingdom and as a consequence throws up a lot, which is where the expression "sick as a dog" comes from. One commercial tells viewers that dogs like liver, another says they like beef, yet another has them wild over cheese – the overall message is that dogs like variety. There is absolutely no proof of this. Dogs bolt their food down; they do not have time to taste it. Clearly, variety is for the owners.

Unquestionably, people overfeed their dogs, which has led to the introduction of special foods for obese dogs. A survey done for Ralston Purina in 1975 revealed that 41 per cent of the respondents claimed their dogs were overweight, which probably matches the human situation. A fat man has a fat dog, or as portly Canadian painter Albert Franck used to say

*Since that article was printed, one manufacturer bit the bullet and announced his product was convenient.

about his lumpy Labrador, "A cricket should never lead an elephant."[16] Specific feeding instructions are printed on the label but even those who bother to read labels do not necessarily comply. People eat three times a day and because of a lifetime of propaganda impressing everyone with how human dogs and cats are, people will feed their pets three times a day, too. Although contra-indicated in pet food commercials dogs really are different from people and they require only one feeding a day.

Pet food manufacturers apply a psychological game to feeding. Since dogs are colour-blind, what difference does it make to them if their food is brown, red, or purple? But manufacturers believe *people* feel better giving their pets "hamburger" that looks like real meat; hence, most canned food is coloured red even though, as some labels may indicate, very often water is the second biggest volume ingredient in some canned dog food. With Gaines Burgers, for example, blatantly humanized in name, shape, and size, the colour is psychologically critical. Not juicy enough to be mistaken for minced sirloin steak, it is a dull brick red, just red enough to resemble meat yet not appetizing enough for humans to toss it on the barbecue. What could be more typically American than sharing the ubiquitous hamburger with the dog? Again, it harks back to guilt: feed the dog what you eat and it will appease whatever guilt you feel about your dog. Not to limit its market possibilities, General Foods also makes cheeseburgers for those dogs which need a change of pace from plain hamburger. They launched the product with a multi-million-dollar ad campaign, telling viewers how much dogs like cheese. Their commercials are misleading for although they exhort the advantages of cheese for dogs, they don't put a speck of actual cheese in the cheeseburger. What look like cheese are actually bits of orange-coloured cereal with artificial cheese flavouring, as the label clearly shows.

There is a definite cultural implication in pet feeding patterns. Sales of commercial pet food in France, Italy, and French Canada, range from low to non-existent. In a pet food survey conducted in Canada in 1974, it was revealed that 38 per cent of French people in Quebec own one or more pets, compared to the survey's national average of 59 per cent, and feeding differences are even more marked. Fifty-two per cent of the respondents in Ontario buy commercial dog food; the figure for French people in Quebec is a mere 4 per cent. In almost every question concerning pet feeding the survey cautioned against using the figures for French Canada due to the small base.[17]

Differences between Latin and Anglo-Saxon temperaments may be the explanation for differences in attitudes toward feeding between these two groups. The Latin, typically emotional and effusive, has more regular release of his feelings. He rages and laughs and loves with ease, unlike the Anglo-Saxon, who characteristically suppresses emotions. The Latin does not need a pet as an object on which to lavish emotion. He has a more practical conception of pets; the dog is an animal not a member of the family, he belongs outside not inside, coddled on a silk cushion by the fire, and scraps from the table are good enough for him. Rather than spend money on dog food the Frenchman would prefer to buy himself a new coat or a new pair of skis, something which gives him instant gratification and status. Quite the reverse of Anglo-Saxons whose dogs, like their old school ties or new cars, are status enough.

There are no easier customers than cat owners for they have been pre-sold at every turn by being told that cats are finicky. Morris, portrayed in a blasé, effeminate voice-over in the commercials, is the archetypal finicky cat who doesn't like this and doesn't like that. He turns up his nose at all food and ambles away except, that is, when 9 Lives is offered. This he eagerly devours. With sales of $113 million – 23 per cent of the canned cat food market – Morris alone has done more for sales than all other ad campaigns put together, if only to persuade the viewer to get a cat in order to enjoy its finickiness.

Cats are more discerning eaters than dogs, but definitely not as finicky as the commercials imply. As a matter of fact, veterinarians say that the natural eating cycle of a cat is to be occasionally picky, eating very little on any given day or two.

However, manufacturers have convinced cat owners that this means dissatisfaction with the present food. The concerned owner rushes out and buys a new brand, by which time the cat is restored to his normal eating pattern and would doubtless eat whatever is placed in his dish. The owner presumes he fancies the new product, and continues to buy it, until the cat enters his next stop-and-go feeding cycle.

Pet food is a unique product in that the purchaser is not the user. To determine how good it is you have to depend on someone else's word every time – the manufacturer's. If the dog or cat doesn't like a particular brand or, more aptly, has trained his owner to think he doesn't like it, then you are at the mercy of advertising when making another choice, which doesn't help you much, since all advertisers tell you your pet will like their stuff.

Formulation

What are all those wonderful flavours that drive the dog into a tail-wagging frenzy? Meat? Bones? Fat? Marzipan? Essence of postman's leg? No one can say for certain what dogs like because, as already mentioned, they will eat anything. Without doubt, taste and flavour are formulated to please the pet owner; he or she feels a little better about serving a dish of ghastly-looking guck if it smells appetizing. Thus, dog food is flavoured with familiar spices and salt, garlic, and onions.

What the product is actually made of is something else. Sweden and the United States are the only two countries which have legislated minimal nutritional standards for pet foods. American manufacturers formulate pet foods by following the Protocols of the National Research Council (NRC), which require that should the label specify, made with "meat by-products," those by-products can only be "non-rendered, clean, wholesome parts of the carcass of slaughtered mammals, such as lungs, livers, spleens, kidneys, brains, stomach and intestines, free from their contents; but must not include skin, horns, teeth, and hooves." Blood and bone may be included. If by-products are derived from animals other than cattle, swine, sheep, and goats, they must be specified on the

72

label. Horsemeat or whale meat, for example, would have to be identified as such.

Poultry by-products are similarly regulated, consisting of non-rendered, clean parts of carcasses of slaughtered poultry, such as head, feet and viscera, free from fecal content and foreign matter, "except in such trace amounts as may occur unavoidably in good factory practices."

Although not obliged to by law, generally speaking, Canadian pet food manufacturers adhere to the American NRC Protocols. The British Meat (Sterilization) Regulations passed in 1969, decreed that all meat, whether obtained from "knackers, condemned by abbatoirs, or imported, must be sterilized," and the Pet Food Manufacturers' Association in England reports that since that time the majority of British manufacturers have, like Canadians, abided by the American Protocols. The Canadian Veterinary Medical Association (CVMA), in conjunction with a community college Animal Care program, is currently analyzing Canadian pet foods, and director, S.N. Ward concludes, "most Canadian pet foods are pretty good."[18] The ones which are not – those available on sale for twelve cents a can, some private brand labels, and occasionally small, local packing-house operations – disqualify because lab analysis reveals raw materials such as hides, hooves, hair, teeth, stomach contents, and, who knows, perhaps even old work boots. And that is the point. No one knows where some companies obtain their raw materials. To date, only one Canadian company, Standard Brands, which manufactures Dr. Ballard's pet foods, has passed the nutritional test and its products bear the notation, "As certified by the Canadian Veterinary Medical Association." Curiously, Dr. Ballard's has failed to give this certification top billing in its advertising. When the country's national veterinary association demonstrates its concern for the health of animals by developing minimal nutritional guidelines for pet food and only one manufacturer adopts them, one wonders why. Ward claims that it costs an additional four cents a case for a manufacturer to adopt the CVMA formulation standards, that is, one-sixth of a cent per can.

The ultimate question is, How good are commercial dog foods? Are you feeding your dog cans of hides and hooves, teeth and hair? Short of laboratory analysis you cannot be 100 per cent certain. Although reputable manufacturers' products are fairly dependable as to ingredients, the processing may combine additives which are destructive. For example, fish catches are frequently treated with antibiotics prior to shipment to the cannery, and over a period of time of ingesting it, the cat or dog may suffer deleterious effects. But then, that is the risk people take eating some processed foods.

Manufacturers argue that only quality raw materials are used in their pet foods; if they weren't the dog wouldn't like the product, and the owner wouldn't buy it again. Not so. A can of food made entirely of decomposed meat may have a processed smell that the dog happens to love. It will no doubt be inexpensive – products of dubious content usually are – and the owner will continue to buy it as long as the dog continues to eat it.

Many veterinarians say that one of the biggest problems they encounter in household pets is malnutrition. The trouble is, even dogs fed expensive commercial food suffer from malnutrition because it may lack the proper balance of nutrients. The commonest feeding fallacy is that dogs need only meat. That is like saying a person can be healthy eating only steak. A dog fed exclusively on a meat diet will soon develop an offensive odour, diarrhea, and bloating, and in time he may succumb to uremic poisoning due to kidney malfunction. Canned dog food must include grains in order to provide a balance of proteins, carbohydrates, vitamins, and minerals. Cans labelled "balanced" or "complete" contain meat and cereal products, giving the dog nutrients that do not need to be supplemented.

There is no nutritional value in water and until the Federal Trade Commission (FTC) recently curtailed such practices, many brands of canned pet food contained more water than any other ingredient. Previously the words "water sufficient for processing" were added at the end of the ingredient list on the label and despite a tough fight the pet food industry failed to impede a ruling by the FTC in June 1977, which stipulated that water must be shown as a regular ingredient. Since ingredients are required to be labelled in descending order, a can of "all-meat" dog food which listed water first (and many would prior to FTC intervention) is not very attractive to the consumer knowing he or she is paying the same amount per pound for water as for other ingredients.

Hip dysplasia and other bone irregularities heretofore considered genetic are being reviewed by researchers, suspicious that improper diet may also be a contributing factor. But answers are a long way off. Many pet food companies are spending more money in researching how their products will outsell their competitors' than in investigating the digestive system of the dog. Funding sources, namely governments, are too overburdened by cancer and heart research to allot money to the health problems of household pets, which is as it should be.

The following table shows the shift in ingredients used in pet foods from 1963 to 1974 in the United States.[19]

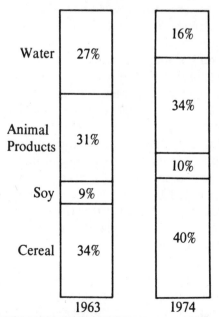

% Ingredients

Fig. 3 Average percentage of pet food ingredients used in canned, moist and dry foods.

Research

Of course manufacturers will not say how much they spend on research, but Quaker Oats, Ralston Purina and General Foods all have vast, multi-million-dollar research facilities, staffed by several hundred persons. Quaker Oats, for one, houses hundreds of dogs and cats in air-conditioned splendour in a country estate occupying 600 acres in Barrington, Illinois. As already pointed out, Gray Summit, Missouri, is the 820-acre nerve centre of Ralston Purina's Pet Care Centre, the world's largest research facility for pet nutrition and research. Bob Mohrman, Senior Manager of R-P's Pet Nutrition and Care Research Department, talked about this end of the business.[20]

Nutritional research is conducted with fourteen breeds of dogs, ranging in size from five-pound Chihuahuas to 150-pound St. Bernards. About 700 dogs are used for experiments at all times. Only purebreds are used because their correct appearance, bone structure, conformation, and general body condition, as established by the American Kennel Club, become the standards for how breeds should be progressing during tests. About 700 domestic shorthairs, Persians, and Siamese, are used to test cat food.

Every Ralston Purina product is tested first of all for palatability, its effects on breeding, growth, and digestion, and how it performs as a maintenance diet. No matter what, the dog or cat must like the food enough to eat it repeatedly. In palatability tests two groups of dogs eat two types of food – one is the control product, Purina Dog Chow, which the company knows dogs like, the other is the new product. Amounts of food left are measured after each feeding, and once four or five days have elapsed a total is taken. If the dogs ate all of Product X each time, obviously they liked it. If not, it's back to the drawing board. To be palatable several things must pass the dogs' approval. The product has to be the right size for biting, the right texture, flavour need be only generally enticing, and can be improved by adding flavour boosters such as onions, spices, herbs, cheese flavouring, salt; it must have an approved "mouth feel," as the industry calls it, and strike the right balance between moisture and dryness.

Once palatability is established the next testing stage is digestibility. Dogs' droppings resulting from the new product are examined for net utilization of nutrients and checked for volume, firmness or looseness. Ideally they are firm and as small in volume as possible. These droppings are measured against those in the control group being fed Purina Dog Chow.

Reproduction tests are next. Again, with the desirable results of the control group for comparison, dogs are bred and numerous factors are studied: the number of offspring produced, their mortality rate, body weight gain, general body appearance and condition, blood chemistry, food intake and how offspring, when weaned, develop on Product X. Throughout gestation and lactation the bitch is examined for body weight gain, quality of milk, and blood chemistry.

Product X is then tested for its growth potential. Puppies from six to sixteen weeks, studied over a ten-week period, are carefully examined for body weight and length gains, for food consumption, general body condition, and blood serum values.

The final test for Product X is maintenance: How healthy does the dog remain? Adult dogs are watched over long-term periods during normal activity in the kennel environment. (Growing, pregnant, lactating, or working dogs are excluded.) Growth tests are monitored over time and additional studies may be made, for example, on the dogs' coats. This is done by cutting a portion of the dog's hair at the onset of feeding with Product X, then comparing the new hair growth to the pre-Product X coat, studying the diameter of hair shafts, rate of hair growth, and sheen. Condition of teeth, gums, and claws are also noted.

In spite of the millions of dollars spent on nutrition research, a Ralston Purina brochure informs, "Our research does not stop here. New products are given in-home tests in randomly selected consumer households before final production begins."

Mohrman reported that it takes an average of twelve to eighteen months from the time a product is conceived until it reaches the market. A notable exception, Tender Vittles, was almost seven years in the making.

Semi-moist foods for dogs, such as Gaines Burgers, were introduced in the early sixties and enjoyed immediate acceptance by consumers, but General Foods, Nabisco, and Quaker Oats all failed to match this success of semi-moist food products for dogs with a similar product for cats. Ralston Purina entered the picture in the mid-sixties and company spokesman Ron Filer explained, "Our main problem was finding a product that would remain stable and that cats would like. Above a certain moisture content bacteria and molds develop. By 1968 we had a product that was bacteriologically stable, but it wasn't palatable enough. Then we came up with a promising preservation method which also helped the palatability." All told, more than 100 palatability tests were done on 2,000 cats.[21] Tender Vittles landed on the supermarket shelves in 1971 and however many millions of dollars this product cost to develop, it was obviously worth while for, by 1975, it had two-thirds of the market sewn up. Sales for Tender Vittles that year were $67,000,000. Quaker Oats' entry in this product category, Moist Meals, lagged far behind at $12,000,000.

It would be heartening to imagine manufacturers of human food spending seven years and millions of dollars developing each new soup or cereal. Why would they, when a cat food brings in $67,000,000 in annual sales? Research money and talent in the human food industry is devoted to market research. The mechanics or selling and distribution, testing the name, package, commercials, and ads to determine consumer response, are major concerns, not how the product tastes or, god forbid, how nutritious it is.

Advertising

In the United States pet food manufacturers spent $170,000,000 on advertising in 1976.* But to accept this as the actual figure is like quoting a mortgage payment as one's total housing expense; a realistic picture includes taxes, heat, light, water, maintenance, etc. The true cost of advertising must

*Whenever figures are quoted for advertising spent they usually denote "placed" advertising, that which appears in print, on radio or on television.

include promotion, public relations, marketing, packaging, professional services, education – there are numerous subheadings under which spreading the company word can be grouped. Hence, the $170,000,000 could conceivably be doubled when taking into account media cocktail parties, market sampling, sponsorship of dog shows, film-making, audio-visual presentations, publishing brochures, and the countless related activities all the major pet food manufacturers are engaged in to promote their products.

The "big spender," by a long shot, Ralston Purina, poured $60,000,000 into pet food advertising in 1976 (out of a total advertising budget of $88,000,000), ranking the company fifteenth out of the nation's one hundred leaders in media expenditures. In second place, in pet food advertising, at about half as much, is General Foods, with $32,000,000, although they led the field with the largest amount spent on a single product – $11,000,000 for Cycle Canned Dog Food, slightly ahead of R-P's number-one brand, Purina Dog Chow, at $10,000,000. Next, Alpo Canned Dog Food with $8,000,000, then Gaines Burgers (General Foods) at just over $6,000,000, followed closely by R-P's Purina Meow Mix cat food at about $6,000,000. These advertising expenditures are distributed among six media – magazines, newspaper supplements, network radio, outdoor billboards, spot, and network television – with 90 per cent going into television. The overwhelming reason why? – television delivers.

Market research studies show that from two-thirds to three-quarters of pet food buyers have heard about the product they are currently buying from television. The second most powerful sales instrument is the package itself. Probably no other consumer product has as much time, money, and as many resources poured into it as the package design for pet food. In the United States, England, and Canada spokesmen for pet food manufacturers were asked how much their respective companies spent on packaging, and without exception they smiled complacently and shook their heads. Each conceded it was "a lot" and one man exclaimed it was a "fantastic amount of money." The marketing manager in a pet food company's advertising agency, who emphasized he wished to remain anonymous, declared, "There are very few products where advertising and packaging create all the consumer interest, and in the case of pet food, you cannot stress too strongly the importance of packaging."

Advertising agencies discovered a long time ago that if you do not have a dazzling product you hire a dazzling spokesman to endorse it, that the celebrity with a stake in stardom, money, sex appeal, or sports, has the ability to transfer something of his famous quality to the viewer. Presented with Product X in a commercial, the consumer will later subliminally be reminded of the celebrity and, for a moment at least, will associate personally with all the stardom, money, and sex appeal of the superstar pitchman.

Ralston Purina had an early lead in the celebrity parade in 1933, when they used movie star cowboy Tom Mix to endorse their breakfast cereal, Hot Ralston. In 1976, Catfish Hunter was featured in ads, posing with four of his (then) forty-four dogs, extolling the virtues of Purina Dog Chow. A guy who is paid a million dollars to play major league baseball is an obvious winner, so if Brand X is good enough for a successful (money) jock (professional athlete) with macho (moustache and big dogs), it's got to be good enough for me, the average viewer deduces. For more than ten years television's best-known second banana, Ed McMahon, has been touting Alpo on the "Tonight Show." He is the perfect pitchman for this product. Since Johnny Carson projects a different image, big old reliable Ed is like a favourite uncle telling you in a no-nonsense, authoritative way to go out and buy the stuff.

In television commercials a woman is invariably the pet feeder. This neatly replicates the human situation, in which the children and husband all want the dog but the mother ends up with the responsibility. One Canadian ad man flatly stated that his agency's commercials are never directed to anyone but women.

Other than breeders or kennel operators, the majority of owners buy pet food at supermarkets. In fact, pet food accounts for more than 1.6 per cent of total supermarket sales.[22] Since the display space in American supermarkets averages 170 linear feet, which approximates from the end zone in a football field to the centre stripe, the person encountering such an expansive array has come to rely slavishly on television messages for help in making decisions. But rather than selecting product benefits the consumer has fallen victim to the commercials' gimmicks, he or she has been swayed by Morris the cat, by the chuck wagon, the darling puppies, the celebrity, and so on.

In their zeal to be convincing, commercials repeatedly distort the facts. They imply that the road to perfect health for your dog is to feed him this or that type of food. In spite of advertising, food contributes only one measure of a dog's health. As Ralston Purina's Bob Mohrman pointed out, "Three factors affect a dog's potential health and longevity. They are genetics, management of the environment, and nutrition."[23] Naturally a dog with good breeding has advantages over one without and the dog in a loving home, where it is looked after and given proper medical attention, will live longer and be healthier than a mistreated or stray dog. And certainly, good nutritious food will benefit the dog's health.

Commercials never convey emotions other than the pleasures of pet owning. Consistently, the dog is the perfect pet, loyal and devoted. The realities of a dog running away, barking all night, tromping over the neighbour's flower beds, and defecating in public places, don't exist. People do not want to see the realistic aspects of pet owning and there would be no magic if the commercials suggested that people leash their dog, tie him up or repair the sofa he chewed. Nevertheless, caged in every humane society or city pound are dogs and cats waiting to be adopted or waiting to die because people were influenced in part by commercials that portrayed the dog as some sort of miraculous creature, magically able to look after itself.

Pet food companies unforgivably violate attempts to control pets by almost exclusively showing dogs running freely without leashes.* One of the most appealing qualities of dogs is the sense of unbound freedom associated with them, and to

---

*A recent pet food example deserves to be singled out – a Ken-L Ration commercial opens with a small boy running with a large, leashed dog.

leash them would shatter an illusion. Furthermore, it might imply that people have a responsibility toward their dogs. Leash laws are in effect in many cities in North America and the United Kingdom, and pet food companies are well aware of the problems caused by uncontrolled dogs. In seminars and symposia throughout the United States, Canada, and Britain, speakers implore owners to control their dogs and municipalities to enact laws or at least to enforce existing ones. Pet food manufacturers and their associations make token endorsements of these positions by sponsoring forums and disseminating findings, yet they still allow dogs in commercials to run free, quite as though leash laws had never creased their consciousness. Perhaps this is overshadowed by their relief at surviving another symposium with the pet's position intact, receiving a reprieve from the anti-dog lobby, or more breathing space from crusading pressure groups. As long as pet food commercials continue to show unleashed dogs these advertisers make a mockery of a serious social problem.

Seldom do small dogs appear in commercials. Irish Setters and Afghan Hounds are romantic favourites, their silken hair flying behind them in a parody of those slow-motion girls in shampoo commercials. As a fashion accessory they serve commercials handsomely; however, there is an ominous suggestibility behind these commercials. Repeated showing of large, splendid-looking dogs creates a desire to own these animals and before you know it Father comes home with an Afghan. Although people want large dogs for guarding, as symbols of status, virility, and power, it is the fashionable appeal of dogs in commercials, movies, and glossy four-colour ads, that accounts for the thousand-fold increase of some large breeds in the United States.*

*During the period 1964 to 1976 large dogs have shown tremendous increases in popularity, among them English Sheepdogs, at 3,148 per cent; Siberian Huskies, 1,365 per cent; Irish Setters, 1,268 per cent; and Salukis, 1,017 per cent. (See Appendix A, for the 100 Most Popular Dogs.) The film, *Serpico*, released in 1974, is said to have been a contributing factor in the phenomenal increase of English Sheepdogs. Al Pacino, the attractive hero-cop, had one certitude in the film: while he single-handedly battled police corruption, endured the breakup of a romance, and was the victim of treachery, his English Sheepdog stood by him, loyal and faithful to the end.

Pet food manufacturers are aware that people regard pets as members of the family. They should be aware; they helped perpetrate the notion through their advertising – and advertising continues to hammer away at the point. One commercial opens with a pleasant young man saying, "This is my boy's favourite food," and you expect to see a freckle-faced boy, but instead, the action cuts to a dog at his dish. The man announces, "He's as much a part of the family as anyone, so why shouldn't he have the best?" Then comes the pitch for Dr. Ballard's Beef Stew. Commercials are not even subtle about portraying the pet as a surrogate child, as in the commercial for Gaines Puppy Meal, in which a woman, probably in her thirties, with an obvious air of being single, takes a nursing puppy away from the bitch, and the voice-over says, "When a puppy leaves its mother's side, you become the mother."

Not only television watchers may find pet food commercials offensive. They are subject to censure by the industry as in the case of an exaggerated advertising claim laid recently against Alpo. In December 1976, the National Advertising Review Board – an advertising industry self-regulatory group – ruled that Alpo commercials were misleading because they implied that their product was all meat, which it is not. In one commercial "Bonanza" star Lorne Greene, in an overblown gesture to dogs lustily feeding, intoned, "Look at them. Every natural instinct tells them that they should eat meat." The commercial also implied that meat is superior to other foods for dogs, which the advertising review board ruled is not true, and as a result, Alpo promised it would "undertake to modify the commercials." (Which it has.)[24]

General Foods came under fire from the Federal Trade Commission in 1974 for "false, misleading and deceptive" advertising by claiming that Gaines Burgers contain "milk protein" that a dog "needs." The FTC issued a cease and desist order against the company to prevent it from making any nutrient claim unless that nutrient is present in the product in a nutritionally significant amount, which the milk protein was not; from suggesting pets have a need for a nutrient which they in fact do not; and from making any nutritional claims unsubstantiated by competent scientific research.[25]

Despite anything else said about pet food commercials, the way they anthropomorphize pets is insidious. Cute or cuddly, ridiculous or obnoxious, pets in commercials, with their humanized voices and mannerisms, behave not much differently from the humans in television shows they sponsor. When a cat does the cha cha in a commercial, regardless of whether the intent is pure fantasy or an attention-getting device, the viewer is given a false impression about cats and once you tally up all false impressions of talking, singing, dancing animals over years of television watching you begin to understand why people have humanized concepts of dogs and cats.

Feeding Scraps

The message implicit in commercials is that if your dog or cat isn't being fed this wonderful product he isn't being properly cared for. In the past pets managed fairly well by eating scraps from the table, supplemented now and then with cod liver oil. The butcher would wrap up some bones for a few extra cents, or at no charge toss in bits of liver for the cat. Of course there is no going back. Old-time butcher stores hardly exist today, and where they do their meat is mostly pre-cut, leaving them with no scraps. To the pets' benefit, more is known today about good diet than ever before. It wasn't many years ago that a seven-year-old dog was an old animal; today that dog can be vivacious and in prime condition, thanks in a large part to improved feeding methods. The cruel irony is that while vast stores of knowledge and sophistication are applied to creating nearly perfect diets for pets, a plethora of junk foods has emerged for humans. Dog snacks are nutritionally superior to the candy, soda pop, and potato chips that are designated as human snacks. Human food processors would argue that their snack products, each one taken on its own, are not intended to supply a full day's nutrients – but they fail to point out that if you eat junk food you should supplement it with real eggs, milk, fish and so forth. While a can of pet food is able to supply a whole day's nutrients, the choices for good nutrition among products for humans are lessening, due to the increasing emphasis placed on convenient and instant foods. The consumer is manipulated through million-dollar advertising budgets to buy packaged, processed foods and is not cautioned about them being nutritionally insufficient.

The Pet Food Institute (PFI), comprising almost all of the pet food manufacturers in the United States, until recently has had an easy time representing its members and lobbying for its own special interests; but of late it has had to answer some embarrassing questions about the ethics of feeding animals billions of pounds of food while one-third of the world starves.

The PFI prepared a set of answers tailored to the party line. The same words are used in interviews, reports, symposia, magazine articles, news releases, and brochures, quite as though spokesmen for the PFI are incapable of spontaneous conversation on the subject. As for the alternative of feeding pets scraps, a PFI booklet categorically states, "There is no way in which a pet owner feeding his pet a miscellaneous diet of table scraps could approach the proper nutritional balance for the pet." The text continues that "one specialist" equated a pet fed on table scraps with a teenager whose diet included only sodas and cookies.[26] This is a shabby argument. The dog on a scrap diet is eating what humans eat, and granted, an overabundance of chili con carne, pizza, and french fries is as likely to cause the dog health problems as it would humans. Nutritional deficiencies in humans and animals can result in obesity, high cholesterol levels, high blood pressure, gastrointestinal disorders, and general malaise, not to mention the more serious vitamin deficiency diseases of rickets and scurvy. To suggest that dogs fed on table scraps are unhealthy is specious; the quality of the scraps should be the argument. Families who eat the required balance of fats, carbohydrates, and protein, supplemented with vitamins are healthy, and if the family dog is given vitamins and eats scraps of meat, vegetables, and cereals, he too will be healthy.

The PFI in the above-mentioned booklet takes a last swing against feeding scraps – economics. An "animal authority" asserts that human food is the most expensive there is, and "if a housewife decided to give table scraps to the puppy, she automatically selects more food than is needed by the family." This implies that dog owning is relatively inexpensive, that it doesn't cost anything to feed a dog – not that it costs more or less to feed table scraps as against commercial pet food.

In England, the only country outside of North America with significant sales of pet food, one-third of the country's processed or cooked food is tossed out as scrap.[27] Canadian restaurants, until the last decade or so, used to sell "swill" to pig farmers, but now it is thrown out – re-cyclers want to be paid for picking it up. The average family wastes hundreds of pounds of edible food each year. Insights into food waste were shed recently in the United States by the "Garbage Project" conducted in Tucson, Arizona, which revealed that each city resident threw out between $80 and $100 worth of edible food a year, or a total of 9,000 tons, enough to feed 4,000 hungry people meat, poultry, and fish for a year.[28] Given those statistics, which surely can apply throughout the nation, how can it be a surprise that Americans continue to spend an additional 3 billion dollars for pet food while in one city they throw away 9 to 11 million dollars worth of edible food a year? But then it must be remembered that waste is the American way of life. Throwing things out is demonstrated proof that one can afford to do so. We even make jokes of it – like the alcoholic, who, when asked if he drinks a bottle of liquor a day, replies, "Hell, I *spill* that much a day!"

The first association dog had with man was eating his scraps and throughout history dog has shared man's spoils one way or another. To this day, slipping the dog a tidbit under the table is a common dinner-time habit, and whether approved or not, perhaps it has its origin with the ancient Persians who decreed that whenever a person eats bread he or she must "set aside three mouthfuls and give them to the dog... for amongst all the poor there is none poorer than the dog."[29]

Unfit for Human Consumption?

What is fit and what is unfit for human consumption is a seesaw situation for pet food manufacturers. On the one hand, they are proud of their quality products, as evidenced by the president of one pet food company who ceremoniously munches on dog biscuits at their annual meetings, or the marketing man of another who, during the Cold War, when Americans were building fall-out shelters in their back yards, stocked his shelter with dog food. On the other hand, manufacturers are embarrassed by the fact that humans eat their products. When the subject was introduced to one pet food man he shrugged and asked, "Where else could they get so much nutrition for thirty cents?"[30] The answer, sadly, is "Nowhere." In areas where the pet population is well identified and the sale of dog food is disproportionately high, there is only one explanation: human consumption accounts for the discrepancy. To what actual degree, no one knows – or is saying – but the fact that pet food is being eaten by humans cannot be disputed. As the years go by the quality of dog food continues to escalate and if it were not too close for comfort a comic opera could be written about pets dining on Beef Wellington and Lobster Soufflé, while their masters cleaned up the leftovers.

Before the United States and Britain revised their manufacturing standards, dead, diseased, and unhealthy carcasses from all manner of animals were processed into pet food, which made it unacceptable for humans. Strictly speaking, this no longer applies, for only healthy animals may be used and if animals other than cattle, sheep, swine, or goats are the raw materials, they must be specified on the label.

Is it so repugnant for dogs to eat certain animals? In the wild under nature's laws they would be eating anything they could catch. As a result of the trend to anthropomorphize, humans demand that animals eat only certain animals. Where were all the animal lovers as far back as the 1920s and thirties when half a million horses were slaughtered annually to feed pets?[31] Marilyn Monroe was never more beautiful or sensitive than in *The Misfits*, when she realizes that Clark Gable and his pals are running down wild mustangs with trucks to sell them for slaughter.

There is little doubt that the average dog almost anywhere in the world is better fed than many humans. People in underdeveloped countries eat as much grain per year as a medium-sized dog in Britain.[32] Grains used in the American pet food industry, in their descending order of tonnage, are, corn, wheat, oats and barley, about 25 per cent of which are by-products, generally defined as bran, wheat middlings, germ, and flour from wheat, corn, barley, rice, and oats. Soy meal adds an additional one-third, about 900 million pounds, to the annual tonnage produced, and this is clearly where industry formulation is heading. The amount of soy meal used has increased 167 per cent since 1963; other grains combined have increased 145 per cent in the same period of time.[33] The PFI concedes that a "relatively small amount" of wheat used in the pet food industry might be taken away from the human food chain, but this is only .38 per cent of the total U.S. production. The PFI rushes to the comparison that in 1974, distillers used 8.8 billion pounds of grain,[34] implying that the pet food industry's 2.6 million is trifling by comparison. Trying to justify their use of wheat for a product of dubious value against yet a more questionable product – alcohol – is sly. The PFI might, instead, point out that its members use as much grain for pet food as Canada shipped to developing countries in 1974.[35]

The real point is, one half of the ingredients used in the manufacture of pet foods are grains and soy products, all of which can be eaten by humans.

In buying meat and grain by-products from packing plants and cereal manufacturers, the PFI maintains that it has created a market for materials that would otherwise be discarded; hence the dollars poured into these industries help keep down the cost of human food. In 1974, the industry paid approximately $320,000,000 for meat, poultry, and seafood by-products, and if it had not, the PFI stoutly declares, the monetary loss for the meat, poultry, and seafood, processing industries alone would "be in the range of $200 million."* The PFI explains that this $200,000,000 loss "would have to be made up in increased costs to consumers of primary food products.

---

*The suggestion is that without the pet food industry as a customer, sellers of by-products would lose $200,000,000 by having to offer their products to rendering plants at prices far below their value as pet food ingredients.

88

And, in the case of processors operating on relatively small profit margins, the loss of a profitable outlet for their by-products could mean the difference between survival and bankruptcy."[36] The implication is that those who criticize the pet food industry want small businesses to go bankrupt.

The PFI claim that its use of seafood and seafood by-products keeps prices down for humans is completely misleading. The very opposite is true. Fresh fish on average has tripled in retail price in the past two years, due in large part to the increasing millions of tons of fresh and salt water fish that are fed to household dogs and cats. (See Fig. 3, Page 75 for the amounts.)

Take, for example, tuna. Pet food manufacturers claim they use "red" tuna, the dark, unappetizing stuff humans won't buy. And why won't people buy it? Because those very manu-facturers, through other divisions of their companies, tell con-sumers in million-dollar ad campaigns that white tuna is prime. An apt comparison, however, would be the difference between light and dark chicken meat. The darker flesh tuna has the same high quality nutritionally and tastes almost identical to the white, but pet food manufacturers, wearing their human-food hats, remind consumers, through skilful innuendo, that dark is inferior.

Both Carnation and Ralston Purina are among the villains here. As manufacturers of tuna cat food – Friskies by Carna-tion and a total of nine different brands by Ralston Purina – they reserve the most expensive tuna for human consumption, Carnation Tuna and Ralston Purina Chicken of the Sea Tuna; products vigorously promoted as "solid white tuna." The "inferior" dark tuna is thus left relatively free for feline con-sumption.

Poultry and poultry by-products used in the industry include the offal, heads and feet, backs and necks. These products are lumped together as unfit for humans. Is all that chopped chicken liver in delicatessens all over the country unfit to eat? Just as well devotees have yet to hear. Along with the countless tempting ways of serving chicken livers, heart and gizzards can be very tasty in stews, soups, and gravies; backs and necks are economical for flavourful soups and stock, and so are the feet, as any good cook will attest.

89

Almost all foods used in the manufacture of pet food could be utilized for human consumption, were it not for the assiduous effort of the industry to jockey certain foods into positions of disfavour. Every ounce of grain and grain by-products used for pet food could be made into palatable, nutritious biscuits and breakfast cereals. When I asked about bran, defined as a grain by-product by the pet food industry, a man from Quaker Oats scoffed, "Why, you can't give bran away to humans!" Where has he been? Bran is close to being a food fad, and one of the few nutritious ones at that.*

What about soybeans, which have the highest protein content by weight of all foods? Soybeans are unavailable in most supermarkets; the majority of sales are through health-food stores. And why won't people eat soybeans? Because unless they read health-food journals or books, they are not likely to know this highly nutritional product is available, and the food processors won't tell them since a consumer demand would threaten this cheap source of raw materials for the manufacture of pet foods. In 1974 the pet food industry used 900 million pounds of soybeans; which represents 21 per cent of the American domestic production for that year.[37]

Technology to produce human foods economically and efficiently flounders because the very industries that are capable of devising new human foods from by-products are already engaged in using them for pet foods. It is their economic base. Quaker Oats, Carnation, Ralston Purina, General Foods, and Liggett & Myers, giants who control 70 per cent of the pet food industry, are also major producers of breakfast foods (excepting L & M and to a lesser extent Carnation). Why would they concern themselves with improved use of grains and grain by-products in their breakfast foods when any lateral deployment of raw materials would only imperil their highly profitable pet food divisions? The total breakfast-food business, at 1.7 billion in 1975, in the United States, is still the baby brother of the 2.9-billion-dollar pet food business.

Blood is one meat by-product successfully utilized in pet

*This remark was made in early 1976. Perhaps since tnen the man has updated his views.

foods in Britain. There is no way of knowing how many millions of gallons previously flowed down the drain, but in 1974 Pedigree Petfoods in England developed a technique which changed the composition of blood, enabling it to be processed into chunks, bits, granules and into any form whatever. Supplemented with nutrients, blood has become a valuable raw material; in addition, this use prevents it from being a pollutant. From 10 to 20 thousand gallons per year are used in the U.K. Dr. Roger Mugford of Pedigree Petfoods insists that the pet food industry is morally obliged to protect the human food chain: "The onus is on us to develop new sources of raw materials for pets in order that we may gradually release materials that could be consumed by humans, in addition to transferring technology to the human food industry."[38]

World Shortage of Protein

There is little doubt that the future demand in the food chain will be for protein. Biologist Paul Ehrlich declared, with breathtaking finality, "The battle to feed humanity is over.... Between 1970 and 1985 the world will undergo vast famines – hundreds of millions of people are going to starve to death." Unless, he noted, plague or thermonuclear war gets them first. He further emphasized, "Many will starve to death in spite of any crash programmes we might embark upon now. And we are not embarking upon any crash programme."[39]

Fifty per cent of the world is undernourished, and there is hardly a country that is not affected. A nutrition study conducted by the United States Department of Health and Welfare was discontinued in 1970 after ten states had been surveyed because the information gathered was considered an embarrassment to the Nixon government. In Texas and Louisiana, 16 per cent of low-income families showed serious protein deficiencies, "some well below the levels normally associated with malnutrition in underdeveloped countries."[40]

Judging from the printed material distributed by the Pet Food Institute, a protein shortage does not exist. Either the PFI refuses to acknowledge it or, more likely, is unable to address the issue with any conviction. More so now than ever before it is incumbent upon the pet food industry to answer a very pressing moral question: do dogs really need all the protein they're getting?

Ralston Purina claims that 16 to 18 per cent protein in the diet is sufficient for a normal mature dog but most mature dogs receive a dry type diet which provides 21 to 25 per cent protein. It is very common for owners to feed in excess of the dog's requirements; how much is anybody's guess. According to Bob Mohrman of Ralston Purina, a dog requires one-third to one-half ounce of dry food per pound of body weight, or two and a half to three times that if he is being fed canned food. Thus a seventy-five pound German Shepherd requires on the average one and a half to two pounds of dry dog food per day, or four to six cans, or 1.75 to 2.5 pounds of semi-moist food per day. But you can get odds from pet food manufacturers that the average dog is getting more than that.

An equally pressing issue, how much protein is used by the animal, is now an emerging concern. Dogs require 12 per cent more calories than humans, provided daily in a combination of proteins and carbohydrates. Humans, in order to obtain complete protein, need eight essential amino acids in their diets; dogs need ten. Pet food manufacturers, such as Ralston Purina, General Foods, Quaker Oats, and Standard Brands, to name those with lavish research facilities, are able to identify and select the ten amino acids in the proteins used; but smaller companies may not be able to do so. How much is actually utilized by the dog is impossible to say. It all depends on the quality of protein. Soybeans contain about 40 per cent protein by weight. Cheese is next, with some varieties, such as Parmesan, containing 36 per cent protein. Meat is third and contains from 20 to 30 per cent protein. However, it is the utilization of protein in these foods that counts. North Americans have always believed in the ultimate superiority of meat as a source of protein, but the body uses only 67 per cent of the protein contained in meat. Egg protein can be assimilated at 94 per cent, the highest on the scale, followed by milk at 82 per cent.[41]

Out of approximately 500 brands of commercially prepared

pet foods on the market in the United States, there is no question that many of them contain poor quality, indigestible protein. There is protein in hooves, hides, hair and teeth, even though it cannot be converted into nourishment. Similarly, carbohydrates may be indigestible cellulose or mineral oils of no value.

So disgusted was one veterinarian over nutrient content in pet food that he concocted a product containing the same number of nutrients as one brand of canned dog food, in which the fat was derived from crankcase oil, animal protein from old leather shoes, and the carbohydrates from wood shavings.

Ralston Purina claims 85 per cent of the protein in their products is digestible. Allowing them the benefit of the doubt, 15 per cent is wasted. Conceivably the percentage could be anywhere from 15 to 75, even 100 per cent, given the wide range of products and types of manufacturers processing pet food. Even though some ingredients in pet foods are unsuitable for human consumption, as fertilizer these ingredients have the possibility of serving mankind; dropping, unused, out of dogs' rear ends they do not.

Protein Alternatives

Sufficient protein alternatives can be derived from plants and grasses to supplement the present supply, but the question is, if they can be extracted and readily utilized in foodstuffs, who is first, pets or humans? As British nutritionist Dr. Robie Fears states:

> Deep-sea fish, oil seed residues and leaf protein may all be under-utilised at the moment, but they have great potential for human diets. It would be distressing if oil-seed residues from countries such as India and Nigeria were used in Britain for feeding to pets in addition to their present use as feeds for farm animals. It is bad enough to waste home-produced commodities in pet foods; it is surely worse to import foodstuffs from developing countries for this purpose.[42]

"Wet farming" is considered an area for future consideration. Research on kelp, one of the world's fastest growing plants, is under way off the coast of San Clemente, California, to discover its potential for use as food, fuel, or fertilizer.

Considerable research has been done by British-Petroleum on the development of artificial protein from petroleum by-products. The Celanese Corporation in the United States has filed a petition with the Federal Department of Agriculture for the use of 1,3-butanediol in moist pet foods. An artificial nutrient, this ingredient tested effectively when 15 per cent was added to the diet of pigs, chicks and rats.[43] It is ironic that even though humans are now competing with pets for food, the alternatives will have them competing for a non-renewable energy resource, such as petroleum.

Regardless of the protein alternatives envisaged to feed pets, humans will be in competition for that food, with one exception. Millions of dogs and cats are killed each year, not because they are sick or dying, but merely because they are not wanted. These are healthy animals and as repugnant as it may be to some people – just as repugnant as dogs or cats eating horses or whales – this is a valuable and self-replenishing food supply for pets. If the average weight of 100 million dogs and cats in the United States is fifteen pounds, and the annual death rate through wanton destruction is 12 per cent, right there is an immediate 180 million pounds of raw material available for re-cycling into pet food.

The unacceptability of this notion is proportionate to the concept of how human one's dog is. It is the rule rather than the exception to think of the dog as a family member, and because a potent taboo for humans is eating human flesh, the attitude translates readily to the family pet, whose owner sees him as more human than animal. Pet food manufacturers wouldn't bat an eye over using dogs as raw materials. (Ten years ago horses and whales were commonly used.) Their concern is the bottom line and they would no doubt consider it prudent, in exchange for such an economical resource, to throw some of their advertising weight into campaigns to pre-condition customers to the idea. Granted, 180 million pounds is not much to this protein-sucking industry, but at the very least it frees 180 million pounds of foodstuffs for human consumption.

There may be no other practical alternative than to convince the public that feeding cats and dogs to cats and dogs is not as cold-blooded as phasing out those pets in the face of global food shortages. Or should severe hardship prevail the animals might become a tantalizing source of food for humans, as has happened in the past – pets were all but eliminated by starving Russians at the time of the German blitz. Actually, the dog-eat-dog concept is not only compatible with the pet food industry's character, it conforms to their current trend to specialization and humanization of pet foods; pets could then eat real hot dogs.

Caloric needs vary from dog to dog, breed to breed, from puppies to lactating bitches, to aging dogs, and the best way to provide proper nourishment for your dog is by the do-it-yourself method. More important, when you know what is best for your dog, you are no longer a victim of pet food advertising. Many veterinarians, unlike doctors, are knowledgeable about nutrition and offer good dietary advice for specific problems but regardless, the average dog owner, presuming he or she desires to feed the pet good food, will do well to follow these simple guidelines:

1. Discard the notion that your dog "needs" meat.
2. If the dog has you trained to believe he likes meat, give him half meat and half dry food so that he gets grain carbohydrates and animal protein.
3. For a good balanced diet buy food that is labelled, "Complete" or "Balanced."
4. For a healthy, active dog, buy canned food which is at least 6 per cent protein, and dry food, at least 18 per cent protein.
5. Except for puppies, which should be fed several times daily, feed the dog only once a day. An occasional dog biscuit snack is permitted.
6. Don't feed the dog dairy products – most canine digestive systems are upset by them.

7. If you feed your dog table scraps, refrain from giving him too much fat.
8. Feed in small amounts, with the option of second helpings, rather than in large amounts which are partly eaten.
9. Keep opened canned food under refrigeration to preserve freshness.
10. Consult with your vet for feeding recommendations if the dog is experiencing a health problem of any kind.

Approved Minimum Standards for Canned Dog and Cat Foods in the United Kingdom[44]

Based on Swedish and American published minimal nutritional standards for canned dog and cat foods, along with the advice of experts in the United Kingdom, the British Small Animal Veterinary Association prepared a set of standards which were accepted as the Association's official view of February 25, 1970. They are as follows:

A. **Types of food considered**
(1) High protein canned foods, designed to be fed with carbohydrate supplements.
(2) Complete canned foods, which do not normally require any form of supplementation.

B. **General objectives of minimum standards**
To ensure that both types of canned food, namely (a) high protein food mixed with an adequate calorific supplement and (b) complete canned foods, when fed as the sole ration, will maintain health and promote normal growth in healthy cats and dogs, without the addition of any substance other than water.

Suggested standards (% wet wt.)
(1) High protein dog foods

Protein	(min.)	10%
Fat	(range)	1 - 5%
Ash	(max.)	3%

Calcium	(min.)	0.25%
Ca : P	(range)	1.5 - 0.9 : 1.0
Calorific value	(min.)	75 kcal/100 g.
Water	(max.)	80%

(2) High protein cat foods

Protein	(min.)	10%
Fat	(range)	2 - 8%
Ash	(max.)	3%
Calcium	(min.)	0.25%
Ca : P	(range)	1.5 - 0.9 : 1.0
Calorific value	(min.)	75 kcal/100 g.
Water	(max.)	80%

(3) Complete dog foods

Protein	(min.)	4%
Fat	(range)	1 - 5%
Carbohydrate	(max.)	12%
Ash	(max.)	4%
Calcium	(min.)	0.25%
Ca : P	(range)	1.5 - 0.9 : 1.0
Calorific value	(min.)	75 kcal/100 g.
Water	(max.)	75%

(4) Complete cat food

Protein	(min.)	8%
Fat	(range)	2 - 8%
Carbohydrate	(max.)	12%
Ash	(max.)	4%
Calcium	(min.)	0.25%
Ca : P	(range)	1.5 - 0.9 : 1.0
Calorific value	(min.)	75 kcal/100 g.
Water	(max.)	75%

6

THE ACTUAL COST
OF DOG OWNING

People have been led to believe by the media and the pet
industry in general, that pet owning is free. The benefits
provided by pets become the overwhelming message, and not
until the new dog or cat is actually in the house do people
realize the amount of money that has to be doled out regularly for food and health care. Collectively this amounts to
billions of dollars annually.

Although few keep records, families who first acquire a dog
or cat, regardless of whether it is a $500 pedigree or a mutt
from the pound, are surprised at how much food alone costs.
In a 1972 study by Statistics Canada, covering urban family
expenditures, it was revealed that one-third of the sample
owned pets and reported spending an average of $58.20 per
year on food.[1] Since pet food has approximately doubled in
price since that time, the cost today would be at least $100.
When vets' fees are added to the simple basics of flea powder,
a leash, dog dish and rubber toy, this would amount to a bare
minimum of another $100. Add one illness or a week's board-
ing fees at vacation time and you've got another minimum
$100. The total, approximating $300, is in keeping with the
Montreal SPCA estimate that it costs an average of a dollar a

day to own a pet.[2] This is one of the primary reasons in today's inflationary economy why many dogs, especially large breeds, are abandoned before their first birthday or end up in an animal shelter to be killed. People are continually conned into acquiring more than they can afford, dogs being just one more item.

The only time pet owning is "free" is in the case of farm dogs who live on a combination of table scraps and the small wild animals they prey upon; but even though these dogs are not pampered like apartment dogs, the odd can of flea powder and a visit to the vet is nonetheless required. "Free" in terms of pet owning implies neglect.

To the devoted pet owner, however, cost is of no consequence. Britain's Consumer Association published results in 1977 of a study which examined the cost-benefit ratio of pet owning. Based on 1,600 owners of 2,088 pets, it was concluded that the initial cost of the pet, its upkeep, and the time and trouble invested in looking after it, as measured against the enjoyment the pet gave its owner made dogs the "best buy" in pets. Horses followed, with cats third.[3]

The U.S. trade magazine *Pets/Supplies/Marketing* annually conducts studies on the cost of pet owning and in 1974, pets – defined here as dogs, cats, birds, fish – were reported to be America's most expensive hobby. Including only food, pet accessories and grooming services, and excluding the cost of the pet itself or vets' fees, in 1974 Americans spent 3.9 billion dollars on pets. This amounted to $18.57 for each man, woman, and child in the country.[4] Looking at pet food expenditures compared to other household items, *Supermarketing Magazine* reported that on an average $20 expenditure in supermarkets in 1974 Americans spent 29¢ on pet food, 29¢ on sugar, 31¢ on cereals and rice, 14¢ on fresh fish, and 21¢ on candy and chewing gum.[5]

Photography, the second most expensive hobby in America, lagged $100,000,000 behind at 3.8 billion dollars, and bicycles were in third place as a 1.3-billion-dollar hobby. Here is how the hobbies stacked up:

pets – $3,900,000,000
photography – $3,800,000,000

bicycles – $1,300,000,000
guns and hunting – $775,900,000
golf – $441,000,000
fishing – $407,000,000
camping – $384,000,000
tennis – $282,000,000
skiing – $275,000,000
billiards – $219,000,000
plastic models – $202,000,000
model railroads – $135,000,000
model airplanes – $126,000,000
bowling – $71,600,000
stamps and coins – $50,000,000[6]

The following table shows basic minimum annual costs of keeping a small dog, a medium-large dog, and a cat. Typically incurred costs to the pet owner are examined in detail. Unless excesses and extravagances are specifically noted, costs reported here are average, never the highest price paid.[7]

MINIMUM COSTS FOR PETS UP TO 5 YEARS OLD

In the pet's first year	Small Dog (10 lbs.)	Large Dog (70 lbs.)	Cat
Food	$ 100.00	$ 150.00	$ 60.00
Veterinary Care:			
New dog care (worming. vaccinations. etc.)	75.00	100.00	50.00
Spaying or neutering	60.00	100.00	40.00
(Average: $40-80-small dogs 50-150-large dogs 25-60-cats)			
Licence (no differential)	5.00	5.00	
Accessories: flea collar. leash. scratch post. brush. toy. etc.	6.00	10.00	7.00
Total – First year of pet owning	$246.00	$365.00	$157.00
From 2nd year to 5th year			
Veterinary Care:			
Minor health problem (no hospital stay)	75.00	100.00	40.00
Total annual cost from age 2-5	$321.00	$465.00	$197.00

MINIMUM ANNUAL MAINTENANCE COSTS FOR MATURE PETS
(over 5 years of age)

Food (feeding less but more expensive. specialized food – i.e. for obesity)	$100.00	$150.00	$ 60.00
Veterinary Care			
Surgery associated with ageing: arthritis. uterine problems. broken bones. etc.	200.00	300.00	100.00
Annual shots	25.00	25.00	25.00
Licence (no differential)	5.00	5.00	
Accessories	6.00	10.00	7.00
Total annual cost for mature pet	$336.00	$490.00	$192.00

Veterinary Care

It is safe to say that people use or abuse veterinary services as they do medical services for themselves. One Toronto veterinarian, Dr. Wally Stonehouse, related what appears to be the universal situation: "When some people get a new dog you come to know it very well before its first birthday, whereas you won't see other dogs more than once a year for their annual shots."[8] There is no way of predicting what amount of veterinary expenses a dog or cat will incur annually – other than the once-a-year vaccination for leptospirosis/distemper/ hepatitis and for rabies at a cost of $15 to $25. If a dog is fed properly, exercised sufficiently and generally well cared for, a rule of thumb is that it may contract a minor sickness once every two or three years. However, various house dogs which are kept on leashes and never allowed to run loose where they would associate with other diseased animals, become injured in fights, or risk being hit in traffic, do not see the vet for anything more than their shots, year after year.

Usually when a person first acquires a dog, especially a puppy, a visit to the vet is not only recommended but is essential to the animal's good health. You could expect to pay at least from $50 to $75 to "get him in shape," that is, for worming, vaccinations, a general physical examination, and advice regarding special feeding.

Once the dog has reached sexual maturity, generally by

eight months of age, spaying or neutering is, for responsible pet owners, the next veterinary expense. This would average approximately $15 to $20 in a municipally subsidized clinic; performed by a private vet the charge would be anywhere from $50 to $150 for a dog or cat, depending on both the size and type of animal, and, as always, on what the traffic will bear.*

For one minor illness or accident without an overnight hospital stay the expense is likely to be about $75; however, should the dog require extensive care, surgery, prolonged treatment and medication, this quite naturally could amount to several hundred dollars.

To be certain of obtaining the best veterinary care for your pet, follow these guidelines:

How to find a good veterinarian

1. Probably word of mouth is the best means of recommendation, as it is for other professionals. If the recommender has been going to the same vet for a number of years and knows others who are similarly loyal, this is a good indication the vet is offering satisfying service.
2. You don't have to like your vet – any more than your doctor, dentist or lawyer – but it helps if you respect the person professionally.
3. To make you feel confident in his or her diagnosis or treatment, the vet must appear to be interested in the animal – and you, its owner.
4. Find out about the hours of service, particularly emergency service. He or she, or his or her services, must be there when you need them.
5. The vet's first examination of the animal will reveal much to you. If the vet examines the animal thoroughly, asks a number of questions and takes tests or suggests they be done, you will probably feel more confident in him or her.

*See more about spaying and neutering on page 179.

102

6. Find out if the vet does only routine procedures, or if full medical, surgical, and difficult cases are handled.
7. Should only routine services be offered, ask whether the vet is associated with an animal hospital or if he or she makes referrals.
8. If the vet practises singly, rather than sharing a clinic, find out if he or she confers with colleagues. It is important to know what communication the vet depends on in difficult cases.
9. Take note of the facilities. Is there an X-ray machine, equipment to do blood tests and eye examinations, etc?
10. Observe if the facility seems to be adequately staffed. If the vet is answering the phone and being receptionist, you may wonder, justifiably, if he or she has enough time to devote to your pet.
11. Notice whether the facility appears neat, well organized, and well maintained. Certainly good medicine may be practised amid clutter, but you don't know that on appearances alone.
12. If you are still not satisfied, determine if the vet is continuing his veterinary education, ask if he or she attends professional conferences, serves on committees or boards, or is otherwise active in the profession, notice if there are current medical journals in the office, if he or she consults textbooks, publishes in the journals, or is involved with research.[9]

There are numerous other both essential and eccentric ways in which a person may spend money on a pet. Here are but a few.

Licensing

Most municipalities have a dog licensing by-law which entails an annual fee, a two or three-year fee, or a one-time fee. Regardless of which, the purchase of a dog licence is considered a mandatory though minor expense averaging anywhere from $2 to $10 a year.

To encourage spaying and neutering many jurisdictions have enacted, and many more are considering, a licence differential for half the price if the dog has been surgically sterilized. Another trend is to extend the differential in the opposite direction, that is, to increase the fee for large breeds or guard dogs, or for more than one dog.

Pet Supplies and Accessories

Although sterling silver dishes, mink coats, mouth wash, perfume and deodorant for dogs may be contemporary eccentricities, accessories of one kind or another have been available for pets since the eighteenth century. One of the earliest companies in the United States, Smith-Worthington Saddlery of Hartford, Connecticut, was established in 1794 and to this day continues to sell and distribute pet products. A corporation still making a wide variety of veterinary medicines, Dr. A.C. Daniels, founded in 1878, offered initially a line of treatments for cattle, horse, dog, and cat ailments and enjoyed the patronage of the legendary Buffalo Bill along with Barnum & Bailey and Ringling Bros. circuses. Sergeant's, a household name as far as pet products and accessories are concerned today, originated with a Virginian named Polk Miller, a pharmacist and sportsman whose hobby was formulating products to treat his hunting dogs' various ailments. By 1868 his modest little drugstore became the focal point of friends seeking advice about dogs, guns, ammunition, and, of course, treatment of canine problems. Eventually he introduced a line of products that he called "Sergeant," after his favourite Retriever.

Flea powders originated through a circuitous route from England. A veterinarian named William Cooper developed a remedy which successfully eradicated a particular scab threatening the entire sheep population in the United Kingdom, and upon its success, a nephew was sent to the U.S. to market Cooper's products. When one preparation, a dip, was used to treat fever ticks in cattle, Texas ranch dogs were routinely tossed in the dip with the cattle, which led to a demand for a new product among dog owners. Thus it was in 1924 that a flea powder for dogs was introduced under the brand name Pulvex—the beginning of what was to become a 100-million-dollar annual business.[10][11]

The pet and accessory business made its first major inroads on retail sales in the 1920s when American chain stores such as Kresge's and Grant's began to stock pets and pet accessories—starting with goldfish, that sold for 15 and 25 cents. Max Stern opened a pet shop in New York which has grown into one of the world's largest manufacturers and distributors of pet accessories. Selling only singing canaries at first, Stern quickly recognized the profit potential in bird seed. Soon he stocked other birds, followed by goldfish and aquariums, whereupon he branched out to small pets such as hamsters and other "pet rodents," and began stocking feeds and a number of appurtenances for pet care. The business, Hartz Mountain, now markets over 1,200 items for dogs, cats, birds, fish, and miscellaneous pets, and Stern's son at the helm has amassed a personal fortune estimated at between $500,000,000 and $700,000,000, according to *Fortune* magazine in 1971.[12]

Hartz Mountain's history is a fair representation of the phenomenal growth of the pet supplies industry. The trade magazine *Pets/Supplies/Marketing* states there are now 8,750 pet shops in the United States whose sales in 1976 totalled $804,000,000.[13] In New York alone there are 750 pet shops compared to 596 drugstores in the city.

In the addled economy of 1974 to 1976, sales patterns reflected that some dog owners may have "stepped down" in purchasing for their dogs, occasionally substituting cheaper dry products for expensive canned foods; yet during that same time, dog owners thought nothing of reaching for a $2 doggie toy, special shampoo, deodorant, flea powder, or a hair brush. And since margin on pet supplies "tends to be high, averaging near 50%—quite a bit above the 15% average for pet foods," according to the trade journal *Progressive Grocer*,[14] pet shops, supermarkets, drugstores, hardware stores, and corner grocery stores, are as eager to stock pet supplies as owners are to purchase them.

One of the fastest growing departments in supermarkets, pet

supplies, are classed by themselves as a lucrative product category, no longer relegated to dinky, slow traffic corners. They now command end-aisle displays and self-contained display racks, and many displays previously four feet in length have been expanded to twelve. Another article in *Progressive Grocer* noted, "With grocery stores selling over 90% of pet food and with pet supplies invariably located so close by only a blind man could miss them, grocery outlets have a perfect tie-in." Nonetheless, supermarkets have only 20 per cent of the total accessories market. The article goes on to quote a pet-supplies marketing man: "Supermarket people don't realize that pet supplies is a much bigger business than toilet soap and about equal to laundry detergent – that is, about $1 billion a year. [The trade estimated the pet supplies market at $804,000,000. See page 105.] They're satisfied with what they're getting, but they should be getting a much bigger share of the market than they are."[15]

As a result of impulse buying and a $10,000,000 annual advertising budget, flea collars are the biggest selling individual pet item today, enjoying $60,000,000 to $70,000,000 in annual sales in the United States. Currently a three-way dispute among manufacturers, the Federal Trade Commission and the Environmental Protection Agency, over safety of design and advertising claims, has the flea collar industry temporarily at a standstill. However, as soon as the problems are resolved the market is expected to get into "high gear," industry spokesmen claim. In low gear at $60,000,000 to $70,-000,000, high gear will surely put it into orbit.

Even with a 20 per cent share, grocery stores do a whopping $200,000,000 in annual sales,[16] yet they are pygmies compared to the giant Gimbel's in New York. *Fortune* magazine reported that in 1971 Gimbel's offered over 10,000 pet items and grossed an astonishing $750,000,000.[17] When I visited the department in December 1976, manager Jerry Finkelstein would neither confirm nor deny the figures, but was very helpful in providing a guided tour of his domain. There were blankets and beds for dogs, leashes and collars, both plain and rhinestone studded – "No, I don't think we've had diamonds" – ribbons and bows for the hair, medicated and tangle-free

106

shampoo, conditioner – "This is pretty good stuff. Lots of dogs have dry, flaky skin, just like people" – brushes, combs, deodorants, odour removers, Happy Breath breath freshener, liver-flavoured toothpaste – "Heh! Heh!" – rubber boots in small, medium and large, in red or black – "We're out of blue, I guess" – birthday cards (to canine companions? owners? the vet?), Christmas stockings filled with rawhide cookies, rubber bones, plastic salami slices and corn on the cob – "We have the largest stock of stocking stuffers of anybody" – rawhide and plastic toys in the form of lollipops, baseballs, slippers (small and large), pipes, T-bone steaks, an extensive line of treats – my favourite was Good Boy Chocolate Drops (I didn't want to know what they were made of). The clothing department featured coats – "We quit making mink a few years ago" – sweaters and tartans were big in December 1976, scarves, ear muffs, caps, and for those "certain days" Sani-pants – "Refills? No, you'd just use a kleenex" – and for a jolt back to reality, row upon row of worming medicines, flea powders, and elixirs for constipation and diarrhea, then off to Disneyland again with cologne and nail polish – "Heh! Heh! I guess we have only green left" – the travelling cases in wicker and vinyl – "Recommended by the airlines" – and a Pooch Scoop for $4.98 – "No, we don't sell too many" – a record called "Talk To Your Dog," a rack of books about dogs (and possibly for dogs – bedtime stories about postmen and dog catchers?) – and ending with a few practical items such as housebreaking aids and wee-wee pads.[18]

If that sounds like fairly run-of-the-mill fare, you might seek out an exclusive pet boutique and select a gold bracelet or earrings, a lamé evening gown, top hat and tails for special occasions, a clown's costume for Halloween, and if the dog's hair is wearing thin on top, like his owner's, he too can have a rug. For vacations there are bikinis, ski suits, as well as skis and ski boots, Dior-type sun-glasses, a raincoat, and an umbrella which attaches to the collar to protect the dog's new houndstooth blazer.[19]

Saks Fifth Avenue in New York has a fashion newsletter, *Dog Toggery*, which it sends out to dogs on its mailing list. One such letter read, in part:

Of course, if you're really into fashion you'll want our Chinese-worker jacket in denim, there's even a matching collar and lead, and for your more formal occasions we suggest a red or grey Chesterfield with black velvet collar. A navy blazer is nice for milder days and on rainy ones you might fancy yourself in our private-eye trench coat. Needless to say, we have collars and leads to complement each of your outfits, including our warmest winter storm coats.[20]

It is estimated that for every dollar a dog owner spends on food he or she will spend at least another on accoutrements, such as the ones just mentioned. Maybe that is why Finkelstein chortled only now and then. I got the impression one part of him was saying, "Yes, this is sheer madness," while another part, the $750,000,000 in annual sales part, reminded him there was nothing mad about it at all. A jovial customer I talked to good-naturedly blurted out, "What the hell! When the world is so crummy and everything so depressing, it's nice to have a little fun on stuff like this." Finkelstein's chortle and the lady's boisterous laughter rang in my ears as the taxi took me to my next appointment, past block after block of dingy New York tenements, where nobody laughed.

Boarding and Kennelling

A person can get a room at the YMCA in New York for $8 a night, which is a dollar less than at the new Kennelworth, a 116-room hotel that opened in November 1975 with a starting rate of $9 a day. The catch is, the Kennelworth is for dogs only. For $9 the owner may be pleased to hear that this covers the dog getting walked four times a day by itself – to avoid catching god knows what from other dogs – gives the dog the comfort of a radio – piped in music was tried but discarded, not home-like enough – and the services of dietitian Bill Griffin, who prepares such daily fare as beef, liver, or tripe stew. The hotel's owner, Les Weiner, is quick to point out that a pet's special needs are not neglected: "Some animals crave certain cheeses, others like a bagel in the morning or before retiring. Some cats like only certain brands of tuna fish – and we see that they get what they want."

Although dogs are colour blind, rooms at the Kennelworth are decorated in various colour schemes because, as Weiner has it, dogs can appreciate the intensity of certain colours. Also included in the friendly service, at an additional fee, is the portrait photographer or artist who paints the owner's dog on travel bags, T-shirts, or what have you, and to make the pet's stay more luxurious there is a grooming parlour and a boutique. Based on the Kennelworth's success, booked to 100 per cent capacity compared to the average New York hotels at about 65 per cent, Weiner is planning on franchising a nation-wide chain of doggie hotels.[21] [22]

A Toronto family can leave the dog or cat at home in its familiar surroundings and pay a service called Feed a Pet to come in and do just that, for $5 a day. The operator of a vacation house-minding service, Pat Norton, says 80 per cent of her service involves feeding the vacationer's cat. In her experience, "Everyone's pet is special. It's just like a child. All the cats I've seen are spoiled rotten. Usually they have one bedroom to themselves in a two-bedroom apartment."[23]

A month at summer camp in the Catskills costs $150 for a dog; but for that price the owner receives a letter from the dog, signed with a paw print.* The *Baltimore Sun* observed that while it costs $80 to $120 to board a dog for a month in Baltimore, the state pays $76 a month to board a child in a foster home.[24]

For the family travelling with a dog, no need to wonder which motels or hotels welcome the pet; one may merely consult Touring With Towers, a directory which lists more than 9,000 independent motels and hotels in the United States and Canada, among them ten major nationwide chains, that welcome pets.

---

*The *New York Times* followed up on this story and found some of the camp's services wanting, but the interesting point is that people were willing to put out that kind of money to send a dog to camp.

Life can be fairly grand for the travelling pet aboard the *Queen Elizabeth*. Owners may visit them (there is space for thirty-five dogs or cats) on the Pooches Promenade, where they are likely to be enjoying some of the comforts of home – for American dogs, an authentic New York fire hydrant, and for British pets, a cast-iron Edwardian lamp post.

Grooming Parlours

In the United States the first grooming accessory, hair clippers, was introduced in the 1920s and by the end of the war a full line of grooming supplies was in production. To this day many people buy special clippers and combs to groom their dogs and cats, but with the affluence and leisure time to indulge pets, grooming parlours for dogs and cats are now big business. If New York, with its 100 grooming parlours, is any indication, Americans indeed take their pet primping and crimping seriously, spending $200,000,000 to $250,000,000 in grooming parlours in 1974.[25] Actually, the amount is higher considering that vets do a certain amount of "grooming," for example, clipping toenails.

A basic shampoo, trim, and comb-out, may cost from $10 to $15 for a small dog, but for a large breed with long hair, $100 is not uncommon. Nail clipping generally runs from $2 to $5, $5 to $10 if the vet does it. Groomers claim that although their service is part fashion and part indulgence, the other part is good professional care for the dog; the same pitch hairdressers have always given women.

In an editorial entitled, "Decadence for dogs," Toronto's *Globe and Mail* noted the introduction of the first "hairdressing salon" in Moscow and mused: "One should always beware of stereotypes, of course, but isn't this a trifle effete, even for swinging Moscow? The Chinese will see it as a fitting refuge for revisionist running dogs; the British will suspect that it is a clumsy diplomatic attempt at ingratiation; the Americans will see it as being absurdly out of character." The editorial suggested that "other high points of Western culture," may not be far behind – "i.e. doggie burial plots."[26]

Dog Shows and Trials

There is no method of assessing how much dog fanciers spend on the business of showing dogs – only individuals who keep accurate records know precisely how expensive a hobby this can be. Over a period of time building the dog up to show quality (calling for extra special veterinary care, grooming fees, training and handlers' fees), could amount to thousands of dollars, and there is still the cost of attending and travelling to and from shows.

A survey conducted in 1974 by a Canadian dog magazine published the results of 1,495 "valid observations" of what dog owners spend attending shows and trials annually:

Respondents	Amount Spent
58.5%	$ 0 – 500
19.3%	500 – 1,000
14.6%	1,000 – 2,000
6.7%	2,000 – 5,000
.9%	over – 5,000[27]

Pet Burial

When you part from your friend you grieve not for that which you love most in him may be clearer in absence.

This passage, quoted from Lebanese poet-philosopher Kahlil Gibran in *The Prophet* is featured in a brochure advertising the services of Aldstate Animal Crematory in Brooklyn. The brochure also notes, "The sorrow of your loss can be softened with a sense of security when you give your pet a respectful and private cremation." In a telephone interview I was told that the service includes removing one's dog or cat from home or hospital, at any hour of the day, including weekends. A variety of urns is available in several colours with a space for the inscription – e.g. "Rex 1975" – or a line of poetry. As for the urns, "Ceramic or metal is the higher cost but it is most durable. You could put it in the ground and if you move, dig it up. It won't corrode or decay," the lady promised. The service cost for dogs is $65 and up, "not under that, with an urn," and for cats, about $55 to $60.[28]

There are 415 pet cemeteries in the United States, and one of the oldest and largest is Bide-A-Wee Pet Memorial Park in Long Island, New York, where, it is claimed, "Every species of animal from a horse to a grasshopper named Gary now rests peacefully on the rolling green land." Among the 50,000 laid to rest at Bide-A-Wee, its honoured inhabitants are "Sarge," the German Shepherd, who saved "several battalions of men at Anzion" (presumably they mean Anzio), "Checkers," Richard Nixon's famous Cocker Spaniel, and pets belonging to former New York Mayor Jimmy Walker and Hermione Gingold.[29]

Founder and executive director of the National Pet Cemeteries Association, Patricia Blosser, and her husband Bob own and operate Paw Print Gardens in West Chicago, which is advertised as "one of the world's most beautiful pet cemeteries." Cremation is available, although burial appears to be the preference, with embalming done on request.

The typical kind of service one may expect from a pet cemetery is outlined here, based on a number of brochures and folders produced by the Blossers. For example, their cemetery has lighted walking paths and "reminiscing benches where one can sit and recapture the past," and a chapel is dedicated to "God's Little Ones" near the entrance to the gardens. Music is piped to all corners of the cemetery and chimes may be heard now and then. "Reminiscence lights, warmly glowing" burn for approximately 150 hours and are lighted on special occasions, such as the pet's birthday, the annual burial date, Christmas, Easter, Memorial Day, and Pet Memorial Day (the second Sunday in September); however, they may be lit on any special day the bereaved pet owner chooses. For $5 annually the grave site is maintained. The printed material does not say what happens to those who don't pay (do they let weeds grow over? is the creature disinterred?), but suggests that a one-time donation will relieve the person of sending in the annual fee each year. Flowers, natural or artificial, will be placed on the site at any special time and winter blankets are available "to help protect the grave site from the bitter winter."

Caskets are priced from $30 to $450, ranging from a simple pine box, a styrofoam casket, noted as "the same used for infants," to others in redwood, steel or the famous Hoegh Pet Casket, the "pioneer in pet caskets," available in five sizes.[30] Deluxe models are described by one manufacturer as, "tastefully accented with luxurious tufted white satin overlay with a down-soft urethane pillow and pad. The exclusive velvet finish, in pink or blue, displays warmth and pride."[31] There is also another type which features, "an attractively quilted mattress and pillow, reversible for pink or blue. The white valance is quilted inside, satin-draped outside and trimmed with delicate lace."[32]

Pet memorial markers are available in bronze, granite, and marble – $52 and up. Generally the pet's name is inscribed, its dates and the owner's name; though one may add a personalized epitaph such as: "Gone But Not Forgotten," "Bye-bye Molly. See You Later," "Chippie – He was a friend and companion to all who knew him." For the uncreative owner there are such suggestions as a popular line from Byron's famous dog poem or one manufacturer's favourite, "If Christ would have had a little dog it would have followed Him to the cross."

All dog guides for the blind and K-9 dogs are given a grave site free of charge because the Blossers feel, "These animals have earned and deserve this tribute." Otherwise sites are $60 or, if chosen in advance on the "pre-need" plan, $50.[33]

In spite of caskets costing up to $450, the annual maintenance fees, and expensive bronze markers, only a handful of the 450 pet cemeteries are sizable, money-making operations, according to a *Harper's* magazine article* covering the National Pet Cemeteries Association convention in San Francisco in February 1976. One successful operator was quoted as saying, "Most [cemeteries] are really labours of love, hobbies."

Yet, he explained, "potentially, it's the biggest growth industry in the country. A multi-million-dollar business. But the average cemetery only gets one or two burials a week, that's maybe $12,000-$15,000 a year.... Most of these people aren't business people at all. They're not even educated. You see, we have no school to learn what a pet cemetery should look like, so everybody has to be an innovator. This is why I talk to them. I'm an innovator, see, trying to discover new ways of making a dollar" – some of them being a dog and cat motel, a "canine college," and a canine beauty shop that earns him a profit of $70,000 to $90,000 a year. Another member gave a sales pitch on advertising and pre-selling pet cemeteries and another suggested applying the jargon used in the human funeral business. "We don't say 'ashes' anymore, we say 'cremaines.' We don't say 'digging hole,' we say 'opening and closing the burial estate.' We don't take them there in an 'ambulance' or 'hearse,' but in a 'funeral coach.'" A casket exhibitor explained to writer Tom Englehardt that her business has doubled each year for the past three years. "It's middle-class people who are really into burying their pets. Some of them – their children are grown up, they're all alone, why, I've seen them carry on more for pets than for people in their own families! Remember, people bury people because they have to; they bury pets because they want to!" And a pet cemetery operator said, "Sometimes I hear people say, 'I don't visit my family's grave as much as I come here.' They get so involved with their pets they even faint in our office."[34]

For persons who may wish to enter this growing business, the National Association offers a seven-point plan for getting under way, emphasizing that "mums the word" until the zoning is cleared ("All you need is one neighbour to object and it could cost you hundreds of dollars and a year's time.") It suggests that when appearing before the zoning board, "use humility" and makes the point that a little "'brown-nosing' could pay off richly." The full ungrammatical program is set out in Appendix B.

Should a pet owner desire that a will be made out in the name of his cat or dog, a sample "Last Will & Testimony" is reproduced as Appendix C, compliments of Paw Print Gardens.

Estate Planning for Pets

Recluse millionaires frequently bequeath giant portions of their estates to favourite pets. Quaker Oil heiress Eleanor Ritchey left a $4,000,000 estate in 1971 to the 150 mongrel dogs she had collected over the years, and although contesting relatives received a $1,000,000 lump sum, the money for the dogs increased to $14,000,000.[35]

The subject of estate planning for pets has recently surfaced and one lawyer, writing in *Trusts and Estates Magazine*, suggests that the question ought to be studied in detail by animal welfare organizations. The difficulty is varying state laws and courts; some consider that those who bequeath funds to animals may "lack testamentary capacity under certain circumstances"; other courts have ruled that money given to pets is not considered a charitable donation for tax purposes since pets "do not benefit a general class of animals which is indefinite in numbers, but only certain specific animals." For example, bequeathing money to a humane society or zoo would qualify as a charitable donation. To add to the confusion many areas have no rulings at all.[36]

Another tricky situation is the burial of pets and masters in the same cemetery. In Oakdale Cemetery in Wilmington, North Carolina, both a heroic dog, who died trying to save his master from a fire, and the man are buried together. In another case, a human cemetery owner's dog was refused burial in a human plot and consequently when the man died he stipulated that he wanted to be buried in the pet cemetery alongside his dog. His wishes were honoured and on his tombstone is inscribed, "Here I am resting among friends."[37]

Persons who wish to provide for their pets upon their demise are advised to seek good counsel, know the applicable local or national sentiments, and avoid such risks as bequeathing a discretionary amount to an executor who, when the time comes, deems it beneficial for the poor bereaved dog to ride around in a new Mercedes or relax by a new swimming pool to grieve its master.[38]

Psychiatric Services for Dogs

What do you do if the dog suddenly starts piddling on the bed, jumping at guests, growling at the kids, and becoming more foul-tempered by the day? When a harsh, "Bad dog!" and a swat with a newspaper no longer work – if they ever did – you might do what increasingly more dog owners are doing; take him to a canine psychologist. It could be that the dog has a problem of "anxiety syndrome," "jealousy syndrome," "secretary syndrome," "dominance frustration," or "psychosexual misorientation." But not to worry. The problem can be solved through a program of behaviour modification.

It is a fact, pets are becoming as neurotic as their owners, and for some of the same reasons: the stress, crowding, noise, and pollution of urban living. Poodles and Cocker Spaniels, long considered ideal pets for children, have been behaving recently in a most uncharacteristic manner; biting and attacking children. This was unheard of ten years ago. In response to animal behaviour problems the last decade has seen the emergence of a new discipline in veterinary medicine – canine psychology. Although there are only a handful of practitioners – e.g. one in Canada – counselling services are offered to dog owners by numerous individuals from PhD psychologists to smooth-talking operators of grooming parlours.

The following is a brief glossary of terms they use:

Anxiety syndrome means the dog is worried about almost anything and acts out the anxiety by biting or attacking people.
Dominance frustration occurs when the dog thinks its master is not manly enough to protect the home, which can be upsetting, man being what the dog gave up his pack for. Therefore the dog feels he must be boss and attacks anyone who comes into the home.

116

Secretary syndrome may result when the master works late at the office and the dog gets cranky because it has not been fed and attended to.

Lover, or new baby, or new car syndrome is much the same thing.

Barrier frustration occurs when the dog gets enraged because he cannot break his leash.

Psychosexual misorientation arises when a puppy has been weaned traumatically and its maladjustment shows up in overeating, excessive scratching, or in a "preoccupation with oral behaviour in general," meaning, he bites.[39]

In 1967, *Time* magazine reported on the establishment of a Canine Behavior Center in California which deals with dog problems and, not surprisingly, movie stars were early patrons. Founder Dare Miller claims Kirk Douglas' poodle has been cured of its "terribly regressive characteristics"; Lauren Bacall and Anthony Franciosa had their dogs' postman syndrome successfully treated; Katharine Hepburn's dog has overcome its dominance frustration; Bob Hope's dogs didn't do too well in overcoming their sibling rivalry, mostly, Miller claimed, because the Hopes did not attend all counselling sessions. On the principle that what you lose on the curves you make up on the straightaways, Miller achieved "enormous success" with former Governor Ronald Reagan's dog who was transformed from a frisky puppy into a mature dog that Reagan is "now able to communicate with."

Good behaviour is chiefly the result of Miller's invention, the Hi-Fido, which is like a small tuning fork that vibrates at 34,200 cycles per second, just above the dog's threshold of hearing. The approach is Pavlovian in nature, for when the dog claws the sofa, for instance, the owner throws the Hi-Fido on the sofa, which distracts the dog and he stops clawing. The routine may be repeated until eventually the whole sofa becomes the distraction by which time the dog will perceive the sofa as a hostile environment and steer clear of it. The unit may be affixed to the dog's leash to correct behaviour when out walking.[40]

Evening house calls are made by two moonlighting New

Jersey psychologists who work during the day for a drug company and counsel families at night regarding problems with their dogs. Once a diagnosis is reached they design a treatment program based on behaviour modification. "If people work with just a minimal effort we can achieve 100 per cent success," one of the psychologists claimed, and added, "Most problems can be handled in two or three sessions, with the owner working from 15 to 20 minutes a day." Their theory is that bad behaviour must be punished, never by hitting the dog, but by repeating the command over and over until the dog gets it right, then rewarding it.[41] Since dogs love to be praised they will change their nasty ways if the owner is patient enough, which, incidentally, is the foundation of basic obedience training.

Training

One could buy a book on dog training and effectively train the animal in simple obedience commands, such as "sit," "stay," "come here," and "heel." Various dog clubs, service clubs, city departments, humane societies and perhaps some community colleges or night schools offer obedience classes which are inexpensive and dependable.

In an effort to encourage professionalism and discourage fly-by-night operators, the United States Professional Dog Trainers Association has been formed and president Dick Maller reported that its 1976 membership had tripled from that of 1975. There are 450 members from forty-four states, and from Puerto Rico, the Virgin Islands, Bermuda, Jamaica, Britain, Germany and Australia. The Association's main objective is certification of dog trainers. An apprentice, with up to a year's experience, works only in obedience; a journeyman, with from one to five years' experience is competent to do security training of guard dogs; an assistant master, with from five to ten years may take on guard and police dog training; while a master, with ten or more years' experience, is qualified for all phases.

An average obedience training course is three weeks and

costs about $290, stated Maller in 1976, which covers kennelling and the dog's food.[42] Guard training could run as high as $1,500 and more, depending on the performance required of the dog.

Countless owners have discovered that training a dog is not difficult. Good dogs can learn thirty to forty commands without any trouble at all, and intelligent German Shepherds have learned as many as 150. The important thing is to avoid confusing the animal. For example, the Royal Canadian Mounted Police use three tones of voice in its dog training program and never deviate from them either in training or in working with the dog. A normal speaking voice is used to issue commands, a softer voice is for praising the dog (after completing the command), and the third voice, a harsh, low tone, is a reprimand. Voice consistency is crucial if the dog is to understand each command, and it is essential that the same words be used each time. You can't say "sit" one time and "stay" the next and expect the dog to understand what you are after. In a training program the dog learns that this is work, not play, and the best programs are conducted in only ten, or so, minute periods to begin with, in order to retain the dog's interest.

Acupuncture for Dogs

Acupuncture, the Chinese medical technique over 5,000 years old, has been used on dogs in California since 1974. Although pooh-poohed by traditionalists, one veterinary proponent of acupuncture, Dr. Richard Glassberg, said, "It is no universal panacea but when it works it boggles the mind. You know by all reason that the needles won't work, but then, having tried everything else, the acupuncturists apply their techniques and time and again you see favourable results."

One couple claimed that when their Dachshund, Boris, whose hindquarters had become paralyzed (a common occurrence in Dachshunds) had acupuncture once a month for five months it paid off. "It's worth it to us. Just to see him running around normally again. The first time the acupuncture was

100 per cent successful. The last time it was not so good and he relapsed quickly. But we live in hope," Boris' owner said. The dog could undergo surgery, which is expensive and not always successful, but at the present time acupuncture is the preferred treatment at $20 a session.[43]

As can be seen, the sky's the limit when it comes to indulging one's pet. Regardless of what an individual chooses to spend it remains a *choice*. Taxpayers, however, have no choice in paying for the problems dogs cause. The social costs, both direct and indirect, are just beginning to be realized, as Chapter 7 details.

7

The Social Cost of Pets

The social cost of pets is treated here both in respect to the actual amount of money pets cost society, as paid out from government treasuries, and the "cost" in terms of the nuisance dogs cause. When a dog tramps down a neighbour's flower garden, the cost of this damage cannot be adequately measured in dollars and cents. After all, how much is a package of seeds? The anger, the frustration, and the breakdown of good neighbourly relations are the real costs.

Not only are more and more public dollars being spent on dogs each year – an official of the Montreal SPCA claimed that ten years ago dog control problems did not cost the local municipality anything since programs were supported wholly by charities[1] – but the hidden cost of wear and tear on the human nervous system, caused by dogs, is escalating at a pace many observers find disturbing. The fateful question no one bothered much about ten years ago is in the open: are pets worth it?

Public Costs

Rises in property taxes to cover improvements in streets and sewers, parks, and schools, are in the proverbial inevitability.

However, when millions of tax dollars go toward killing surplus dogs and cats and building new animal shelters, increasingly more taxpayers are becoming outraged. There has always been a certain amount of hostility in childless couples who pay school taxes; yet that position is effectively defended by the argument that an educated citizenry is for the common good. Pets, as many taxpayers are beginning to protest, are not.

Most communities, with the exception of small rural areas, sponsor an animal control program, or the local government contracts a humane society or other animal welfare organizations to provide animal services. In the United States the breakdown is about 450 animal shelters operated by private animal welfare organizations and 2,000 operated by local municipalities, about 900 of which would handle a minimum of 1,000 animals a year, according to the Humane Society of the United States.[2] The City of New York's animal control program, that is, impounding, adopting, issuing licences, and killing, is administered by the American Society for the Prevention of Cruelty to Animals (ASPCA). Regardless of which body administers the program, the local municipality subsidizes if not 100 per cent then at least part of the total operating cost, leaving the balance to be derived from private fund raising.

What sort of tax money is spent on pets? In 1974, it was estimated that city and county treasuries in the United States doled out $500,000,000 for animal control, primarily for impounding and killing animals. The figure does not include ridding streets annually of one million carcasses of dogs and cats killed by automobiles.[3] At an average handling cost of $10 to kill a dog, the near 15 million that are killed annually cost taxpayers $150,000,000.

Next to gonorrhea, dog bites are the most common reported health problem, at one million victims annually in the United States. But before accepting the one million figure, bear in mind that health authorities believe only one-quarter to one-half the actual number of bites are reported. Some say the real figure is more like 2 or 3 million.* At the present time,

*See more about dog bites on page 169.

122

dog-bite treatment costs Americans an estimated $100,000,000 a year.[4]

In the free-wheeling, high-rolling days of the sixties a multi-million-dollar animal shelter was lost among the clutter of multi-million-dollar recreation centres, concert halls, botanical gardens and museums that sprang up seemingly without end. But in the present time of economic restraint, when essential social services are being cut back, any million-dollar public expenditure comes under the taxpayers' close scrutiny. In Toronto a $4,500,000 animal shelter has been proposed – $1,500,000 to be contributed by the city – and while this expenditure would have gone virtually unnoticed ten years ago, now it is resented. A woman whose retarded child died, apparently due to a lack of a proper treatment facility, as reported in an inquest investigating the death, said her situation was "downright unfair." She pointed out, "The humane society can spend $3,000,000 on a place for their dogs and I could not find a place for my son."[5]

Another substantial and ongoing municipal expense is that of disposing of tons of animal carcasses each day. Pathological incinerators, in order to accommodate the growing number of animals destroyed by pounds, animal welfare organizations, and private practice veterinarians, are unable to handle their present capacities in many municipalities. The secretary manager of the British Columbia SPCA, Jack Homes, reported in 1976 that waste disposal in Vancouver's four pathological incinerators had increased by 500 per cent in the past five years, "a cost that has been completely ignored by many," he said.[6] Although actual costs of such services are difficult to obtain, the incalculable social cost, as measured in terms of air pollution and the consumption of non-renewable energy resources, is nevertheless just as offensive as the actual cost.

The extra time and work put in by city sanitation crews to clean up garbage scattered by dogs is also not quantifiable. Neither is the burden on sanitation systems caused by tons of feces and millions of litres of dog urine that are shed into the environment every day, nor how much of it contaminates city water systems. With the smog above and the dog below, environmentally the human being is the filling in a sandwich of crap.

Livestock and Wildlife Destruction by Dogs

Sheep farmers in many parts of the world suffer severe losses to livestock by attacks of feral dogs. In Canada and the United States much of the damage has heretofore been attributed to coyotes and only recently has the dog been indicted, based on wildlife field work which readily identifies predators. Robert Henderson, wildlife damage control specialist with Kansas State University said, "When coyotes make a kill, they generally take only one animal or what they can eat. Free-ranging dogs, on the other hand, will often kill several animals in one session – a kind of blood craze." And he ventured, "I'd say at least 25 per cent of livestock losses blamed on coyotes are actually caused by free-ranging dogs."

Wanton killing of livestock costs the United States an estimated $10,000,000 in compensation to farmers each year. In Canada costs are difficult to compile on a national level since it is the local municipal governments which compensate farmers for livestock losses caused by dogs. Five hundred and fifteen Ontario municipalities paid farmers $160,000 in 1973 for sheep, cattle, poultry, and swine killed or injured by dogs. (The actual amount is more; not all municipalities replied to an Ontario government Ministry of Agriculture and Food survey which provided this information.)[7]

That a pack of marauding, hungry animals will prey on other animals is an undeniable fact of nature; it is also a fact that domestic farm dogs become killers in an instant under certain circumstances. Sheep farmer Robert Walker, a representative of the Ontario Sheep and Livestock Farmers, claims that damage to livestock occurs when two or more dogs are running together. "It starts off as a game of chase but quickly turns into a pack of carnivores intent to maim or kill." There is one more explanation, merely, "A dog is a dog is a dog," Walker says.[8] For this reason he and other Canadian sheep farmers will shoot on sight any strange dog near their livestock, and by law this is their right.

The English Report of the Working Party on Dogs stated

that in 1973, 4,280 sheep were killed by dogs, and 3,618 injured, figures which are described as typical "for recent years." (This represents 1.6 per cent of the total sheep population.) The report claimed the attackers were "genuine strays," but conceded many were owned dogs not kept under control.[9]

It is believed predation by dogs is seriously curtailing sheep farming in Scotland, as it is in other parts of the world. Eight counties in Ohio showed a decrease from 760,000 sheep in 1940 to 131,000 in 1970, and the damage caused by dogs is cited as a major reason for this decline.[10] A New Brunswick government agriculturalist claims similar decreases are being seen in that province's sheep population and states, "There is no geographical area where damage does not occur, except of course in areas where flocks have ceased to exist."[11] Predation of domestic sheep in Alberta in 1974 was estimated at 4.4 per cent of all ewes and lambs, with dogs accounting for 18 per cent of the damage; coyotes were the biggest killer by far. An official stated, "Most of the dog predation resulted from the producer's own dog or a neighbour's dog. As far as I can determine, feral dogs are essentially non-existent in Alberta." He noted that, overall, the 360 ewes and lambs killed by dogs in Alberta in 1974 is a "relatively insignificant problem, province-wide."[12] Whether it is insignificant or grievous by number, no amount of compensation can pay for the loss of prime breeding stock, and a dog on a night expedition, as any sheep farmer knows, does not discriminate.

Alongside the Old West's gunslinger villains, there was a "Wanted" poster tacked up in post offices and general stores in the West for fourteen years for a dog named Dakota Three Toes. It was claimed he destroyed thousands of livestock in his day and rewards were offered for his capture, dead or alive, just as they were for Jesse James.[13]

Dogs are proving to be a serious threat to the deer populations of Canada and the United States. In northern Ontario a farmer claimed seventeen deer were killed by dogs in the county over one winter[14] and although actual numbers are not possible to secure, wildlife authorities maintain heavy damage is done by dogs. The problem is getting worse in Ontario, claims Dr. Murray Smith, a deer biologist with the Ontario

Ministry of Natural Resources, who said, "Although it is sometimes difficult to determine the initial cause of death, especially when the deer is frozen or poorly eaten by other scavengers, there is no question that the incidence of dog-related kills has increased in some parts of Ontario." Three kinds of dog do the killing: coyote-dog hybrids; feral dogs who roam the countryside in packs; and domesticated dogs. "We know that a lot of dogs involved are house pets," Smith stated. "They travel either singly or in a pack and run deer as sport during the daytime." These are city dogs people bring with them for winter weekends at the cottage. When conservation officers first identified house dogs as attackers of deer their owners did not believe their pets could be involved in such bloody activities. As Smith said, "They would say, 'It can't be my dog, he's been sitting on the front porch all day,' but they didn't notice he was gone for a couple of hours."

No one seems to know for certain why dogs are attracted to deer but Dr. Smith states, and he emphasizes it is an impression not necessarily a scientific fact, that the reason is probably due to dogs being carnivores, predatory by nature and quick to revert to the wild state.[15] The Kansas wildlife expert mentioned earlier reports, "There is something about a deer's scent which is irresistible to dogs. The temptation to chase these animals is so great that even well trained hounds occasionally 'break trail' to follow a hot deer track." Deer must devote large portions of each day feeding and if an excessive amount of time is spent running from predators they suffer from malnutrition and hence become easy prey. Also, if overheated during a chase, deer have a tendency to jump into a river or stream or lake and if the water is cold, severe shock may result.

February and March are the worst months for deer. They start to go through the snow crust while dogs are still able to run on top, and to compound the deer's plight, by that time of year, after a long, hard winter, Dr. Smith reports that they have "very little reserve left, they are on the thin edge, less capable of defending themselves."[16] In addition, does are frequently pregnant at this time, which slows them down. Attacking dogs have plenty of advantage, as is apparent.

Along with disrupting the quiet of the countryside, snowmobiles are an indirect mortality threat to deer. Their hard-packed trails through the woods provide quick access for dogs to close in on feeding deer. Even cross-country skiers, gentle folk by nature, are at fault. They bring their dogs along with them and it is not uncommon for dogs to bolt off the trail, following fresh deer tracks.

Car Accidents Caused By Dogs

Loose dogs are a common cause of car accidents and near misses, as the personal experience of numerous drivers and passengers attests to. No one knows exactly how many dogs cause accidents because the information is not broken down statistically in motor-vehicle accident reports. In the United Kingdom the 1976 Department of Environment Report of the Working Party on Dogs estimated that "dogs are reported to be involved in some 1,500 personal injury road accidents a year," and stressed that the number is likely higher since the dog that caused the accident, if not injured or killed itself, would certainly flee the scene and not be implicated.[17]

On the other hand, although millions of dollars in personal and property damages are paid out by insurance companies to accident victims, it is estimated that one million dogs and cats are killed by cars in the United States each year.[18]

Threat to the Eco-system

It is firmly established that dogs threaten the individual, in terms of his or her peace of mind and good health, as well as saddle taxpayers with enormous costs. Now the disastrous ecological effects of the overpopulation of dogs are beginning to be realized.

One research team estimates that dogs excrete 3,500 tons of feces and 36 million litres of urine into the environment every day in the United States.[19] This is a commonly quoted set of figures but is in fact a conservative estimate. If one accepts the lowest estimate of the dog population in the United States at 42 million (see page 36) this number, excreting an average of one half a pound of feces on streets and lawns each day, would deposit a daily total of 10,000 tons of feces. In New York City, with an estimated dog population of up to one million, by giving the benefit of the doubt and allowing 750,000 dogs, at one half a pound per day per dog, 187 tons of feces would be dropped in the city each and every day. This is about the equivalent of a stack of hamburgers a million and a half high. In Great Britain the daily deposit of 4.5 litres of urine and 500,000 kg of feces is equivalent to having an additional four million people in the environment.[20] While great strides have been made by environmentalists to clean up our air and lakes and streams, no corresponding force has rallied to combat the pollution of the environment by dogs. That this form of pollution is tolerated in an age of conservation-consciousness is obscene.

There is no question dog excrement is a health hazard capable of spreading disease, especially to children who play in parks or sandboxes where dogs and cats have defecated. Many serious health risks are at stake, including loss of an eye, impairment of vital organs, high fevers, and severe skin conditions, and these problems are worsening each year due to an increasing number of dogs shedding an increasing amount of infective feces into the environment. The diseases most commonly transmitted by dog and cat feces and urine are toxoplasmosis, visceral larva migrans, and leptospirosis.*

Notwithstanding feces being an assault to the sensibilities and a disease-carrying contaminant, dog feces and urine are destructive to grass and trees. Whenever dog excrement is deposited on grass, a patch of dead grass results. Urine marks lawns, causing unsightly yellow patches in otherwise beautiful green expanses. As for trees, University of Toronto Forestry Department expert John Andresen claims that urine sprayed on tree trunks is "eroding the cortical and suberized layers of juvenile bark. Before the advent of contemporary urban pollutants (including dog urine), urban trees persisted for forty to

---

*These and other pet-transmitted diseases are detailed in Chapter 8.

fifty years; currently, their life expectancy is ten to twenty years." Andresen notes that the City of New York is placing cylindrical metal shields around trees, which of course adds to the cost of tree planting, in each case, by $5 to $10.[21]

Dogs both directly and indirectly are an increasing threat to other forms of animal and marine life. Directly, feral and domestic dogs prey on deer, as already stated, and indirectly dogs and cats threaten marine life due to pet food manufacturers' ingredient usage. In the early 1950s, before meat sources other than beef, lamb, sheep, or pork had to be specified on the label, the wild horse population was decimated by the use of horsemeat in canned pet food. Whale meat was a major raw material until the early 1970s when public outcry prohibited its use. As of 1968 herring shoals have been fished almost out of existence since half the world's fish catch is being fed to animals.[22] Tuna fishermen, responding to the enormous demands of the pet food industry, use huge purse-seine nets that trap porpoises along with tuna, and although the U.S. Department of Commerce estimates that the number of porpoise victims has dropped from 1974, due to the protest of various animal welfare organizations, the tuna industry in 1975 nevertheless killed 150,000 porpoises.[23] Lawsuits are pending to halt this slaughter.

Dognapping

Cocktail chatter over muggings is likely to be blown right out the room by the trendiest new American crime – dognapping. Recognizing the enormous emotional attachment to pets, petty thieves, assorted junkies and street-gang kids have taken to snatching expensive-looking purebred dogs off the street and calling the owner on the phone to demand a ransom for the dog's return. If the dog is not wearing a tag the thief will run an ad in the paper with a detailed description, claiming the dog has been found and that he or she will accept a "reward" for its safe return. One animal welfare worker said, "In our experience they usually ask for five hundred dollars for Yorkies, Siberian Huskies and other purebred dogs. That's about the going rate. Of course, there are cases, too, of junkies ripping off the dogs and just looking to make a quick fifty or hundred dollars."[24]

And less. In Toronto a blind woman left her dog guide tied up outside the supermarket, as was her custom, and when she finished shopping the dog was gone. A few hours later a man in a bar was talked out of $20 for the dog. "I should have known better," the man said, "but I'd had a few drinks and I'm a sucker for Labradors." The dog was not wearing the traditional dog guide harness so neither the thief nor the purchaser would have known it belonged to a blind person. After hearing a radio report that a guide dog had been stolen the man returned the dog immediately, vowing if he should ever meet the thief again, "I'll punch him. I don't like dog-nappers."[25]

Since petty thieves have no monopoly on petty crimes, it has been rumoured that big boys have moved in on dognapping, seizing dogs by the dozen and selling them to research labs.* One sure-fire method of a quick roundup, related by the animal welfare worker quoted above, is for the dog dealer to turn a bitch in heat loose in a neighbourhood and wait until five or six males break away from their owners. The bitch then heads back into the van, followed by the males, the door is slammed and the van speeds across state lines.[26]

Animal welfare organizations, obviously distressed about dognapping, recognize that no amount of sympathy will get the missing dog back and urge owners to license and tag their dogs or have them tattooed for easy identification. Missing pets are usually reported to the police and distraught owners will keep an eye on animal shelters to see if their dog turns up, but without effective identification one black Labrador is barely distinguishable from the next.

Police have to contend with the problem and there is not much they can do; even if the dognapper is caught with the dog it may be difficult to prove the person stole it. The suspect could convincingly say he or she found the dog and was attempting to locate its owner. One lady saw a man shove

_____

*It has been said that the reverse occurs, whereby cleaners and helpers in the lab (not researchers) steal dogs from the lab and sell them on the street.

her Doberman into a car and drive off. She took down the licence number but when the police apprehended the man the dog was nowhere in sight, hence no charge could be laid. This and many similar stories were told by Bob Frank, a concerned citizen who since 1975 has operated a hotline in Chicago, the Society of St. Francis, for missing, lost, and stolen pets. Frank said, "Teenagers, adults, and even entire families are dognapping throughout the country," as well as "lots of amateurs out to make a buck." He claims that along with selling stolen dogs to research laboratories thieves will sell to a person wanting a low-cost purebred. Like hot colour television sets, there is a market for hot dogs.

German Shepherds and Dobermans are stolen and sold to guard dog training schools where they fetch a top price. "There is a tremendous market for guard dogs," Frank said.[27]

Barking Dogs

You are sound asleep and suddenly awakened by a siren. Chances are, you mutter and go back to sleep, acknowledging that the sound is an inevitable irritant in contemporary life. On the other hand, if you are awakened by a barking dog, getting back to sleep depends on how long the dog barks and how long it takes your fury to subside. Unlike the siren, a barking dog usually serves no useful purpose.

Noise is an environmental issue of concern at all levels of government, and legislation has been passed to produce quieter settings on the job and in communities. Investigators have found that community noise is not only a night-time disturber of sleep, in the daytime it interferes with communication, causes aggravation and tension, occasionally induces fear (as in the case of sirens which produce anxiety-provoking association), interferes with concentration and greatly affects an individual's peace of mind. Noise researchers report that a sudden sharp sound – such as a dog bark – is more aggravating than a steady noise. Also, the noise of a barking dog is much more noticeable at night without the muffler of traffic and the usual daytime distractions of a city at work.

Neighbours are often at war with one another over a barking dog, as some people have a lower tolerance threshold for noise than others. In one study, undertaken in California involving barking dogs as an environmental problem, researchers interviewed owners of noisy, barking dogs and discovered that some owners were oblivious to the barking while neighbours were at their wits' ends. One's tolerance for noise depends on one's general nervous condition, the predisposition of headaches, insomnia, and of course, acuity of hearing.

Measuring the noise level of dogs in a "confinement area," such as dog pounds and private kennels, these researchers found it to be well above the level set by the Occupational Safety and Health Act for "continuous occupational exposure." However, barking is a series of peak noises frequently of short duration, although some may be prolonged. This type of noise is "permissible," whereas a continuous sound of the same level would not be permitted under the OSH Act.[28]

Public health researcher Jeff Lewin, in a study on the effect of barking dogs in veterinary hospitals reported that, though bothersome, the stress imposed on persons from barking may also result in "possible gastrointestinal or cardiovascular irregularities." Veterinarians subjected to the noise of barking dogs all day long were affected in varying degrees. Out of eighteen vets, seventeen said they were annoyed by the noise "to some extent, on the average about twice a week," four of whom were "significantly annoyed," and all reported that the noise, when bothersome, mainly interfered with their concentration or made them irritable. One doctor was so concerned with the effect of barking on his clients that he frequently excused himself in order to go and quieten the dogs.[29] Dogs, of course, can be irreversibly silenced by surgically removing their voice boxes, which calls to mind the claimed-to-be-true case of the woman who wanted the vet to de-bark her dog so that it would remain quiet at the opera. Failing that, she requested he tranquillize the dog, in which case she could wear it to the opera around her neck.

The amount of money an individual pays for the privilege of pet keeping, and the millions of dollars public treasuries all over the country hand out to pay for the problems dogs cause, continue to increase. Also on the rise are social costs, even though these amounts are difficult to measure and are not necessarily in dollar value. When half the people in society own dogs, all of society pays in terms of the increasing pollution caused by dogs, their inroads into the human food chain, their threatening behaviour, destruction of other species and plant life, and the nuisance they make of themselves generally. Compounding the costs are the increasing numbers of diseases dogs contract from other dogs and animals and pass on to humans, and the alarming number of dogs who bite people, especially young children, and inflict serious injury. Once disease and dog bites are taken into account the social cost of pets becomes staggering.

8

Diseases You Can Get From Your Pet

Twenty years ago Fran Lee started her career as a consumer activist and in 1970 founded an organization called "Children Before Dogs" to bring attention to the many serious diseases children can contract from dogs. An energetic New York grandmother, she is still going strong, organizing public meetings, appearing on talk shows all over the country and, almost without fail, the moment she quotes the number of children who have lost eyes because of dog diseases, the war is on. Audiences begin to harass and insult her, and on a number of occasions the police have been called in to quell fist fights. At a public meeting in New York in 1972 she was pelted with dog feces; her personal life has been disrupted by picketers outside her home, yelling insults long into the night and a court order was required to stop them.[1]

Fran Lee's plight is not an ugly extreme. Emotionalism rages whenever the word "disease" is uttered in the same breath as "dogs." As far as dog lovers are concerned there is nothing more inflammatory than suggesting that the dog's position at man's side is less than poetic.

Diseases transmitted from animals to man, called zoonoses, have existed as long as both species have shared the earth and out of a total of 150 to 200 known zoonoses, twenty to forty are considered major. Inexplicably, while people are prepared to accept that a hairy, vermin-infested creature stalking the jungle or perhaps a cow in a barn could transmit a serious disease to a human, a puppy causing a child to go blind is unthinkable. The idea rams into the brick-wall mind of the average dog owner who will not accept anything negative about dogs, even when his or her own children are at stake.

How serious pet diseases are and how many persons are affected depends on who you ask. Veterinarians, dog breeders, pet food manufacturers, humane society workers, animal rights crusaders, and anyone with a vested or commercial interest in the future of pets, claim there is as much risk of getting a disease from cats and dogs as catching flu at the office. They trot out statistics that attribute only 2 to 4 per cent of zoonoses to pets and invariably sum up their arguments with the fervent declaration that they would prefer their children to live with the benefits of pets and risk minor ill effects (they can't bear to say "disease") than to live petless. On the other hand, public health officials, pediatricians, and epidemiologists feel that pets are potentially more dangerous to people than has been realized.

Diseases transmitted by pets are definitely on the upswing, and although experts disagree over the rate they express concern about the implications for the future. If dog and cat populations continue their explosive growth and produce the attendant problems of disease, bites, and accumulated tons of feces in city streets and parks, the health of people in cities is in increasing jeopardy. American writers first publicized the matter of dogs as a public health problem in magazine and newspaper stories that started to appear around 1973. Several zoonoses cause a whole range of symptoms from mild to acute to fatal, but it was *Toxocara canis* and toxoplasmosis that captured the public's attention. These two diseases contracted from dogs and cats can cause serious illness or death, and produce congenital defects such as mental retardation, blindness, and nervous system disorders. No ages or races are exempt, and children are particularly vulnerable.

Diseases transmitted from animals to man are primarily parasitic (except rabies, a notable exception, which is a viral

135

infection), and although reported the world over they are rampant in hot climates and where living conditions are unsanitary. People in Third World countries are as conditioned to worms, ticks, and fleas as people in North America are to pimples and dandruff.

Any number of 880,000 classified parasites can be infectious but we are concerned here with six parasitic groups common to dogs and cats (the vectors): protozoa – single-celled organisms which multiply by division; helminths – common worms that develop through egg and larval stages; arthropods – bugs such as ticks and mites; mycotic agents – i.e. fungi, bacteria, and viruses. Both ectoparasites (mites, ticks, fleas, etc.) which live on the skin and produce infestation, and endoparasites (worms) which cause infection by invading the body and penetrating organs, can be transmitted from dogs and cats to man.

In 1626, Francesco Redi, the grandfather of parasitology, proved to an incredulous scientific audience that worms were both male and female, and that through sexual contact they produced eggs which developed into the larval stage and thereafter into adult worms. From this discovery the medical discipline of parasitology evolved. It thrived throughout Europe during the great plagues, tapering off by the twentieth century. The Second World War reawakened interest in the subject for countless hitherto unaffected persons – British, American and Canadian troops – became victims of tropical diseases. A resurgence in the practice of parasitology is now under way. Places with low incidences of parasitic diseases, such as Europe, Britain, Scandinavia, the United States, Canada, Australia, New Zealand and some Balkan countries, are showing sharp increases. When Lassa fever, endemic only to Nigeria and Liberia, was suspected in Toronto in 1976,* it was as incongruous as hearing that scorpions were thriving on Arctic ice floes.

More and more disease anomalies are coming to light for several reasons: jet travel exposes people to exotic countries

* A Canadian woman, who had been in Africa years previously, was returning from Europe when she was suddenly stricken with what appeared to be Lassa fever. The hospital was quarantined, but after five days Lassa fever was discounted.

and their exotic bugs; immigration is often accompanied by alien parasites that find new hosts in the new country; environmental disruptions cause shifts in wildlife populations, bringing animals closer to people; many countries have discontinued or cut back use of insecticides; and city people are exploring the countryside and interacting with wild animals that may bite them and pass on infections.

Nevertheless, in North America the main cause in the rise of parasitic diseases is the increase in the dog and cat population. It is estimated that if dogs continue to proliferate at their present explosive rate of 2,000 to 3,500 per hour (compared to the human reproduction rate of 415 per hour), their numbers will double by 1984. One estimate yet to materialize is how sick or healthy these animals will be, and how much greater a disease risk this represents to humans.

Some people complain that a sick dog gets better care and attention than a sick person. One disgruntled American vet insists, "ninety per cent of American dogs enjoy better medical care than half the people in the world." A similar view is shared by Dr. Crawford Anglin, Chief of Infectious Diseases at the Hospital for Sick Children in Toronto, who says society is better geared to look after pets than children "in insuring they are immunized against infectious diseases."[2] Dogs, with improved feeding and veterinary care, are living four to six years longer than they were fifteen years ago, yet in Britain the rate of infant mortality in coal-mining and factory towns is among the highest in the western world. Until some of these inequities are dealt with and zoonoses are regarded as more than regrettable misalliances, like being unlucky in love, many more humans will in one way or another be tragic victims of dogs and cats.

The following outlines some of the more common diseases transmitted by pets to humans.[3]

Toxoplasmosis

It is estimated that half a billion people in the world have toxoplasmosis. That is over one-eighth of the world's population, ranging from 20 to 100 per cent in many tropical countries. Yet most victims do not even know they are infected. So what is all the fuss about? one might ask.

Newspapers and magazines are now reporting birth deformities and severe illnesses caused by toxoplasmosis, a disease that was barely mentioned in the popular press five years ago. Sensational stories have since appeared with frequency. However, in the case of toxoplasmosis, even the most extravagant accounts do not exaggerate the damage it is capable of causing.

A parasitic disease previously thought only to be transmitted placentally to the newborn from an infected mother or from eating uncooked or rare meat, scientists now have hard evidence that also indicts the household cat. Since no one likes to hold the pussy cat responsible for causing such severe afflictions as blindness or brain damage there has been strenuous resistance by both the public and the medical community in accepting the fact that today cats are common vectors of toxoplasmosis.

First reported in 1908 in a North African rodent called the *gondi*, the parasite *Toxoplasma gondii* was found late that year in man, and subsequently in cattle, pigs, sheep, dogs, monkeys, mice, rabbits, opossums, racoons, skunks, and pigeons. Significant research on toxoplasmosis was undertaken between the years 1927 and 1942 and it was universally held that the disease in humans was a result of eating raw or lightly cooked meat, a finding long supported by the high incidence of toxoplasmosis reported in those cultures with a passion for raw meat – the French with their steak tartare and the Arabs with kibbe. However, there was a missing link. Strict vegetarians and herbivores such as cattle, sheep, goats, chickens, and many bird species, were also victims, and it wasn't until the mid-1960s when simultaneous evidence by researchers, W.M. Hutchison of Glasgow and Jacob Frenkel and J.P. Dubey of the United States supplied the missing link. They discovered that feces from infected cats could transmit toxoplasmosis and the barn cat became the new villain. Barn cats enjoy free range in selecting their places to defecate, including the grain bin. Here we see the infectivity cycle of cat to cattle to human. The cat defecates in the grain bin, cattle eat the infected grain whereupon their musculature carries the toxoplasma parasite, a person eats rare or raw beef (there hasn't been enough heat to kill the parasites), ingests the parasites, and becomes infected.

When *Toxoplasma gondii* parasites invade man's cells runaway multiplication is normally halted by the human body's natural defence system which musters a special army of antibodies to fight off attackers. This is how one can be infected and not know it: parasites in the body are held in check by antibodies and may remain in this dormant stage for months, years, or even the rest of one's life. The presence of toxoplasmosis in humans is determined by testing a blood sample for the presence of antibodies and if positive a titre (the amount or level of antibodies found) is said to be present; if the test shows a negative titre there is no antibody level, hence no evidence of infection. A toxoplasma positive titre is good news – up to a point. It is akin to having measles as a child and thereafter being immune. However, a positive titre can be dangerous if a severe illness or the administration of drugs such as corticosteroids halts the body's manufacture of antibodies, and should that happen, the toxoplasma parasites, up to now held in check, are suddenly freed. It is as if the army, the natural antibodies, is successful in barricading the enemy, the parasites, until the gates are stormed by a new marauder, illness or drugs. In this eventuality, toxoplasma parasites are released and begin to multiply rapidly and that is when trouble begins. They will attack almost any cell but seem to favour the eyes, brain, and spinal cord.

Much information about toxoplasmosis is still guesswork, not the least of which is its diagnosis. The disease often slips by physicians because its symptoms are vague and frequently resemble viral infections, and to make matters worse, general practitioners, except those in the tropics, have virtually no experience with or knowledge of parasitic diseases. The patient may have a slight temperature, swollen lymph glands, and feel washed out. Chances are, the doctor prescribes bed rest and aspirin. In more severe cases the person may experience malaise and lethargy for a matter of weeks, in which case the diagnosis is likely to be mononucleosis; and in time it, too, passes. However, acute toxoplasmosis may result in heart failure, blindness and brain or central nervous system damage for the unfortunate individual.

Treatment is a hit and miss affair and some of the consequences have been disastrous. Infected persons treated with corticosteroids for, say, arthritis, have been known to die suddenly of toxoplasmosis. The only reason this does not happen with alarming regularity is that corticosteroids administered to persons with a toxoplasma positive titre are accompanied by drugs that kill off the parasites, rather than the host.

In spite of many imponderables, scientists are now fairly certain about how a person may contract toxoplasmosis: either by indirect transmission, that is, through eating raw or undercooked meat which contains the parasites, as already discussed, or by direct transmission through ingesting them in cat feces.

This is not as unlikely as it may seem.

A cat with toxoplasmosis harbours the causative organisms clumped together in a protective covering, like thousands of grains of sand in a plastic bag. These "grains," called oocysts, are defecated by the cat and although fecal passage of the oocysts may last only two or three weeks in a cat's lifetime, during this stage the cat may defecate several million of them. They are tenacious. They can survive for as long as a year in the earth and freezing temperatures do not necessarily kill them. Being highly resistant to chemicals standard household disinfectants offer no sure prophylaxis. And since cats cover up their feces, this tidy streak of theirs safeguards infective oocysts on the ground. The point is, humans become infected immediately upon inadvertently ingesting infective oocysts contained in cats' feces. This happens when hands come in contact with infected feces through changing kitty litter, gardening in soil where infective cats have defecated, and by children from playing in sandboxes that are shared by infected cats. The hands get in the mouth – especially true in the cases of thumb-sucking youngsters, persons who bite their nails, or those who don't wash their hands before eating – and the person is infected.

Toxoplasmosis would be dismissed as minor were it not for

140

one very high risk group – pregnant women. In 40 per cent of women who contract toxoplasmosis for the first time during pregnancy, one-third to one-half of the babies born may suffer irreversible brain damage, spinal cord damage, central nervous system disorders, or blindness. Dr. B.H. Kean, professor of tropical medicine and parasitology at Cornell University in New York, estimates that one hundred New York babies are born annually with toxoplasmosis. In a study involving 5,000 pregnant women the incidence of toxoplasmosis was higher than the combined number of babies born with defects from congenital syphillis, rubella, and phenylketonuria (PKU), a common cause of mental retardation.[4] But the disease is capricious. Of those one hundred babies perhaps 40 to 50 per cent will reveal obvious deformities at birth, while others are perfectly normal except for a positive titre. However, parasitic cysts present in the newborn may be activated years later, quite frequently affecting the eyes, liver, lung, brain or muscles.

Researchers claim that the incidence of toxoplasmosis increases 10 per cent with every decade. That is, 10 per cent of persons age ten are positive, 20 per cent at age twenty, 30 per cent at age thirty, 40 per cent at forty, levelling off at about 50 per cent in western countries. In tropical countries 100 per cent of the population is commonly infected. Even though the rate of infectivity may be high the incidence of clinical disease is generally low. (This is an important distinction to keep in mind regarding zoonoses generally.)

Veterinarians, physicians, parasitologists and epidemiologists maintain that neither the incidence nor the effects of toxoplasmosis is cause for alarm, except in regard to pregnant women. Here the potential risk is real and serious. Yet in reviewing the medical literature on toxoplasmosis only one author suggested that pregnant women should get rid of the cat. Veterinary parasitologist Dr. J.P. Lautenslager of the Ontario Ministry of Agriculture and Food, Veterinary Services Branch in Guelph, Ontario, offered some practical advice: "I tell women, 'if you are pregnant, consider sending the cat away for a nine-month holiday. If that's not acceptable, keep the cat inside and never give it raw meat, or eat raw meat yourself. That would be a fairly safe situation.'" He also said that if a titre on the cat showed positive it would be reassuring to pregnant women.[5] Positive, remember, is an indication of immunity.

If personal experience is ever a valid measure, doctors may now be on the alert. When I asked my family doctor what he told pregnant women about their cats, he allowed, "Well, I guess I'll have to start telling them *something*."

Preventive measures

1. In the extreme, get rid of the cat to reduce the potential risks.
2. Never feed your cat raw liver, or any other raw meat.
3. Avoid eating raw meat yourself, or meat that is lightly cooked. Beef, for example, requires cooking to an internal temperature of 150°F to kill toxoplasma parasites. This is about medium done, just a trifle pink in the centre.
4. If you are pregnant stay away from free-roaming cats. To help your cat remain toxo-free, keep it indoors, or on a leash when outdoors, admittedly curtailing its natural instincts. Whenever cats hunt for mice and birds they are subject to contracting toxoplasmosis.
5. Pregnant women should never change the kitty litter. It is no guarantee against infection, however; infective oocysts could be in the carpet.
6. Under normal circumstances change kitty litter daily. One researcher suggests baking it for an hour to kill infective oocysts.
7. Don't throw kitty litter on the garden. If it contains the infective parasites they can survive for as long as a year; dispose of it in tight plastic bags or incinerate it.
8. If you are really concerned, have a toxoplasma titre determined on both you and your cat. Reputed to be one of the most reliable tests in medical history, the Sabin-Feldman dye test (Sabin, the researcher of polio vaccine fame) will reveal the presence and level of toxoplasma antibodies. If the results are negative you are vulnerable; if positive you are immune to re-infection;

however, there is the possibility you may experience problems should a serious illness occur. (See page 140.)

9. Don't allow children, especially crawling, thumb-sucking youngsters near kitty litter or cats' feces. Also, keep cats out of children's sandboxes and cover them when not in use.

10. Whenever you or your children see the doctor about a vague illness, be sure to mention if you have a cat, or any other household pet.

Toxocara canis (roundworm)

Every time the young mother brought her two children home from a city park on Sundays she'd spend half an hour scraping the dog droppings off their shoes. Finally, in desperation, she phoned the city health department and asked if her children could get *Toxocara canis* from the mess dogs left in the park.

One warm summer night a young couple picked up some chicken after work for a picnic in the park. A piece of chicken fell to the grass, and when the man brushed it off and began to eat it, his girl friend gasped. "Don't eat it," she exclaimed, "you could get that dog disease."

Two years ago, in all probability, neither the mother nor the girl would have considered dog feces a health risk. Yet more and more people living in cities the world over, particularly in North America and England, are becoming aware of this danger. They have heard the rumblings, and recall a sensational case or two of a child dying or having an eye removed, and although not exactly sure of the details they distinctly remember that it had something to do with dog droppings on city streets and parks.

Is it true? Can dog feces spread disease? And if so, how serious are these diseases? The immediate answers are "Yes, Yes" and the disease *can* be very serious, although most of the infections contracted from dog feces are minor. *Toxocara canis*, the roundworm, and by far the most commonly present parasite found in dogs, and its companion *Toxocara cati* in cats, can be transmitted to man. When humans are infected by the worm *T. canis* or *T. cati*, the disease is called visceral larva migrans.

It is not uncommon for half and as many as all litters of puppies to be born with *T. canis*, transmitted from the bitch during gestation. Baby worms are passed in the feces of new-born puppies, and the bitch in a maternal clean-up after whelping eats the puppies' feces, thus re-infecting her body with baby worms that grow into adults and reproduce by laying eggs. Hence the bitch seeds the environment with infective eggs shed in her feces. Even if the bitch is wormed after whelping, larvae remain in her muscles and may be placentally transmitted to the next two or three litters, at least, and the re-infection cycle repeats itself once more.

How many times is the cuddly new puppy handed over to the crawling child? In this endearing picture, millions of sticky, gooey, infective *T. canis* eggs may cling to the puppy's feet and fur and readily stick to the fingers of the thumb-sucking child. The infected child may develop a tummy ache and be cranky for a couple of days, at best; at worst, partial blindness may result, and in rare cases, the child could die. To take pleasure in watching the little puppy with the toddler can be an expensive sentiment.

Not only puppies are infected. Surveys undertaken the world over reveal from 1.3 per cent to 93 per cent of dogs studied were found to have *T. canis* worms. An Ontario survey showed that an average of 21 per cent of puppies and mature dogs were infected. (See Tables 1, 2, and 3, pp. 151-155).

Eggs excreted in fresh feces on the ground are not infective for humans. It takes an incubation period of from three to eight weeks (depending on heat and moisture conditions) for the eggs to develop into the third—and infective—larval stage. Newly passed dog feces are therefore "safe"; it is those dried-up, harmless-looking sausages that are the danger.

Eggs are normally associated with fragility, but not so the *T. canis* eggs. They have been tested for survival in a temperature of 5°F and 100 per cent lasted for three weeks; at four weeks the survival rate dropped to 98 per cent; by two months it was 43 per cent and in four months, none had survived. Another test, alternating freezing and thawing daily for ten days, resulted in an amazing 90 per cent survival.[6] The implications are that in a cold climate such as Canada, where this study was undertaken, and in the northern United States and Europe, infective eggs could conceivably be passed in dog feces in the fall and be preserved until spring if the weather did not reach prolonged below-freezing temperatures. It has been estimated that eggs may remain infective for up to two years.

When *T. canis* eggs are ingested by man they develop into the larval stage and migrate to various organs (the viscera), which is why in humans the condition is called visceral larva migrans. Larvae migrate from the intestine to the liver, lungs, heart, kidneys, brain, retina of the eye, and then fan out to the muscles. In muscle tissue they are dead-ended, usually causing no harm, and in time they die or the host kills them off. (They have, however, been known to survive for ten years or more.) It is when the larvae penetrate an organ that trouble may develop, especially if the affected person is predisposed to allergic reactions. Bronchial conditions may result from larval irritation to the lungs; various blood conditions occur (notably eosinophilia, a white blood cell imbalance which usually signifies parasitic infection); and larvae are capable of detaching the retina, causing blindness.

As with toxoplasmosis, diagnosis of *T. canis* infection is erratic because symptoms are usually not acute. The danger is that by missing the diagnosis infective larvae may be pursuing a steady course of attack on the body's organs, especially the eyes.

In 1978 an Irish journalist, Inez Heron, wrote an account of her eight-year-old son's heroic battle against the disease. He appeared to be suffering from appendicitis, was operated on, another three operations followed, his condition was diagnosed as terminal cancer and he was given only a few days to live. Fifteen months, six operations and several radium treatments later, it was discovered the boy's trouble was a result of the *Toxocara canis* parasite. By this time he was blind in one eye.[7]

Numerous cases are documented of surgeons removing eyes

145

from children after mis-diagnosing the problem as a potentially fatal retinoblastoma (a malignant tumour on the retina) that later proved to be a lesion produced by *T. canis*. In 1950 in the United States, twenty-four of forty-six eyes were enucleated (removed by surgery) because they were thought, erroneously, to be cancerous, with repeated instances occurring in 1959, 1960, and 1961. Similarly, eyes were mistakenly enucleated in Britain. Ophthalmologists who detect doubtful lesions on retinas now test for parasitic infection before they jump to carcinogenic conclusions and the likelihood of such mistakes happening again is, thankfully, remote.

Resulting in a handful of deaths per year, a few dozen cases of blindness, some lung and blood changes, countless vague illnesses, especially in children who have difficulty defining symptoms, the medical community's lack of concern with *T. canis* up to now has been deplorable. It is true serious illness or debility from visceral larva migrans in humans is infrequent. Tell that to the mother whose child has been blinded by a dog's worm; she is not consoled that it occurs less frequently than glaucoma or cancer.

Preventive measures

1. Have lactating bitches and the new puppies wormed before the pups are eight weeks old.
2. Keep children away from puppies before they have been wormed.
3. Beware of dried dog feces on streets and parks; they could be infective.
4. When cleaning up after one's defecating dog – as responsible dog owners do – use a plastic bag as a glove so that feces do not touch the hands.
5. At the very first worm noticed in the dog's feces or vomit, have the dog wormed immediately.
6. Since *Toxocara canis* does not develop to the adult worm stage in man, a child will not pass toxocara worms, (human worms, yes). Thus worm-free stools are no indication that the child is toxocara-free.

7. When the child has a persistent cough, a kidney infection, bladder troubles, or eosinophilia, tell the examining physician if the child has a pet, or if he or she has recently been around pups or if the child crawls where dogs run and defecate.
8. Cover the child's sandbox to prevent the dog or cat from defecating in it. Infective eggs of the cat roundworm, *Toxocara cati*, are also capable of causing visceral larva migrans.

Cutaneous Larva Migrans (creeping eruption)

Creeping eruption occurs when parasitic larvae, rather than being ingested, penetrate the skin. An eruption results which shows the path of tunnelling larvae underneath the skin, travelling at a speedy several millimetres a day. Before long the condition resembles tightly condensed varicose veins without the swelling.

Transmitted by at least four known species of parasitic worms, cutaneous larva migrans (CLM) is widespread in the southern United States, southern France, Spain, South Africa, India, the Philippines, Australia, and South American countries such as Brazil, Uruguay, and Argentina. A disease associated with poverty, it is prevalent wherever conditions are extremely unsanitary and humans and dogs crowd together, infective feces incubating in the sun. Canadians who flock to tropical paradises to avoid the long, cold, winter have commonly brought home dysentery among their souvenirs, but cutaneous larva migrans is an increasing risk. A Toronto man returned from Barbados in February 1976, his back and chest actually infected with CLM, having done what all other tourists do – lie on the beach. He had no way of knowing the particular beach was infected.

Skin eruptions appear on hands and feet after persons have either walked in infective dog feces or touched them, as frequently happens with children who play in the dirt. Since larvae do not reach the adult worm stage in man and reproduce, they die under the skin – sooner or later.

Preventive measures

It might be said there is no cure for cutaneous larva migrans until poverty is eradicated. In the meantime:

1. Don't walk barefoot where dogs defecate. (Or, as parasitologist Dr. J.P. Lautenslager tells his students, "If you're going to walk in dog shit, put your shoes on.")
2. Keep children away from playing in sandboxes or areas known to be running places of dogs.
3. Always lie on a towel when suntanning, not directly on the sand, particularly on an unfamiliar beach or if you notice dogs.

Ancylostoma caninum (hookworm)

Although there are four common hookworms found in man, *Ancylostoma caninum* is the only one transmitted by dogs – the others depend on human to human transmission.

Larvae penetrate the skin, causing cutaneous larva migrans, or they may reach the blood stream and travel to the lungs and brain, where they may live for as long as a year. Since this hookworm species is very common in dogs the world over (see Tables 1, 2, and 3, pp. 151-155) transmission to humans occurs by walking in infected dog feces or by touching feces with the hands and ingesting the larvae.

The infected person may feel nauseous, headachy, have diarrhea or constipation and be subject to malaise. An extremely heavy, long-term worm burden in children may cause mental or physical retardation, and although deaths have occurred they are usually caused in combination with another infection.

The preventive measures for CLM, above, would also apply for *Ancylostoma caninum*.

Hydatid Disease (tapeworm)

Canids who eat the offal (organs such as liver, kidneys, etc.) of infected animals, for example sheep, may contract the parastic hydatid cyst which becomes a tapeworm. The disease thereafter progresses as cysts develop into mature tapeworms *Echinococcus granulosis*, which shed their eggs in feces and are then transmitted to man who may accidentally ingest the eggs. This is the familiar route of transmission of other parasitic diseases. With children who have ingested eggs, cysts may advance over a period of several years and appear as calcified growths in X-rays. Growths the size of grapefruits have been discovered in the liver and lungs of adults infected as young children.

The disease is serious in many parts of the world, especially in the Middle East. In Uruguay, a country of about three million people, sixty deaths a year are reported and as many as 600 surgeries are performed annually to remove enlarged hydatid cysts.

The sheep-dog-sheep cycle of transmission is most prevalent almost everywhere except in North America. The disease appears in northwest Canada in a moose-wolf-moose cycle. Sled dogs, eating the offal of those infected animals, become infected and transmit the parasite to man. In Australia a similar dog-kangaroo-dog cycle prevails.

Preventive measures

1. Be certain that farm dogs have no access to offal of infected sheep or other animals.
2. Known or potentially infected dead animals should be buried deep in the ground.

Dipylidium caninum (dog tapeworm)

Dogs who bite at their fleas may ingest infections along with the flea, one of them being *Dipylidium caninum*, a tapeworm whose eggs are eliminated in the feces of dogs and cats. Children may become infected by ingesting fleas present in the dog's fur, or infected fleas may be passed from the dog's mouth by licking the child. Although fairly common in dogs and cats, the tapeworm is also present in the fox and wild relatives of canids and felines.

The following tables show some random incidences of hookworm, roundworm, and tapeworm found in dogs. It is important to remember that puppies have a high incidence of worms and the figures in these tables, although interesting, can be misleading when the ages of the dogs examined are not known. As can be seen in the Australian study of *Toxocara canis*, 100 per cent of the puppies were infected, compared to only 9 per cent of the adults. The asterisked footnotes offer some clues, but each study would have to be examined closely before it could be determined precisely how representative these figures are, with the exception of the Ontario study, which reports the ages of dogs examined.

TABLE 1

Incidence of Various Gastrointestinal Worms Found in Dogs in Several U.S. Areas[8]

	Hookworm (*Ancylostoma caninum*)	Roundworm (*Toxocara canis*)	Tapeworm (*Dipylidium caninum*)
Ohio State University Area (over 20 year period) (Goss & Rebrassier, 1922)	18%	23%	—
Washington, D.C. (Wright, 1928)	50%	33%	—
New Orleans (Hinman & Baker, 1936)	42.5%	1.9%	—
Columbus, Ohio (Doutz & Rebrassier, 1942)	—	16.09%	—
Florida (Donaldson, Steele & Scatterday, 1949)*	86.1%	—	—
Ohio River Drainage Area (Ehrenford, 1957)	—	21%	—

*Based on recovery of adult on necropsy.

	Hookworm (*Ancylostoma caninum*)	Roundworm (*Toxocara canis*)	Tapeworm (*Dipylidium caninum*)
New York City (5 Metropolitan Areas with Contrasting Environment) (Dorman & Van Rostrand, 1958)*	6.8%	13%	—
New Orleans (Beaver, 1959)*	51.07%	7%	—
New Orleans (Vaugh & Jordan, 1960)*	51.8%	8.2%	—
Cornell U. Vet. College (Annual Report, 1951-56)	7.3%	9.3%	—
Hawaii (Ash, 1961)**	71%	23.4%	85%***
Bermuda Islands (Williams & Menning, 1970)*	54%	38%	9.29%***
Chicago, North Side (Jaskoski, 1970)*	3.78%	2.01%	—
City of Houston,			

* Based on examination of stools collected from sidewalks, lawns and vacant lots.
** Based on recovery of adult on necropsy.
*** More than 100% reveals multiple infection.

	Hookworm (Ancylostoma caninum)	Roundworm (Toxocara canis)	Tapeworm (Dipylidium caninum)
West Suburb, 1975	39%	6.6%	—
City of Houston, 1975 (Steele)	85%	13%	42%*
Montreal (Choquette, Gelinas, 1950)	9.5%	52.6%	—
Indiana (Ehrenford, FA, 1956)		21%	—
Eastern & Southeastern U.S. (Mann & Bjotvedt, 1965)	60%	12%	11%

*More than 100% reveals multiple infection.

TABLE 2
Prevalence of *Toxocara canis* in Dogs in Other Countries[9]

Country	No. Dogs Examined	Percentage Infected
India (Calcutta) (Maplestone & Bhaduri, 1940)	100	82%
France (Thienpont, Vanparijs, 1969)	—	17%

Country	No. Dogs Examined	Percentage Infected
Australia (Brisbane) (Sprent, English, 1958)	29 pups 35 adults	100% 9%
Italy (Thienpont, Vanparijs, 1969)	225	79%
Bermuda (Williams, Menning, 1961)	71 pups 366 total	66% 38%
Poland (Thienpont, Vanparijs, 1969)	—	21%
Germany (Thienpont, Vanparijs, 1969)	1,642	10.6%
Mexico City (Styles, 1967)	120 pups	93%
England (London) (Woodruff, 1970)	300	20.7%
Nigeria (Wiseman, Woodruff, 1971)	72	37.5%
Malta (Wiseman, Woodruff, 1971)	52	28%
Kenya (Nairobi)		

Country	No. Dogs Examined	Percentage Infected
(Wiseman, Woodruff, 1971) Great Britain	35	5.7%
(Bord, Woodruff, 1973)	800	24.4%

TABLE 3
Toxocara Canis in Dogs in Ontario[10]

Age of Dog*	No. Dogs Examined	No. Infected	Percentage Infected
no age given	264	45	16%
2 weeks – 2 months	57	32	58%
2 months – 6 months	299	120	42%
6 months – 12 months	133	21	16%
1 year – 2 years	129	12	10%
2 years – 4 years	137	9	7%
4 years – 7 years	83	1	1%
7 years – 10 years	48	1	2%
10 years – 15 years	23	0	0%
"mature"	6	0	0%
"various"	370	92	28%
Totals	1,549	331	21%

*By reporting the age of dogs examined it can be seen that the incidence of Toxocara canis decreases with maturity.

Leptospirosis

The contagious bacterial disease, called leptospirosis in animals and Canicola fever or Weil's disease in humans, was first reported in animals in 1915. Researchers in Norway discovered that rats and other rodents are the principal hosts of the leptospores that cause the disease, but it wasn't until 1948, after an outbreak in dogs, cattle, and swine in the United States, that leptospirosis was identified as a zoonotic disease.

European physicians are well acquainted with Canicola fever, as it is contracted relatively frequently from farm and pet animals. In North America from 15 to 35 per cent of the cases are caused by dogs, and the potential risk is growing due to the increasing numbers of dogs in the environment. In most instances the disease is not serious, except in acute cases where jaundice-like symptoms or symptoms similar to those of meningitis are produced, and the victim may be left with central nervous system disorders or permanent kidney or heart damage. In cases such as these a fatality rate of up to 20 per cent has been recorded.

Leptospirosis, together with toxoplasmosis and *Toxocara canis*, are the three big diseases of pets that concern public health officials today. Spread by urine (from ingesting infected animal urine), leptospirosis is rarely contracted directly by humans. Transmission usually takes a secondary route. The tiny bacterial organisms thrive in soil and water and, like all unsafe water that can look deceptively clean, the prettiest babbling brook may harbour contaminated leptospires from urine of untold numbers of sick animals.

Although the exploding dog population accounts for part of the steadily climbing rate in North America, another explanation is the changing patterns of leisure activities. Hordes of city people flock to the countryside, day-tripping, weekending, and vacationing. Campsites are big business for the tourist industry and skyrocketing sales of mobile homes and campers reflect the increasing numbers of North Americans who are camping, picnicking, swimming, boating, hunting and fishing, as never before. Over the past decade public health officials are noticing some of the inherent risks of these excursions to the country, one of them being contracting leptospirosis from contaminated streams, ditches, creeks, ponds, and from the soil itself.* But avoiding the countryside and languishing in one's own backyard does not ensure immunity. A person could be plucking weeds out of flower beds and be exposed to leptospirosis from a dog who had urinated there as long as three weeks ago. Children are at a risk, too, playing with infected puppies that accidentally urinate on them.

By calculating the current average weight of the American dog, and the average daily amount of urine passed, a veterinary journal calculated that the United States has 9.5 million gallons of dog urine deposited on it every day.[11] The implications of such quantities of disease-free dog urine gushing through city sewers, to be re-cycled into the drinking water, are disquieting in the extreme, but the possibility that even one per cent of the urine may contain leptospires is frightening.

Large dogs take the brunt of the blame for most problems under discussion, but in the case of leptospirosis the small and young dog is frequently the guilty party. Dogs with short legs and long hair, such as Terriers, Dachshunds, Pekingese and Spaniels, drag their bellies through puddles and may pick up leptospires. By licking their hair they ingest the organism and the developmental cycle of the disease begins. Microscopic organisms stick to the fingers of individuals who play with dogs by rubbing the belly or places where urine has sprayed, and should those hands find their way into the mouth (especially likely in the case of children) infection is under way.

The World Health Organization reported 73 cases of Canicola fever in Russia in 1955. The outbreak was due to well water contaminated with dog urine. Such large-scale attacks come to public attention periodically, but thousands of individual cases are never reported because symptoms mimic many other disorders. Furthermore, even in reported cases, quite frequently the vector is unknown, although it seems

---

*Although dogs are responsible for increased incidence of leptospirosis, it is far more commonly transmitted by swine, cattle, rodents, and wild animals.

fairly certain that transmission from infected farm animals, rats, or wildlife far exceeds that from dogs.

Vector notwithstanding, the outlook is pessimistic. More dogs, more city people in the country, increasing interaction with wildlife, more polluted water and soil, shifts in animal populations caused by such ecological disturbances as land reclamation projects, forest removal, highways bulldozing through farmlands, creation of drainage and irrigation ditches – all these conditions invariably result in new leptospiral reservoirs.

Contaminated water and soil pose unavoidable risks to the individual, owning a dog constitutes risk by choice. The combination of dog-owning and swimming in a dubious stream sets up the perfect double risk situation for contracting leptospirosis. Yet what could be more typical than a boy and his dog splashing about in a stream on a hot, sunny day? These are the golden moments of youth. Unhappily, it is now acknowledged that on a growing number of these occasions, leptospirosis could be one of the not-so-golden consequences.

Preventive measures

1. When camping never drink stream or lake water, no matter how clear and tempting it looks.
2. If water must be used for drinking or cooking, boil it at least twenty minutes beforehand.
3. Give your dog a good bath after a day's woodsy outing, especially if he has been in the water.

Rabies

Literature is replete with hair-raising tales of mad dogs frothing at the mouth, drunkenly unsteady on their legs, lunging to bite a small child. Yet, in spite of how horrific some of the stories are, they don't distort the truth as far as rabies is concerned. A rabid dog, capable of whipping a community into a frenzy, is frightening to behold.

Once a dog contracts rabies (from another rabid dog or wildlife animal) it is doomed. If a rabid dog bites a person and the victim contracts rabies (only about 30 per cent of people bitten by a known rabid dog get the disease) and no treatment is administered, the person inevitably dies. The reason for its deadliness is that viral particles in the saliva of a rabid dog penetrate the victim's skin, as in the case of a bite, and incubate in the tissues, then travel with great speed and efficiency to the central nervous system. Should the infection reach the brain before rabies vaccine has been administered and the body begins to produce antibodies, death results from acute encephalitis.

There are three stages of rabies recognizable in dogs. The first is characterized by a voracious appetite and generally peculiar or erratic behaviour. It is in the second stage, the one that has created legends, that there is frothing at the mouth, followed by convulsions and delirium. In the third and final stage the animal becomes quiet, almost paralyzed. By this time it has usually crawled off somewhere to die.

History has demonstrated that rabies has waxed and waned at about one-hundred-year intervals since it was first recognized in 2,300 B.C. Today the spread of rabies by dogs has been controlled in many countries through elimination of strays and by vaccination. A classic case of eradication through vaccination occured in Malaysia in 1952. Of a dog population, including a high proportion of strays, 18,000 were vaccinated, 12,000 were destroyed, and the incidence of rabies plummeted. In July of that year thirty-five cases were reported; control measures began and by December there was not one more case.

Worldwide, dogs transmit rabies to humans more frequently than any other animals do, although most biting mammals may be vectors, i.e. foxes, coyotes, wolves and jackals, cats, skunks, racoons, mongooses, and bats. In North America, however, dogs account for only about 5 per cent of cases – the fox, skunk, and bat, are the common vectors. Vampire and insectivorous bats of Mexico, South and Central America, the United States, Canada, Europe, and Southeast Asia, have been known rabies vectors. Exposure is generally by means of a bite, although in the caves of Frio, Texas, which house thousands of bats, rabies occured in 1968 in three persons through aerosol transmission.

Rabies is found throughout the world, in the arctic, temperate, and tropical, regions of both hemispheres. At the present time twenty-three countries are rabies-free, among them Australia, New Zealand, Japan, Hawaii, and other Pacific Islands, some of the West Indies, Great Britain, Ireland, Norway, and Sweden. The World Health Organization reports that 15,000 persons in India die of rabies each year, about 35,000 Americans require rabies post-exposure treatment annually, and rabies treatment is given to half a million people per year in the world. The situation is worsening in many countries, for example in Korea, Vietnam, and in other Asian locations.

Quarantines have proved effective in controlling rabies in several countries, notably England, Denmark, Finland, Ireland, the Netherlands, and Norway; but there is no panacea. After being rabies-free for the past seventy-five years an outbreak occurred recently in Denmark. Quarantines are imposed on dogs entering these countries for a period of six months. The British, who adore movie celebrities, made no exception for luminaries Elizabeth Taylor and Richard Burton, who, when filming in London, were compelled to lease a yacht and moor it on the Thames in order to be able to visit their six dogs.

Probably no nation is as preoccupied with rabies as Britain is. Rabies had been eradicated in 1902 but broke out after the First World War when returning soldiers smuggled dogs and cats home with them from France. In 1918, an outbreak of 318 cases was reported, which took four years to eradicate and Britain has been free of rabies since 1922. Authorities are keeping a nervous eye on the European situation where, since the Second World War, rabies has moved across the continent from the east at a rate of twenty-five miles a year.

The British are near panic-stricken at the thought of rabies reaching their island; one rabid dog was reported in 1969, which resulted in a government Committee of Inquiry on Rabies. Among its recommendations to Parliament in 1971 were strictly tightened quarantines and a stepped-up public education program. Some people think the scare tactics have gone too far. Advertising campaigns with lurid headlines, such as "Rabies is a killer," or "Smuggling pets could bring rabies into Britain," and showing the skull of a human supposedly shrunken by rabies, are complemented by television commercials of a person in the throes of a rabies convulsion. Citizens have responded by reporting suspicious-looking stray dogs or tourists in coastal towns who might be suspected of trying to smuggle pets into the country. Vigilantes seek out boats that they suspect have cats aboard and seaport people spy on their neighbours, looking for smuggled pets. Rhetoric surrounding the current wave of near hysteria is distinctly sabre-rattling. Gavin Strang, Secretary for Agriculture, Fisheries and Food, recently announced, "I want to say clearly, loudly, and convincingly, that the government is meeting the rabies threat with resolution and vigour. Our primary aim is to keep this dreadful disease out of the country. We shall strive to the utmost to achieve this. Our contingency aim is to be ready to contain and eradicate any rabies outbreak should it nevertheless occur. We do have contingency plans. We stand ready." Indeed they do. In Kent the county council has a supply of protective clothing for dog control personnel, visors, goggles, cat nets, dog rings, collapsible steel cages, animal muzzles that dog owners must use, feeding tins, and leashes for cats and dogs when confined.[12]

Rabies can be eradicated, as twenty-three countries have recently demonstrated. But a good piece of legislation is meaningless unless it is strictly enforced.

Preventive measures

1. At first sight of a staggering, glazed-eyed dog, get as far away from it as you can as quickly as possible. Then phone the responsible local authority: medical officer, police, dog control officer, etc.
2. If bitten by any animal, clean the wound immediately with soap and water. Report it to your doctor at once or have it checked in the emergency department of the nearest hospital.
3. If bitten by a dog, try to see where the dog goes in order that it may be caught and tested. In the event of a bat bite, if possible attempt to capture it for testing.
4. Never pet a racoon, skunk, or any wild animal, no matter how cute it is. Fact is, if a wild animal that is

normally wary of people, such as a racoon, skunk, fox, or wolf, comes close to you and seems very friendly this is generally uncharacteristic behaviour and can be a sign that the animal has rabies. The virus has reached its brain and the creature is disoriented.

Although it seems heartless, one would relieve its suffering by shooting a rabid animal – but not in the brain. The local animal or wildlife authority should be contacted because the brain may be used for laboratory tests and positive identification of rabies made.

Ringworm

In European countries in the nineteenth century children with ringworm were forced to wear thick, heavy hats resembling football helmets to prevent the spread of their condition to other children. As the disease was difficult to treat (and still is) the ugly red round patches on the scalp persisted sometimes for months. The jeers and taunts of malicious children must have caused severe emotional strain. Ringworm is still a stigma. Some islands in the South Pacific harbour a species of the disease which causes large body sores that last for years, seriously hindering a person's chances of attracting a spouse.

Ringworm is a fungus disease; the fungi, known as dermatophytes (often called "skin plants"), occur in three basic types: one is infective man-to-man only; the second type occurs in man and animals; and the third is specific to the soil. As many as fifty species of fungi are agents of the infection of animals and man.

Despite no recent large-scale epidemics in humans, the disease has shown a steady progression over the past decade and is now the most common fungal disease reported. In Britain more than half the reported fungal infections in humans are of animal origin, but authorities claim the actual incidence is much higher, especially over the past decade which shows an outstanding increase in the pet population.

The species of ringworm transmitted from dogs and cats to man is *Microsporun canis*. In about 90 per cent of vector dogs and cats the skin appears normal and ringworm is diagnosed only after examination under an ultraviolet light and laboratory culture of the organism. Humans may therefore become infected due to close contact with a dog that shows no visible signs of the condition. In the other 10 per cent of cases there are clinical signs: lesions appear on humans as they do on animals – in circular scaling patches on the skin, frequently on the scalp. The spread to humans is from tiny active arthrospores that live on the animal's skin or may be shed in the hair. Hence, hairs in the rug that the vacuum cleaner doesn't pick up, those in cat blankets, and even the straw in the barn where cats sleep, have proved to be infective for many months.

Ringworm was first reported as a zoonosis in 1820 by a Swiss veterinarian who diagnosed a young farm girl's condition as having been transmitted from cattle. Since that time four types of ringworm have been identified: the scalp type described above; a body ringworm that may be contracted from dogs and cats, but is most frequently transmitted by cattle, horses, or other farm animals; a foot type, known as "athlete's foot," and a type which affects the fingernails. Out of the four types, three (the scalp, body, and fingernail type) are transmitted from both dogs and cats, but it is obvious that wherever animals are, ringworm is a hazard.

Fleas

From the dawn of civilization fleas have tortured men with insufferable itchiness. In ancient times, when people lived and slept in the same clothes for days or weeks, when sanitation was unheard of, small wonder that fleas were a raging, cursing, scratching part of everyday life for peasant and king alike.

In North America alone there are sixty-six genera of fleas, and some 230 species and subspecies, compared to fifty-five species east of the one hundredth meridian. For this reason North America has been described as a parasitological paradise to flea fanciers.

The commonest flea found on humans in North America

163

and Europe, *Pulex irritans*, occasionally finds a host in dogs, rats, mice, cattle, pigs, and badgers; but infection is spread from human to human in unhygenic, crowded conditions. No matter how one lives, humans are also attacked by the dog and cat species of flea, *Ctenocephalides canis* and *C. felis*.

Aside from being irritating, fleas are killers. Rat fleas are the principal vectors of bubonic plague, which wiped out one-quarter of the European population in the fourteenth century. The "Black Death" has recurred in several epidemics, most drastically in the Great London Plague of 1665, in Manchuria in the nineteenth century, and as recently as 1900 in San Francisco where 133 cases were reported over a four-year period, 121 of them resulting in death. Until recently bubonic plague was a serious health problem in India and Burma. Several thousand cases were reported in South Vietnam in 1962, recent epidemics have hit Indonesia and Nepal, and to this day about two cases a year occur in the United States.

Displeasing though fleas are, a certain grudging admiration is due them. Some species can live for over 500 days without food; they have a robust sex life – with copulation lasting anywhere from three to nine hours; and fleas don't clutter up their homes with eggs or bother rearing their young. Since much of their lives is spent being carried around on a warm dog or cat the only threat to their existence is the occasional assault by a hind foot or a blizzard of flea powder.

Both dog and cat fleas feed by pricking the skin of their host and sucking the blood, and both species can live happily ever after on dog or cat or, in their absence, man. After the adult fleas breed fertilized eggs are dropped to the ground where they hatch into larvae in about nine to fifteen days (but eggs have been known to survive for many months). As fleas' eggs are most likely to be dropped when the dog or cat stops moving, the pet's bedding or sleeping place is likely to be infested with them.

Fleas inside pupae are stimulated to hatch by warmth, vibration, carbon dioxide, and the smell of a dog, cat or human. Therefore an unhatched flea has only to wait until a host with these characteristics comes along. Although it prefers a dog or cat, a flea will settle for a person's ankle if no more suitable host happens by. Called the "kangaroo of insects,"[13] a flea can leap eighty times its height and 150 times its length, which allows for little or no defence against an ambitious flea.

Every fall veterinarians are beset with scratching dogs and cats, and their owners. A common scenario is this: the fleas have hatched their eggs, which have fallen around the dog's sleeping place and here and there on the broadloom. The family leaves for vacation, taking the dog with them or boarding it out, leaving the house empty. During the two- or three-week vacation the larvae have developed into baby fleas inside pupae, but there is no available host to feed on. Then, the moment the returning vacationers come in the door the fleas hatch and pounce, hungry for a meal of real blood. Whoever enters first is the victim. The Arabs derived a cunning method for dealing with this problem: when houses had been left unused for any length of time the slaves were sent in, then after a safe interval the family followed. Parasitologists advise a similar strategy when people come home from vacation: send the dog in first, then give him a flea treatment the next day.

One of the infuriating things about fleas is that because they spend a great deal of time off their host, de-fleaing the dog may not necessarily keep your house free from fleas. Often no course of action other than fumigation throughout the house will kill the larvae. Obviously, people have no protection against flea eggs which have dropped in the park, on the sidewalk, or on their lawn.

The flea plays yet another nasty role – it can be the intermediate host for transmitting the tapeworm *Dipylidium caninum* (see page 149) to dogs, cats, and man. Eggs are eaten by flea larvae and cysts develop which remain in the flea through its entire life cycle. If a dog or cat gets annoyed by the flea biting him and takes a nip of his own hide, he will likely swallow the flea containing the tapeworm cyst. In the dog's intestine the cyst grows into an adult tapeworm. Then the dog has to be de-wormed as well as de-flead.

To the average person a flea bite is merely irritating. Scratching often causes a papule, a reddened area at the bite, which swells but soon disappears. However, in an allergic person, especially a child, the bite may produce suppurating sores that swell to the size of hens' eggs and take several weeks to heal.

Rocky Mountain Spotted Fever (tick-borne typhus)

A number of rickettsial diseases (infectious fever diseases) the world over are transmitted by ticks, mites, and fleas found on mice, rats and other small rodents and animals. Rocky Mountain spotted fever is of concern here since it is transmitted to humans by dog ticks.

An ancient enemy, ticks were nonetheless believed to serve many useful purposes. Linneaus, the father of scientific nomenclature, believed ticks prevented children from contracting very serious diseases and for centuries the Chinese were convinced ticks prevented smallpox. We may call it superstition or voodoo but they believed they had a cure: "Mix white cattle ticks, one for every year of age, with rice powder and make a cake. Let the child take it with an empty stomach. When a foul stool is passed, the child will be immune from smallpox for his entire life."[14]

Rocky Mountain spotted fever is transmitted to man by an infected dog tick, *Dermacentor variabilis*, which bites the person and sets up an infection characterized by high fever, headaches, chills, and a rash that covers most of the body. The disease is effectively treated with antibiotics and usually results in no lasting debility. However, if untreated the fatality rate is about 20 per cent.

This disease, which for years was reported mostly in the states of Virginia, West Virginia, Maryland, and North Carolina (despite its western name, where it is now least reported), also occurs in western Canada and some parts of Mexico, and Central and South America. Public health officials, such as Dr. Alan Beck, are becoming alarmed at its recent spread to eastern American cities and by the sharp increases seen generally in North America during the last ten years.[15] The United

States Centre for Disease Control in Atlanta, Georgia, reported a 19 per cent increase in Rocky Mountain spotted fever from 1976 to 1977 in the United States, with 42 and 40 deaths respectively. Health officials could not account for the increase.[16]

Scabies (sarcoptic mange)

Scabies is widespread wherever the daily bath is unpopular. It thrives in undeveloped countries, with troops in wartime, and in virtually all unclean places where people are crowded together, as in prisons or labour camps. Transmission is by direct contact with an infected person or dog.

Scabies is a disease caused by small mites, *Sarcoptes scabei*, which burrow into the skin and cause maddening itchiness. It is almost impossible not to scratch – the compulsion intensifies at night – which aggravates the area, causing a fluid to be released, which dries and leaves unsightly scabs on the skin.

Dog-to-dog transmission occurs as a result of direct contact with mangy skin; for example, pups from two days to two weeks old commonly contract the condition *Demodectes canis* (or "red mange"), from the abdominal skin of an infected bitch. If your dog is infected and you have a friendly romp with him, you are certain to contract scabies. Merely rearranging the dog's bedding makes infection possible.

If untreated, the disease usually lasts no longer than four to five weeks (in the absence of reinfection), which suggests that the canine species of mites that cause scabies does not reproduce on the human host. Although the major route of infection is by human to human transmission, there is no doubt that scabies may be transmitted from dogs to man.

Preventive measures

1. Avoid a dog with mange.
2. Do not share towels, clothing or the bed of a person with scabies.

167

Other Diseases Transmitted by Household Pets

Allergies: A person allergic to dogs and cats develops a hypersensitivity to the protein material of the animal's hair shaft, or, more frequently, to the dandruff on the outer skin, which is constantly being sloughed off. Even if the animal is not present in a room the affected person may react to the hair on sofas, in rugs, in the pet's bed or even in the air. Symptoms generally include puffing of the eyelids, watering of the eyes, nasal congestion, sneezing, and respiratory discomfort, and especially with asthmatic persons, wheezing or coughing. When one child in a family is allergic it commonly happens that the family continues to keep the pet anyway while the allergic child undergoes regular injections of an antigen, even though this is not always successful.

Cat scratch fever: As the name implies, this disease occurs from a scratch or bite by a cat, and although the symptoms can be merely a painful sore, a slight fever and flu-like feeling, in severe cases it may lead to convulsions and encephalitis.

Cryptococcosis: A species of fungus found in cities and places where great quantities of pigeon droppings accumulate. It is a rare condition, but dangerous to persons with immunological problems.

Giardia lamblia: A form of dysentery transmitted to humans from dogs, especially in poor areas where fecal contamination is widespread. Stomach pains, diarrhea and vomiting may be acute but symptoms are generally short in duration.

Multiple sclerosis: Two reports in the British medical journal *The Lancet* in early 1977 suggested a possible link between multiple sclerosis in children and house pets. This is seemingly another rendition of a now familiar and recurring old tune. Although two researchers stressed that their findings should be interpreted with caution until others confirmed their results, they did not have long to wait. A New Jersey researcher, studying fifty multiple sclerosis patients found that forty-six had been in close contact with a house pet, usually from within five to ten years prior to the onset of multiple sclerosis. Even though the early research was hailed as a discovery of "monumental importance," the New Jersey researcher also called for more studies.[17]

Psittacosis (parrot fever or ornithosis): A disease characterized by fever, headache, and cough due to pneumonic involvement. The effects range from mild to acute; death is rare. Usually by aerosol transmission, it is contracted from pet birds that may be seemingly healthy, or from places where pigeon or other bird droppings have accumulated in a confined space.

Dog Bites and Attacks

In June 1976, in upstate New York, a mother left her German Shepherd dog alone with her new baby while she went shopping, and when she returned the dog had attacked and killed the infant. Dr. Alan Beck talked of the public reaction in his office of the Bureau of Animal Affairs in New York City. "We had phone call after phone call," he related, "and they were much the same tone. One lady screamed at me, 'What did that child do to annoy the dog?' I told her, 'Lady, the child couldn't have done very much, he was only two months old.'"[18]

This incident typifies the dog owner's immediate reaction to biting – there has to be provocation in order for a dog to bite. At the very most an owner might admit some dogs bite – but never his.

Every year in the United States one million people are victims of dog bites and attacks; some say it is much more. Because there is no accurate or standardized system of reporting, authorities agree that reported dog bites generally represent half the actual number, in some cases, one quarter. A dog owner seldom reports that his own dog bit him and were it not for the endless rabies scare probably even fewer bites would be reported. The situation is worsening month by month, year by year. Many public health officials are beginning to regard dog bites as a major urban problem, some going so far as to claim it has reached epidemic proportions. In large American cities dog bites are second only to gonorrhea as the most reported disease or injury.

Dr. Alan Beck, in his pioneering study of stray dogs in Baltimore, done in the early seventies, found that the problem of dog bites and attacks merited serious attention and followed it up with an investigation of dog bite injuries in St. Louis.[19] Around this time similar studies were under way in other U.S. cities, notably Norfolk and New York, as well as in Britain, Japan, and Israel. The American cities reported an average of twice as many bites as in the previous five years, which was consistent with Israel, Canada and France, but dog bites appeared to be slightly fewer per capita in England – possibly because there were fewer strays, more dogs on leashes, and fewer guard dogs in Britain than in other countries. About 40,000 people annually in New York are bitten seriously enough to require medical attention, with severity ranging from nips on the ankle to mutilation necessitating stitches or reconstructive surgery. According to epidemiologist William Winkler of the U.S. Centre for Disease Control, Atlanta, Georgia, family pets or neighbours' dogs killed at least eleven people* in the United States in 1974 and 1975, all but two of whom were children six and under, or infants.[20] In those same years not one person was attacked and killed by wild bears.[21]

Following on the heels of Beck's research a study of dog bites as a social phenomenon and matter of public concern was published in 1974 in New York. The authors, Harris, Imperato, and Oken, reported that for about twenty years after the Second World War the annual incidence of dog bites was

---

* Dr. Winkler notes that due to a lack of comprehensive surveillance the true number of deaths is unascertainable and suggests that these eleven cases "undoubtedly represent only a portion of the actual number that occurred during the reporting period."

fairly static; then around 1965 the situation changed noticeably. From 1965 to 1970 an increase of 33 per cent more bites were reported and from 1970 to 1972 a further 37 per cent were reported. (Beck found that in Baltimore the number doubled from 1955 to 1972, with the big jump occurring between 1970 and 1972.) At the time of the New York study, citizens were preoccupied with the tons of dog droppings on the streets and parks and the authors felt attention paid to this problem obscured the much more serious problem of dog bites. Dr. Beck agreed with them, stating, "While I don't want to underrate the need to stop the pollution of our streets and parks by dog wastes, as a public health problem it is minor compared to dog bites."[22] In the opinion of Harris *et al*, "Public concern has been focused on the wrong end of the dog."[23]

Changes in the size and characteristics of the dog population were noted in the New York report. The trend in New York is toward guard dogs, large, aggressive breeds such as German Shepherds, Doberman Pinschers, and Great Danes,* owned by persons who desire protection against rising crime. Guard dogs are trained to be aggressive, and bites occur when children reach for them as they would a pet dog. In fact so dangerous are guard dogs that they are designated a bio-hazard and like poison must be properly labelled in New York.**

Poor breeding is responsible for the increased irritability of certain pets, as evidenced by the numbers of unscrupulous breeders who cross certain wolf species with German Shepherds to produce a fierce guard dog. In the Arctic such crossbreeding occurs naturally and frequently between huskies and wolves, and these unions can produce unpredictable dogs. A lady in Yellowknife who owned this type of mongrel became victim at an Eastertime 1978 dogsled race. Three kilometres along the ten-kilometre course the five-dog team attacked and

* From 1964 to 1976 the American Kennel Club registration increased 1,423 per cent for Doberman Pinschers and 473 per cent for Great Danes. (See Appendix A, 100 Most Popular Breeds.)

**See more about guard dogs on p. 215.

killed her. No one could say why.[24] The very make-up of city living, with all the stresses and strains of crowding, noise, and pollution that erode people's levels of tolerance have similar effects on dogs. When a dog that by nature should be running and leaping through fields and chasing groundhogs is instead locked up all day in a New York apartment and only goes for an evening walk in Central Park, it is quite likely to be as ill-tempered as its owner might be, after a pressured, anxiety-ridden day at the office.

It came as a surprise to many observers that the dogs who did the biting were not the beasts who snarled and skulked in back alleys. As Beck's two studies (Baltimore and St. Louis) reported, almost half the bites occurred on or very near the owner's property and 79 per cent of the persons bitten knew the owner of the dog. Increases were recorded of children under nineteen years old being bitten, and an increased number of bites occurred on the face. This was explained as due to the growing number of large breeds which stand level with a child's face. Provocation as the reason for a dog biting a person was firmly discredited, in the St. Louis survey, which revealed that 74 per cent of the bites involved no prior interaction with the dog, that is, the victim was not on the owner's property and his or her behaviour was not directed toward the dog. Although German Shepherds are often accused of being the canine Public Enemy No. 1 no specific breed is shown to be more vicious than another. However, most studies reveal that large dogs are more involved in bites and attacks than are small dogs.

While the preponderance of dog bites in the United States are inflicted by owned dogs, in Japan the reverse is true. Noted observer of the dog as pet in Britain and Asia, Dr. A.H. Carding found that most of the dog bites in Japan were from strays, whose population there is unequalled anywhere, and accounts for the majority of the dog population. In Tokyo 25,000 persons were bitten in 1972, compared to the 40,000 in New York that year, and 180,000 complaints had been received in Japan.

There are still people who believe that every dog is entitled to one bite. Until such outdated, witless folklore is finally laid to rest the incidence of dog bites will not subside.

Preventive measures

In order to prevent a bite, it might help to be able to recognize when a dog is intending to bite. Some of the signs are: barking (it is not true that a barking dog never bites), snarling, teeth-baring, and a straight, standing-up tail (don't trust an unknown wagging tail either, sometimes this can be a hostile sign).

Should you encounter such an animal:

1. Stop and turn sideways from the dog. Never face him head on, or look him in the eye – this to the dog is a threatening gesture.
2. You might startle him out of his nasty intentions by saying sharply, "Go home!"
3. If that doesn't work, raise an arm in front of you to distract the dog. Rattle your purse, car keys or jewellery to divert his attention.
4. Try not to freeze, even if you are afraid. A still, unmoving pose indicates to the dog that you want to fight.
5. Do not run, unless you are absolutely certain of outdistancing the dog and of reaching a safe place.
6. If the dog has bitten you, try not to scream (admittedly, easy to say) for this may scare the dog, causing him to bite again. Try to put something near his mouth, such as a newspaper, your gloves, scarf, a stick, anything you can manage. Better he bites it than you.
7. A useful disorientation is to grab the dog by the tail and spin him around, if it can be done.[25] (Don't try it with anything larger than a Toy Poodle.)
8. Without fail, report the bite immediately to the local health officer and secure the identity of the dog wherever possible. Although the risk of rabies is slight, it cannot be ignored.
9. If you suspect the dog is rabid, wash the wound as soon as you can with soap and water, then go directly to a hospital emergency department. In this case it is very important to be able to identify the dog.
10. Children must be taught never to reach out to pat a dog, especially a large breed. Chances are it is a guard dog and definitely unfriendly toward small people.

11. If there is a threatening dog in the neighbourhood, talk to its owner (and be prepared for a confrontation) and make certain children know it is dangerous. Should the dog continue to be a threat, report it to whomever is responsible for animal control – the city pound, humane society, police, etc. It is also a very good idea to bring the matter to the attention of your local elected representative.

One can easily see how some zoonoses and dog bites are becoming a major concern, research into the causes and effects of zoonotic disease falls lamentably behind that conducted in other disciplines of medicine. Funds for studying human disease are easy to come by in comparison to cutting up a few thousand cats' worms in a lab, and as long as researchers and granting agencies are attracted to the more glamorous medical conquests like sewing a severed limb back on rather than investigating why an almost invisible creature bites a person on the ankle and causes death, zoonoses will continue to remain in the shadows.

Without any doubt at all, family practice doctors in America, Britain, and many European countries are in urgent need of upgrading their knowledge of zoonoses. Veterinarians and parasitologists attending a pet symposium in Toronto in 1976 were critical of the short shrift given by medical schools to the teaching of parasitology and zoonotic diseases, and unanimously agreed that the average general practice graduate almost anywhere in North America is woefully ignorant of the diseases which are transmitted from animals to man. Must a zoonotic epidemic occur before the medical community is jolted out of its present state of complacency?

People have not been educated about some of the factual risks they face by associating with pets. There is no argument that animals in society ought to be protected from cruel and inhumane treatment by humans, but on the other hand, who is protecting people from animals? The humane societies are not. Pet owners are not; not when 21 per cent of pet dogs in Ontario, for example, harbour the parasite *Toxocara canis*, which is potentially dangerous to humans. How discomforting to know that one-fifth of a dog population is infected with a disease that humans may contract. And this is a *known* risk. What about the unknowns?

Time is running out. It is essential that research be accelerated, family physicians upgrade their knowledge of zoonoses, humane societies and veterinarians educate people about the realities of pet-related diseases, and pet owners themselves take the initiative in keeping their animals healthy. If not, more and more humans will become needless victims of animal diseases and dog bites.

9

Planned Parenthood for Pets*

Having looked at some of the social, financial, and health costs incurred by the overpopulation of pets today, one may wonder what is being done about it. Regrettably, not very much.

If the total pet population lived in the wild it would be held to controllable limits, as all animal populations are year after year, century after century, by four common mortality threats: predation, starvation, disease, and accidents. Since pet animals live in apartments and houses, none of these circumstances has any noticeable effect on their numbers, and now that their numbers are becoming a problem, external methods of control are being applied. At the present time these are: mass killing of surplus pets, spaying and neutering, and administering contraceptives.

Mass Killing of Surplus Pets

By far the most popular method of birth control in practice today is killing pets, but since 72,000 a day would have to be

---

*This was the title of an article by Djerassi, Israel, and Jochle that appeared in the *Bulletin of the Atomic Scientists* in 1973 and first examined some of the evidence supporting the dangers of the overpopulation of pets.

killed – about twice the present amount – to maintain zero population growth, this would be costly and, one would hope, morally calamitous. So far, killing 13 to 15 million pets a year seems to be acceptable.

That the annual slaughter is unaccompanied by public outcry has already been established, but what can be heard are those who protest against the method of killing, not the extent of it. Whether the animal dies more humanely by sodium pentobarbitol injection than by decompression or electrocution is apparently the more pressing concern. In Dallas in 1975 a grand jury indicted the SPCA as a result of a citizens' pressure group for misuse of a decompression chamber, alleging that the shelter manager had "intentionally and knowingly confined animals in a cruel manner."[1] But where were the crusaders protesting the killing of the animals in the first place? The reverse of the Dallas situation has arisen in Mount Pearl, Newfoundland, where the local SPCA president complained that animals which had been dead for a week had not been removed from their cages. The society is threatening to sue the city for showing "a flagrant disregard of our animals."[2] Such concern is thought provoking. Are the society members outraged because their anthropomorphized concept of pets demands that dead animals be treated with the same dignity as human corpses? or are the bodies taking up space required to kill more dogs? I suspect the carcasses symbolize for them the whole problem of people abandoning and mistreating animals, and whoever has the nasty job of killing should at least dispose of the bodies swiftly so as to bury such a devastating reminder of the problem.

Euthanasia is a subject of ongoing discussion and debate in the humane movement for it involves trying to select the ideal method of death, one which is the most humane for the animal and the least upsetting for the operator. The animal may have been the victim of inhumane treatment throughout its lifetime but once at the shelter the last few moments of its life are considered; that is, it is of paramount importance how quickly the animal dies and how little pain it experiences. Examining some methods of euthanasia briefly, the most prevalent in the United States is by high altitude decompression, whereby animals are placed in a chamber, atmospheric pressure is reduced and animals black out "somewhere between seven and sixty seconds, with total euthanasia resulting within three minutes," states the manufacturer of one such decompression chamber.[3] The decompression method is used in 320 communities in the United States; however, it has never been acceptable in the United Kingdom. The Humane Society of the United States rejects it due to the fact the animal suffers severe, albeit brief, pain just prior to death, and instead favours injections of barbiturates which produce a quick and quiet death. This method is used by most private practice veterinarians although it is not entirely suitable for public shelters since these are potent drugs and subject to strict controls. They must be administered intravenously or intraperitoneally by a veterinarian, the cost can be higher than many other methods, and because many of the drugs are potentially addictive, they have the potential for abuse by staff. In the U.K. and Canada the most common method of killing is electrocution, conducted by an apparatus which passes an electrical charge through the brain to stun the animal, then through the body to fibrillate the heart. The animal is rendered unconscious and insensitive to pain immediately.* Anesthetic inhalants such as chloroform and toxic gases such as carbon monoxide, cyanide and carbon dioxide, to name a few, have specific applications, although they pose some risk to workers. Shooting the animal in the brain is likely the most humane method of all for the animal. It produces instantaneous unconsciousness but is distasteful for the operator.

Researchers continue their search for ideal deaths, veterinary journals report on their findings, international seminars are held, and the humane movement continues its debate. Regardless of the sincerity of purpose the fact remains that one method of killing is merely selected over another, which in the end achieves little more than tacit endorsement of the mass slaughter of animals to deal with the problem of overpopulation.

*Electrocution is capable of producing a painless death. However, as reported by the World Federation for the Protection of Animals in 1976, a careless operator and an electrical cabinet not built to proper specifications may cause extreme pain for twelve to twenty seconds prior to death.[4]

The mass killing of dogs as a method of population control was practised as early as the 1830s in New York City and it didn't work then either. Dogs, along with pigs, rooted through garbage in the streets and became such a nuisance that a bounty of fifty cents was paid per dog. This lasted for about twenty years. The bounty applied only to specific times – the daylight hours in the summer, the "dog days of August" when, superstition holds, dogs are mad. As a result a summer bloodbath in the streets ensued, "jarring the sensibilities of many citizens," described a public health history of New York. The author quotes an early *Daily Tribune* newspaper report of how bounty seekers, young boys, "scarcely so tall as the far nobler and more intelligent quadruped they assailed, went about the streets during the Summer, staggering under clubs as heavy as themselves, striking down and then horribly mangling with many blows every dog they encountered."[5]

Since then society has come a long way. We no longer pay a fifty-cent bounty to young boys for clubbing dogs to death in the streets; we round up dogs in an orderly fashion, stuff them into vans, and pay a local pound an average of ten tax dollars per dog to systematically suffocate, electrocute, overdose, or gas them.

Spaying and Neutering

Municipally subsidized spay and neuter clinics began with a City of Los Angeles experiment launched in 1971; and opponents say it should end there. These clinics have caused a series of violent confrontations that are going on to this day. On the one side animal welfare societies print posters and pamphlets urging citizens to spay and neuter pets at the clinic, and on the other side veterinarians and some public health officials oppose spay clinics on the grounds they are costly and have no effect on reducing the pet population.

A brief review of the Los Angeles spay and neuter program, as furnished by the city's Department of Animal Regulation, shows that in its first year of operation, with spaying costing $17.50 and neutering $11.50, it incurred a slight deficit. By the end of the second year two more clinics were added and the program was declared self-sustaining. Even so, it came close to being curtailed in 1973-74, mostly due to budget and staff problems, administrators claim. Nevertheless additional clinics have been established in the state and elsewhere, based on the Los Angeles model.

Critics who insist the clinics are costly failures are persuasive and have many people convinced. For one thing, operating at full capacity, a Los Angeles clinic is able to perform a mere twenty-one surgeries a day. Objectors also claim that the public is not behind the project and that all taxpayers should not be obliged to pay for the problems created by a few.

Right from the beginning the veterinary profession raised hell. Veterinarians regarded sterilizations sponsored by a municipality as an encroachment on their territory, insisting that reduced fees would subsequently result in a lower calibre of work performed by paramedics. Fearing that municipal clinics were the first step toward socialized veterinary medicine, they objected to the use of ovariohysterectomy (removal of ovaries, or spaying) and orchidectomy (removal of the testicles, or neutering) as the only alternatives to preventing conception. Veterinarians also complained about freeloaders coming to the taxpayer-supported clinics when they could afford the higher vets' fees. Regardless, if all vets spayed animals eight hours a day, five days a week, they insist it would not make a dent in the pet population.

The City of Los Angeles steadfastly maintains the program is "thinning the ranks of the animal population," and offers proof by citing the reduced traffic in the city's animal shelter system. It dropped 8.5 per cent the first year the spay clinic was in operation, 3.6 per cent the following year, and by 1976-77, the decrease was 6 per cent. One of the best arguments waged in support of spay clinics is that they reduce the number of animals killed in shelters. The Los Angeles program reflects a modest annual decrease. In 1970-71, out of the total number of animals handled, 76.6 per cent were destroyed; in 1976-77, with decreases ranging from 3 to 8 per cent in the previous six years, they still destroyed 72.7 per cent of the total animals handled.[6]

When a million animals are killed in a state annually and

one of its cities shows a decrease averaging less than 6,000 a year the event is given a typical Hollywood klieg-light star treatment. As a consequence, some of the other factors contributing to a possible reduction are eclipsed, such as the stricter enforcement of leash laws, the incentive of owners to sterilize their pets and thus pay half the licence fee, and an increased public awareness of the overpopulation problem. Attributing a decrease in the number of animals killed in shelters to spay and neuter clinics appears to be legitimate; however, there is no proof that clinics reduce the pet population. The argument is not against spaying and neutering – every responsible person agrees this should be done on a large scale – it is against spaying and neutering being subsidized by the local government.

A persistent and winning case against municipally-sponsored spay clinics is that they do not reach the intended customer, the irresponsible pet owner. Responsible owners have always had their pets spayed or kept them confined during periods of heat and avoided unwanted "accidents" one way or the other. The target groups at whom spaying is directed, those who allow their animals to breed indiscriminately, would not go to the spay clinic even if it were free. The American Humane Association surveyed pet owners on a national scale and discovered that only 50 per cent of dogs were licensed. If people will not abide by the law and purchase a licence for their dog for from $2 to $10, it is naïve to expect they will have the animal spayed or neutered at a clinic for $12 to $20.

Clearly, the message is not getting through. Pet owners are not being informed that it is socially unacceptable to add litter upon litter of puppies and kittens to species which are seriously overpopulated. Unfortunately, the ones who should be co-ordinating public education programs, the veterinarians and animal welfare groups, are not on speaking terms.

As the journal *Modern Veterinary Practice* stated, "The mere thought of *spay clinics* has many veterinarians and most associations up in arms." That is putting it mildly when one reviews the number of law suits, arrests, injunctions, and other legal arenas in which the veterinary profession has tangled with animal welfare and citizen groups. Vigorous campaigns against the Los Angeles program resulted in two animal societies having an injunction placed on the Southern California Veterinary Medical Association for attempting to disenfranchise members who co-operated with the municipal low-cost spay clinic. Similar fights are under way in New York, and according to *Modern Veterinary Practice*, two other humane organizations are considering taking court action against veterinary associations for their efforts to block subsidized spay programs. And in Florida a veterinary association is planning to file suit against a spay and neuter clinic for advertising its services. Antagonism between the two factions appears to be unbridgable.

Veterinarians dub their opponents "little old ladies in tennis shoes," whose sole aim is socialized veterinary medicine, and citizens' protest groups feel veterinarians are driven only by personal monetary concerns rather than by consideration of the threats to public health and welfare caused by the pet overpopulation. One animal welfare executive stated that veterinarians "have consistently opposed public low cost spay-neuter clinics with all their might, in much the same fashion as the AMA opposed Medicare. This has not hurt the incomes of human doctors in the least, and there is no reason to believe the clinics would hurt the incomes of veterinarians."[7] The fact is, with growing awareness of spay programs, many private practice veterinarians are doing a booming business in sterilizations.

Surgical sterilizations require professional medical personnel, expensive equipment, all housed in multi-million-dollar facilities – and the work is painstakingly slow. Consider the twenty-one sterilizations performed a day in a single Los Angeles clinic. One must acknowledge this produces a reduction in fertile animals, but even if the number is multiplied by those in a hundred more clinics, the results are still minuscule. It has been statistically calculated that if 90 per cent of the males in a freely associating population were castrated, and no females spayed, the reproduction rate in that given population would be the same as if nothing had been done. On the other hand, if 90 per cent of the females were spayed and no males altered the reproduction rate would be cut down to a mere 10 per cent.[8] Without doubt there would never be enough manpower to spay 90 per cent of the female dog population.

The odds are against a clinic's success when an animal shelter next door provides pets for adoption without a sterilization proviso. In Los Angeles in 1971-72, 2,781 sterilizations were performed, but over 20,000 unspayed and unneutered animals were released from shelters in the same period.[9] One intact adoption defeats as many as five to ten times the number of sterilizations. It's like raking leaves in a windstorm.

Many pet owners are confused, superstitious, and just plain misinformed about spaying and neutering. The benefits of spaying are based on medical fact; the alleged disadvantages are not. Once a bitch is spayed she no longer enters the estrus (heat) season twice a year, and this spares the owner the nuisance of wiping up vaginal drips; but more than that, male dogs no longer hang around. Without estrus they are not attracted. Spaying also helps to control the cancerous breast and reproductive organ tumours that female dogs frequently develop in later years.

A neutered dog does not travel in packs after bitches in heat, is less prone to fighting, and is protected from the prostate problems that beset older, unaltered, male dogs.

As for spaying cats, the advantages are similar to those for spaying dogs, and in addition, the neutered male cat no longer sprays, filling the house with an offensive odour.

Spaying and neutering makes better pets of dogs and cats, generally speaking, because they are disinclined to roam; this helps to alleviate troubles that arise with neighbours. There is also an economic benefit. Many municipalities charge a lower licence fee for spayed or neutered animals. In Los Angeles, where it is $7 for intact animals, $3.50 for those sterilized, licences would cost $42 over a pet's twelve-year life span, instead of $84.

Looking at the reasons why people refuse to sterilize their pets offers a revealing glimpse into their psyches. Some object on the basis of mutilation, others want their pets to produce at least one litter, some, under the banner of animal liberation, desire that their pets enjoy a normal, unsterilized sex life, others claim altering makes the pet fat and lazy, and some say they cannot afford sterilization fees.

There are animal lovers who define mutilation as anything from spaying and neutering to stress or suffering in laboratory experiments to tail docking and tattooing. Although their reasons may appear illogical to some they devoutly and unswervingly adhere to the mutilation concept.

Too many believe a bitch is not complete until she has had one litter. With global concerns zeroing in on overpopulation, food shortages and environmental protection, supporting the idea of more birthing in any species, excluding those destined for extinction, is not kindheartedness to animals, it is ignorant, self-serving, and soulless. Those with "just one litter" propensities are reminded that one half of all puppies born in the United States and one third in the United Kingdom are put to death before their first birthday. These statistics are swatted aside like bothersome gnats by eager breeders who promise to find happy homes for the litter. Are they going to ensure that the happy homes agree to spay or neuter the animal when the time comes and not to abandon it when its newborn cuddliness wanes or it piddles on the broadloom just once too often? If not, then who is going to be responsible for the future litters of those puppies and kittens? If they all survived, one bitch could theoretically produce 67,710 offspring in six years.[10] Under tight controls, breeding the animal once a year and permitting only two puppies to survive in each litter would still produce 254 puppies over seven years. When upwards of 50 million puppies are born annually in the United States many of those who were quick to promise responsibility are slow to follow through.

Humane society workers claim men resist castrating their animals because they identify with them and to these people castration is a threatening procedure. They regard animal sex as real and natural, perhaps some of the things human sex is not. Could it be that these men vicariously enjoy the dog's freedom to indulge in sex as a purely instinctive act, something they themselves may only fantasize about? Guy Hodge, director of information and legislation for the Humane Society of the United States, claims male resistance to castration prevails even among many humane society officials and veterinarians. He allows, "It would be funny if it weren't such a terrible problem."[11]

Ever watched a loose female dog in heat? She is mounted by one dog while four or five others stand by waiting their turn. Is that what dog owners mean when they claim they want their bitches to enjoy a free sex life?

Some argue that a spayed or neutered animal becomes fat and lazy. But there is a distinction to be made here between domestic farm animals and cats and dogs. If the neutered pet is curling up on the sofa at night instead of carousing, and is still being fed the same amount as before, quite naturally it may gain weight. However, as an isolated factor spaying is not usually a valid reason for weight gain in dogs and cats.

People who say they cannot afford to sterilize their pets arouse no sympathy today. The animal welfare movement continually reminds people, "If you can afford a pet, you can afford to spay it." For communities without low-cost spaying and neutering programs there are several animal welfare organizations that assist those on limited incomes to have their pets spayed at bargain prices. Movie stars, such as Doris Day, Gretchen Wyler, Kim Novak, and Brigitte Bardot are strong supporters of animal welfare and Zsa Zsa Gabor and Shirley Jones lent their names to the cause of Love Unlimited, a group formed in 1972 by producer Milo Frank in alliance with the South California Veterinary Medical Association in which vets agree to do a certain number of free surgeries per week for indigent pet owners. In the first six months, 2,000 sterilizations were performed at reduced prices.[12] Other organizations, such as the Pet Assistance Foundation and Mercy Crusade, Inc., in business for the past twenty years, recruit vets to spay and neuter animals for one half to one third of their regular fee and the two groups made 43,000 referrals in 1972 alone.[13] Celebrating their twentieth anniversary in 1977 of spay assistance programs, Friends of Animals, with the help of 450 volunteers and 700 vets, who reduced their fees, now subsidize 50,000 sterilizations annually.[14]

This raises the question, Does the family on social assistance have the right to the luxury of a pet, supported by tax-payers? Owning a pet is a luxury, not an individual right, anymore than owning a Rolls Royce is or having chicken every Sunday. The family that accepts government subsidies, for whatever reason, twists a privilege into a right when demanding that social assistance provide food and medical care for a dog or cat. The extension, then, of welfare recipients' attitudes and taxpayers' tolerance of them, is that social largesse will soon cover car payments. That is not as preposterous as it first appears, if a pilot program in Toronto is any indication. One welfare agency included in its supplements a weekly appointment at the hairdressers for mothers who battered their children, on the assumption that a little pampering and an improved appearance may bolster the woman's self-esteem above the level of frustration or despair that drove her to beat her child.* If people on welfare are entitled to hair-dos, anyone who would deny them a toy dog is an unspeakable tyrant.

As of July 1973, the official position of the American Veterinary Medical Association, with its 30,000 members (one third of whom are in small animal practice), does not endorse spay clinics for some of these reasons: [they] "are highly recommended, but provide an extremely ineffective solution to mass reproduction control of animals"; "have proved to have contributed an infinitesimal solution to animal population control when compared to the overall number of pets"; "can never reach a wide enough segment of the animal population to be effective. On the other hand, responsible pet owners have always used spaying and neutering to prevent birth of unwanted pets"; and they "have proved more costly than anticipated and have frequently required subsidization at a high cost to the taxpayer." The association suggests that efforts of concerned citizens' groups ought to be directed toward other

*Every woman appreciates that a new hair-do or new dress is an effective morale booster. No woman appreciates paying for someone else's, even though social workers would warn, if you don't pay a pittance for this hair-do, you might pay considerably more in the long run for hospitalization, incarceration, or plain human suffering. Presumably the child who is being beaten to death would agree; his mother should look nice.

solutions, namely "safe, inexpensive, and effective non-surgical sterilization methods."[15]

There has been some talk of following the example set in Norway where spaying and neutering are prohibited altogether, on the grounds that if one is to enjoy the rewards of pet companionship and loyalty one must accept the nuisance of female discharges, the attraction of males to females in heat, and males that roam. The Norwegians feel that altering a dog surgically is succumbing to one's own shortcomings and acknowledging that the pet owner is unable to assume full responsibility for looking after a dog. Oddly enough, this is precisely the rationale behind the introduction of spay and neuter clinics in North America.

Pet Contraceptives

The contraceptive pill has been "just around the corner" for quite a number of years. Ovulation suppression was successfully tested with injections of the hormone progesterone in rabbits as far back as 1937 and in canines from 1952, but as yet it has not been widely accepted for pets because the hormone (male) produces adverse biological effects in female cats (queens) and dogs (bitches) that pet owners will not tolerate, such as endometritis, elevated blood glucose, stimulated mammary nodules, raised blood cholesterol, gall bladder problems, clitoral enlargement and masculinization of the female puppies, to name a few.

The Upjohn Company of Kalamazoo, Michigan, in June 1978, launched a non-progestational contraceptive called Cheque, which halts estrus in both bitches and queens for as long as it is administered. In Canada the drug is expected to be available either in Carnation canned dog food or in a pure liquid form, pending Department of Health and Welfare approvals. The drug has been tested for two years (within a twelve-year birth-control test program) on 700 bitches. Its developer Dr. James Sokolowski states that the biological effects have not adversely affected the health of test animals and he gives it "a very acceptable risk:benefit ratio."[16]

Obviously there could be alarming consequences if contraceptives were readily available in commercial pet food. What about people who eat dog food? Sokolowski was ready for this: "First, the labelling would prominently read, 'Not For Human Consumption,' the label will look medicinal and a further deterrent is price. It will cost a little more than a high quality high meat canned pet food." As for accidental ingestion by children, Sokolowski assured that little girls would not develop peculiar appendages. At a later date he modified his position slightly: "Based on our current knowledge we can say that a single 30 mcg. dose would not be toxic to humans and should not cause lasting biological effects," but he admitted, "We cannot speak specifically to the antifertility effect." After testing toxic doses on rats, Dr. Sokolowski stated that to receive a lethal dose a person would have to consume 3,733,310 cans of the contraceptive dog food at one sitting.

One objectionable side effect of the drug is that when bitches are withdrawn from it to breed, all puppies born are male. "Even the females," Sokolowski allowed. When asked if he considered his product to be effective in reducing the pet population, Sokolowski smiled and said, "No." But quickly added, "Our product is only one part of the control of the pet population. The first step, killing unwanted pets, has not controlled it. The second step, spaying and neutering, has not. Ours is the third step. And once you have a variety of these three choices you will see a difference."

Paralleling the human situation, nearly all the research and experimentation has been done on females. Why not males? Dr. Sokolowski was asked. He replied, "We stopped our research on males because by the time contraception occurred the dose had killed the dogs. We had a lead with Cheque and had to take it."[17]

Sokolowski's English colleagues would argue the point. Several years ago the Glaxo Drug Company in London developed similar non-progestational steroids and subsequently abandoned them to exclusively produce progesterone contraceptives administered by a veterinarian. Dr. Jim Evans, developer of Ovaban (called Ovarid in the U.S.), Glaxo's progesterone estrus inhibitor, spoke of pet owners administering drugs and the problems encountered: people can't read labels properly; they forget to give the dose; the dog doesn't eat all the food hence doesn't get the required dosage, and owners don't like the side effects, particularly the one which produces all male puppies and/or masculinized females. "This is the sort of product that has to remain in the hands of the veterinary surgeon if it is to be effective," Dr. Evans contended.[18]

Also going against Cheque is price. To supply correct dosage to a twenty-five pound dog is costlier than spaying in a municipally sponsored clinic. Even so, the contraceptive is only 90 per cent effective at this time. Being a little bit pregnant is one of the unattractive side effects.

Unlike spaying, which is irreversible, chemical contraceptives can be stopped if the bitch is to be bred, a valuable advantage to breeders of show dogs. Contraceptives help prevent mammary tumours and, similar to replacement hormone therapy in menopausal women, they act as a biological pacifier in the dog's later years.

Other methods have been tested with varying degrees of success. Tubal ligation is one, the intravaginal device another. The pill implant and the "morning after" pill are under study and have been for some years. Lloyd C. Faulkner, a Colorado University researcher noted for his work in developing unique contraceptive methods, is currently working on a project involving immunizing dogs and cats against the reproductive hormones. Another approach is chemical vasectomy in dogs. Each method has its specific application, but the difficulty is no single contraceptive is universally acceptable and probably none will be when considering the demands of pet owners. Some want the contraceptive to prevent births, others to eliminate the nuisance of heat and mating behaviour, some want the agent to be reversible, others demand permanent sterilization without adverse effects. Faulkner admits, "We are hampered in our efforts to find alternative methods of contraception by our ignorance of the mechanisms of reproductive function in dogs and cats. The biological clocks that regulate reproductive cyclicity in these species are unknown."[19] Such paucity of knowledge is echoed by veterinarians, humane society officials, and a concerned public, and until researchers' pleas for added funds materialize, a birth control method which is safe, effective, available, and acceptable, will be around a ten- to twelve-year corner.

As readily acknowledged, the biggest problem with dogs in society today is irresponsible pet owners, and it has been suggested that sterilizing aggravates the situation since people tend to view spaying or neutering as a licence for the animal to roam freely. A sterilized dog will not add to the population, but it will still bite kids, foul the streets, bark, cause car accidents, and spread disease. People seem to forget, although they are reminded now and then, that the safest method of birth control, one which is reversible, has no side effects, and is available in any supermarket for two or three dollars, is the leash. Unfortunately for us all it, like any birth control method for dogs and cats, is just too much bother.

10

Dogs or People?

Can society afford dogs? The answer is No. But if the question is, Does society want dogs? the answer is probably Yes. Reason lies between the two viewpoints, as always, and resolution will depend on whose rights are deemed more important, those of dogs or people.

The real measure of freedom within a society is the government's regard for citizens' rights, those of the individual and of groups bonded by race, religion, occupation, age, or sex. One of the most respected documents in the free world, the Declaration of Independence of the United States, acknowledges that man is endowed with certain "inalienable rights," among them "Life, Liberty, and the Pursuit of Happiness," and in 1776 the American colonies pledged to guarantee these rights. History has shown that whenever the government has violated any of its citizens' rights, revolution, which in itself is an "inalienable right" of the American people, has resulted.

Rights evolve as a nation's social conscience matures. Black Americans, who for years accepted being discriminated against, rose up in massive protest in the 1960s and now demand equal rights with white Americans. Women, long prejudiced against in jobs, are fighting to achieve wage parity, and even non-smokers have the right to eat in restaurants without cigarette smoke wafting under their noses. Non-dog owners are now demanding their rights.

A revolution, granted a quiet one, is shaping up over the rights of dogs as against the rights of people; dog owners versus non-dog owners. The conflict is basically between those who believe dogs have the right to run free and behave on instinct and those who feel dogs should be under the owner's control. In the early stages of researching this book I asked a dog owner why he didn't tie his dog up during the day while he was at work and the man looked at me as if I was out of my mind. "Because that's not natural," he protested. "Dogs have to run. They've got rights, too, you know. How would you like to be tied up all day?" For the countless times I continue to ask the question the answers don't change much. Owners have romantic visions of their dogs playing in the sun, frolicking in the park, dozing luxuriously under a shade tree, being free, exercising their rights. In effect, owners are condoning the dog's right to foul your lawn, overrun a park, bite your kid, cause you to have a car accident, strew garbage all over your place, jump up on your white pants, sniff your crotch, and all the while you have no right to challenge the dog's nature. Or if you do, you are insensitive and without respect for animals' rights.

There is no disputing the contribution certain dogs make to society. Thousands of blind persons would lead less productive lives were it not for dogs; lost children might never be found alive without the aid of dogs; many streets would be unsafe if there were no police dogs on patrol; children would miss them and old people might wither piteously on the vine of neglect without the companionship of a pet dog. But is that enough? Do these few circumstances justify half the population owning pets and indulging in a useless extravagance at the expense of all of society? In the United States it costs taxpayers about $500,000,000 a year to pay for problems caused by dogs – treatment of diseases transmitted by them, bites and attacks, sanitation, destruction of livestock, and animal control programs. The figure does not include subsidizing spay and neuter clinics, picking up dead dogs off the streets, or education programs. Paying $500,000,000 merely to clean up after dogs is scandalous when there are people who live in shacks and don't get enough to eat. That $500,000,000 could renovate 17,000 houses all over the country; it could buy 10,000 kidney dialysis units and full-time treatment for a year.[1] And going to the extreme of allowing public funds to nourish the creative spirit of man, the Metropolitan Opera, the National Gallery, and the New York Public Library, could benefit handsomely by sharing $500,000,000 annually. Nonetheless, this $500,-000,000 in public money is small change compared to the 3 billion dollars people spend annually on pet food and the additional 3 to 4 billion dollars they spend on rhinestone collars, false eyelashes, grooming parlours, and the myriad other frivolities lavished on pets.

Ironically, the money expended to keep dogs is perhaps the least costly expense incurred by them. Although dogs have always bitten people, transmitted disease, defecated indiscriminately, and aggravated human life in various ways, it has not been until their numbers started to escalate into the millions that their habits became costly social problems. We are now past the stage of considering only the physical problems. More crucial is the ethical question of dogs using manpower, resources, energy, and food, for which humans the world over are competing.

Society is the victim of an overpopulation of pets and yet this same society, quite paradoxically, is responsible for creating a greater reliance on household pets than ever before. The past twenty-five years have produced more social changes than the previous 150, and growing numbers of people depend on dogs to assuage the abrasions these changes are producing – the alienation of city life, the soaring divorce rate, crime in the streets, the Women's Liberation Movement, the Gay Liberation Movement, more children living with single parents, and more couples choosing not to have children – in all of these circumstances a dog is a handy, dependable, loyal, an unconditionally loving human substitute. From a moral viewpoint one begins to wonder if the value of dogs in society is beginning to exceed that of humans. Already there are ominous indications that this is occurring. When the photograph of former President Lyndon Johnson holding his Beagle by the ears was flashed across the country he received more mail that month from irate animal lovers than he did from parents of men who were dying in Vietnam. Records show that the two heaviest loads of mail British Members of Parliament ever received both involved animals. Look at some of these recent facts:

- In 1975 the mayor of Pisa, Italy, banned dogs from the centre of town because of fouling, and he received a murder threat.[2]
- A New Jersey yachtsman was charged with manslaughter in the drowning deaths of two crew members when he refused to throw his Labrador overboard to make room for the men in the lifeboat. He was acquitted.[3] [4]
- A sixteen-year-old California girl was rescued from her home in 1977, starving, having been locked in a room for four years, and weighing only sixty-three pounds. In another room two Great Danes were found, healthy and well fed.[5]
- Based on a policy revised by the Anglican Church in Canada in early 1976, two Anglican bishops refused to baptize two infants whose parents were not regular churchgoers, while in that same diocese a bishop baptized cats and dogs in the annual blessing of the animals service.[6]

Go back a little further into history:

- In 1867 Henry Bergh, founder of the ASPCA inaugurated a horse ambulance two years before the first human ambulance was operated by Bellevue Hospital in New York.[7]
- When Queen Victoria granted a royal charter in 1840 to the SPCA (founded in 1824) the East India Company was still in the slave business. The first animal protection act was passed in 1822, eleven years before the abolition of slavery and another twenty-two years before children were exempted from working in the mines.[8]
- In America the first Society for the Prevention of Cruelty to Animals was founded in New York City in 1866, eight years before a similar organization for children. Because there was no law at this time to protect children, an

abused nine-year-old girl had to be declared at least equal to an animal in order that her parents could be charged under the SPCA act. This celebrated case led to the formation of the Society for the Prevention of Cruelty to Children in 1874.

The first Canadian SPCA was founded in Quebec in 1869, followed nineteen years later by the Protection of Neglected Children Act, passed by Parliament in 1888. The Toronto Humane Society, founded in 1887, showed no discrimination; it dealt with prevention of cruelty to both animals and children.

At what stage does the frequency of events indicate a new social trend? Citing a few examples and implying they denote the global situation is dangerous; yet the fact is, day by day, there are an increasing number of incidents depicting animals taking precedence over man. When British MPs count animal issues as generating top priority concern from voters, this is surely indicative of a prevailing attitude.

Solving the problems that pets impose on society today is an awesome task, mostly because the first hurdle one has to overcome is the personality of the pet owner, especially the dog owner. Bearing in mind one's own dog is never at fault, dog owners will acknowledge, sometimes under pressure, that "dogs" – a bizarre species quite unrelated to their precious little Muffy – might cause problems, but not *their* dog. (Spelled backwards, remember, it is god.) Ordinarily nice, respectable people have blind spots concerning their dogs. They can't see it gnawing at the postman's leg; they don't notice the dog relieving itself in the neighbour's driveway. I'm convinced some dog owners rate defecation with some sort of benevolent public service, that the feces are reconditioning the gravel, fertilizing the park, rejuvenating the sidewalk, providing an interesting colour relief from all that boring green grass. Classically, dog owners are deaf to their own dog's barking – this is well established. And the dog's God-given right to run free is the rule not the exception.

The next stumbling block is politicians. Elected to serve the common good, politicians ignore their responsibility toward controlling animal problems for obvious, although contemptible, reasons – half the voters own dogs or cats. And since regulations and controls are regarded as "anti-dog" by dog owners, politicians who support amendments to bylaws or introduce new legislation that deals with dog problems automatically alienate one-half of their voters. If politics is the art of the possible, seemingly it is impossible to campaign for dog laws and remain in office. An alderman in a small town in British Columbia told me both he and the mayor were defeated on what he called environmental issues: the town's garbage and tougher animal control bylaws. When I asked a Canadian government cabinet minister, who enjoys great popularity in his half-urban, half-rural riding, and whose campaign literature includes the dog in the family photograph, if he would vote for tough animal legislation, he smiled and said, "No way!"

Yet it is fairly easy to get politicians to vote for a subsidized spay and neuter clinic, chiefly because it lets them off the hook. They appear to be doing *something*. Having supported a safe item on the pet agenda, which pays lip-service to the whole overpopulation problem, this allows them to coast for a while, avoiding the controversial issues of leash laws, stoop-and-scoop laws, rights versus privileges, heavy fines for infractions, and so on. Meanwhile, they endorse a costly failure. It is not as though politicians fail to hear complaints about dogs. In a 1974 U.S. survey to determine what are the major urban problems facing municipal governments it was revealed that the number-one complaint mayors received from citizens was in regard to "dog and other pet control problems." Tax rates were ranked fifth, crime eighth, and fourteenth and last was fire protection. When asked to rank what they considered the major urban problems mayors cited refuse and solid waste as number one, streets and highways second, law enforcement third, and out of a total of twenty-eight urban problems dogs were not even ranked.[9] One can only conclude from this survey that although people do, mayors do not regard dogs as a problem. This incongruity was also noted in a random survey of elected aldermen in the City of Toronto. A worker in one local constituency office stated that by far the biggest complaint he received from constituents involved dogs and dog problems. However, when the alderman representing that ward was questioned he admitted the problem was serious but claimed dogs "were not a big issue" in his ward.[10]

Even if people in cities wanted to do so they are legally prevented from keeping chickens to lay eggs for them to eat. Yet for their sheer pleasure they could have a dozen dogs in the back yard and an alligator in the bathtub. A person with a contagious disease must be quarantined, yet that same person is under no obligation to keep his or her pet disease free or confined when it has a contagious disease (the exception being rabies). Politicians must be made to answer for these double standards, especially now that the growing population of household dogs and cats is imperiling public health and slashing giant slices out of the public tax pie. To those politicians who have the courage to put forth meaningful animal control laws, voters must pledge their support at the polls.

At the rate the dog population is growing, by 1984 it will double in the Western World. (The human population is expected to double by the year 2019.) Can you visualize double the number of dogs running loose on your street or in the parks? Feeding the world's population is a subject of grave concern and as more and more authorities project death by starvation for millions of people in the Third World in the decade of the 1980s, and serious food shortages in developed countries, will any nation with a public conscience tolerate pet animals consuming double their present amount of food? Checks and balances have been initiated by an enlightened citizenry and committed persons in public life, but one of the dangers inherent in today's dog crisis is that emotionalism tends to pit one group of fanatics against the other, with the result that neither is taken seriously. On the one side is the hysterical dog owner whose dog doesn't require controls because its right is to be free; on the other is the equally hysterical dog hater who won't be satisfied until men in brown uniforms march in and snatch dogs right off the laps of little old ladies. Dr. Anthony Carding, the British authority familiar with the worldwide problem of pets, claims that public hostility toward dogs "is greater in England than anywhere else in Western Europe,"[11] which, for a nation famous for its fervid devotion to animals, comes as a surprise. In the United States and Canada anti-dog movements are gathering momentum; outraged citizens are calling for strict dog controls in letters to the editors, and whenever local authorities attempt to change animal bylaws one visit to the council chamber at the time of debate is a convincing demonstration of the anti-dog lobby in full-blown fury.

Anti-dog activities are beginning to produce results. Pet banning, for one, is a burgeoning fact of North American and British life. An urban renewal project on Roosevelt Island, New York City, prohibits both automobiles and dogs. More and more apartment and housing units for families and senior citizens throughout the Western World are clamping down on pet keeping, and new developments, fairly extensively, have pet restrictions written into leases. In England, 46 per cent of public rental authorities prohibit pet keeping, but the percentage zooms to a high of 75 per cent when renting from private landlords.[12] Over fifty years ago dogs were banned in Reykjavik, Iceland, because it was felt they jeopardized the public health and sanitation standards of the city. The shortage of food was the reason the Chinese banned dogs from cities in 1963, on the basis that food eaten by dogs is subtracted from what is available for human consumption. Chairman Mao had plans for a healthy populace.* Pigs were banned from the streets of New York only in 1863 because they had become a nuisance, running loose, causing horse-and-buggy accidents and fouling the streets, and if anyone is complacent about dogs in today's society, these historical facts may serve as an ominous portent.

Fran Lee, the Children Before Dogs activist ("We tried education, placation and all we got was defecation.") is convinced banning is on the way. Once environmentalists get around to declaring household pets pollutants,** action is

---

*Despite Mao's all-pervasive power, shortly after his demise pets began making a comeback.

**A pest control symposium held recently in Detroit referred to urban dogs as "vermin."

bound to be swift. Just as the automobile industry was forced into installing pollution control devices in cars, soft-drink manufacturers were compelled in many areas to put only returnable bottles on the market, and as anti-litter laws gain more widespread enactment, and industry is restricted more and more from polluting the air, lakes and streams, dog owners too will be forced into tighter controls and restrictions.

Many municipalities have already enacted get-tough bylaws. In a perusal of bylaws from twenty-nine Canadian jurisdictions twenty-one of them have since 1974 updated their animal control legislation in respect to pets. One of the notable amendments regarding pet ownership is the limitation of the number of pets a resident may own without a kennel licence to two, and in some cases to three or four. In Windsor, Ontario, the limitation also includes cats, restricting ownership to no more than two dogs and two cats per household. Some other Canadian cities with restrictions on ownership are: Edmonton, Alberta; Victoria, B.C.; Humboldt, Sask.; Montreal, P.Q.; Charlottetown, P.E.I.; and in Ontario, Ottawa, Sudbury, Windsor, and some boroughs of Metropolitan Toronto.[13] As of early 1976, dogs were banned from fifteen Toronto parks and playgrounds. This trend has been noticed in other bylaws in respect to specific places where dogs are not allowed.

Controls on breeding, although not widespread, are beginning to appear in municipalities in the form of a spay and neuter clause for adopting animals from a shelter, and a licence differential on altered animals. Some municipalities have raised licence fees, especially for sexually intact animals. A gentle beginning, but at least a response to the problem.

Combined with the gradual updating of animal bylaws the only other measures that attempt to combat the dog problem are killing surplus animals and establishing low cost or subsidized spay and neuter clinics. But these measures are not working. Instead of pouring hundreds of thousands of tax dollars into unproved experiments such as spay and neuter clinics, municipalities would be better off to:

1. encourage the notion that it is anti-social to be an irresponsible pet owner;

2. launch a vigorous education campaign of responsible pet ownership, especially in the schools;
3. amend bylaws to induce responsibility and penalize infractions.

First, the matter of irresponsible pet owners being anti-social. Shame, the emotion everyone responds to, is an effective change agent, and though it is only a beginning, people have been shamed out of, if not outlawed, from smoking in elevators, pitching pop cans out of car windows, and littering parks. Quite possibly the same pressures might be capable of modifying pet owners' beliefs that their pets have the right to run loose.

Dogs that are unleashed and run loose, that leave their excreta on public and private property, that bite and bark and annoy people in countless ways, are behaving "naturally"; yet, for humans, such activities are anti-social, since they violate the safety, peace, health, and well-being of people. And who is responsible? Not dogs, certainly, for they are incontinent animals. The sole responsibility for the anti-social behaviour of dogs must rest with the owner. Whenever a dog owner stands by waiting for his or her animal to relieve itself (can there be a more ludicrous sight?), without cleaning up after it, he or she is committing a crime against society by allowing the environment to be polluted, and thereby insulting the senses of its citizens. Dog owners, avowing there is nothing cleaner than a dog's tongue, will let the dog lick their face, even though the animal may have just licked its genitals or anus; yet people squirm at the thought of scooping up the dog's dung. Perhaps our use of language is one of the problems. If we ceased using euphemisms and called dog excrement by the dirty word it is – shit – perhaps it would be taken more seriously. Shit is offensive; it offends people and nature. Dog owners feel inelegant stooping and scooping, although on the other hand they may derive a perverse satisfaction in depositing shit everywhere via their dogs. In an act of hostility and rebellion they may be getting back at bosses, the unions, the government, taxes, high and mighty relatives, their sullen kids, or whomever else is dumping on them. Whatever the reasons,

200

they can no longer be of any consequence. It is time for a threat: if you do not clean up after your dog you may lose the privilege of having one.

Owners must accept the responsibility of birth control for their pets. If each individual owner of a household pet, one way or another, prevented his or her female from producing offspring and the male from fertilizing females whether by control, through drugs, or by spaying and neutering, this would show a decline in the pet population in the long term. Perhaps most important is the short term. Such responsibility would reduce the number, which presently stands at 13 to 15 million, of animals that are put to death every year because they are surplus.

The prospect of educating today's adult pet owners to be responsible for their pets' behaviour is dismal, for thousands of years of history have to be counteracted in order that people may re-evaluate the role of pets in society and think of them as animals with special needs, not humanoidal freaks that are more important than people. It is like coming upon a tribe of savages and trying to talk to them about sanitation, public health, pollution, and social responsibility. And since today's adult pet owner refuses to acknowledge that his or her individual lack of responsibility contributes in any way to the collective problem, the hope remains with educating future pet owners.

It is essential that the anthropomorphizing and idealizing of animals be eradicated from animal education. The Lassie syndrome – in which such traits as loyalty and dependability are exaggerated to an unrealistic extent – must be obliterated. Not that books and movies outrightly lie; more to the point, they omit reality. Lassie on film never dumped on a neighbour's property, no one ever picked burrs out of her coat or de-wormed or de-fleaed her, and Lassie never kept anyone awake with her barking, she was too busy bounding photogenically over fences and fetching little boys out of creeks.

And then there is Walt Disney. Probably no single individual or organization has distorted the truth about animals more than Walt Disney. From animal cartoons to documentary shorts to full length movies, Disney films are gaucheries of exaggeration and deception. Disney's preoccupation throughout his career (although he died in 1966 the Disney Studios carry on its founder's aims) was to present animals in situations that concentrated on the most unattractive human characteristics of aggression, sadism, and stupidity. Given that the humanized animal chases, clubbings, ceaseless stumblings, and banana-peel pratfalls, may tickle and fascinate children, there is no serious objection to the violence of Disney – obvious violence being obviously phony to most children. The real quarrel is that in his drive to perfect film technique, through tricky visuals, editing, and sound effects, Disney ridiculed wildlife. Penguins slipping on the ice to idiotic musical sound effects become vaudevillian pratfalls not creatures coping with their environment. The true examination of nature is either not filmed or is left on the cutting room floor. Intellectually, Disney films have a this-is-it tone, that if one bear cub cuffs another over the head and the sequence ends with an amusing sound effect, it is like the punch line of a joke and that's the implied end of the matter, all you need to know about bear cubs.

In traditional children's animal stories ownership of a pet animal fails to imply a responsibility toward the animal. This is an educational deficiency that must be reversed.

Legislation is the last step, for if people cannot be shamed or educated into being responsible pet owners they will, sad to say, have to be legislated into it. But no matter how many bylaws are conceived and debated and finally written into the books, if not enforced they are more offensive than the offences they intend to curtail for they presume citizens can be bought off with words, not action. Enactment of stringent bylaws and their enforcement must be a municipal priority – and it is up to citizens' groups to insist that it is.

Attitudinal changes, educational programs, and bylaw enforcement, are all very important and the money required to enact these changes is there, although perhaps in the wrong hands. When municipalities are presently taxing their citizens to the limit, clearly what is required is an infusion of new money. How this can be achieved is discussed in Chapter 11.

11

A Few Modest Proposals

Dog owners, aggravated non-owners, the pet industry, breeders, veterinarians, the media, the animal welfare movement, and our lawmakers, must all make contributions toward solving the dog crisis if the relationship between pet animals and man is to remain stable and the rights of both respected. The demands are high. At the very minimum, an attitudinal change is essential, then effort and money are required, before it is too late. No single endeavour will significantly reduce the problem. What is necessary is a combined program to educate people to become responsible pet owners, to control the breeding of pets, and to support the enactment and diligent enforcement of tough animal control laws. Only then will results be seen.

This chapter deals with some starting points:

Education

The crucial philosophy to be conveyed is that pet ownership is a privilege not a right. And every pet owner earns this privilege by abiding by a code of behaviour which safeguards the dog while preventing it from interfering with or placing at risk the health and well-being of humans or other forms of plant and animal life. Here are some suggestions for ways in which education about pets may be fostered:

1. Humane societies, animal welfare groups, veterinarians, dog clubs, and public health officials, must be called upon to give classroom instruction in the junior grades on responsible pet ownership.
2. An effective place to teach responsible pet ownership to youngsters is within their wildlife or natural history studies.
3. Funds generated by the pet industry must be devoted to classroom films, slides, pamphlets, workshops, and adult seminars, which should concentrate on responsible pet ownership and on eradicating the tendency to anthropomorphize animals.
4. Concerned parents and teachers must control the tendency to anthropomorphize animals in school texts the way the women's movement works toward removing sexism and racism from school texts.
5. Education must arrest the Smokey the Bear syndrome, which caricatures the bear as an attractive, cuddly pet that is quite humanized. Despite zoo signs which read, "Do Not Feed The Bears," people delight in feeding these animals and when a bear's paw swipes out at a child and forty stitches are required to close the wound, everyone is horrified. The teddy bear turned into a savage.
6. Naturalists must be allowed to present their side of the animal education story to children in an effort to counteract the sugary, one-sided, distorted world of Walt Disney.
7. Visits to animal shelters should be made by school children so they can see first hand how many animals are waiting for a home, or worse, waiting to be destroyed because they are surplus.
8. Animals must not be brought into the classroom as a learning experience unless the teacher has a guaranteed

home for them at the end of the study term. Every June humane societies are called upon to dispose of classroom pets no one wants.

Dog Owner Responsibility

The very act of bringing an animal into the home as a pet places the owner under an obligation to properly feed and care for it, to protect it from abuse and from abusing others. This constitutes the earned privilege of pet owning, and failure to abide by the code must result in loss of privilege. (See #2, page 219.)

Before owners may be legislated into responsibility, or conversely, out of pet ownership, these standards of basic human decency and consideration toward their fellow man must be adopted:

1. All pet dogs must be licensed.
2. All dogs must be leashed when off the owner's property. Any owner whose dog is found running at large ought to be subject to penalty.
3. Pet dogs must be spayed or neutered, licensed breeders exempted.
4. Owners are required to clean up their dog's defecation.
5. Bitches in heat must be confined.
6. Every pet dog must have obedience training courses and prove to be under the control of its master.
7. Once a year the animal must be vaccinated against leptospirosis/distemper/hepatitis and rabies.
8. Keep crawling children away from puppies. The risk of the child being infected by puppy worms is too great. (See *Toxocara canis*, page 143.)

When you come right down to it, not very much is asked of pet owners. If keeping a pet is important, the eight preceding suggestions must be followed.

Limiting Pet Ownership

It is essential that municipalities impose limitations on pet owning if problems caused by pets are to be held in control. This can be done, assuming pet owning is established as a privilege and not a right, by the following considerations:

1. Limit households to two pets (either dogs, cats or one each). More than that would require a kennel licence.
2. Impose size limitation. Three Great Danes with only a ten-foot patch of garden is not a satisfactory situation, regardless of how well-behaved the dogs are. A large dog must have a minimum amount of running space and if a family can't provide it only a small house dog or cat should be allowed.

Pet Industry Tax

One of the logical sources to tap for funding animal control programs is the pet industry. Certain companies would argue they are contributing their share toward public education through printing brochures and pamphlets and by sponsoring dog shows and symposia. However, a cursory investigation reveals that in many corporate endeavours brand name identification is the primary objective of sponsorship. This is not good enough. So highly profitable an industry has a moral obligation to repay the society upon which its good fortune depends. Using the United States as an example, consumers spend 3 billion dollars annually on pet food and an additional 3 to 4 billion dollars on pet supplies, accessories, and services. Let us say the manufacturer's cost to put pet food and supplies on the market is half the retail cost, which would be about 3 billion dollars. If a mere one per cent tax were levied at the manufacturer's level this would generate $30,000,000, which could be allocated to animal control programs. Here is just an idea of how much that kind of money could buy:

100,000 classroom posters	$ 75,000
1,000,000 brochures	500,000

Production of ten fifteen-minute educational films – 1,000 prints of each	750,000
Production of five one-half-hour educational television programs	500,000
Ten grants of $100,000 each for pet contraceptive research	1,000,000
500 information officers to present responsible pet ownership education programs in the schools and to special adult groups	750,000
500 bylaw enforcement officers	750,000
Total	4,325,000

And there is more than $25,000,000 yet to spend.

Pet Food Alternatives

If the projections of market analysts Frost and Sullivan materialize, the pet food business in the United States will reach the 12 billion dollar mark by 1986, four times what it was in 1977.[1] And by that time it is also predicted that food and water supplies will be on the top of government agendas the world over.[2] With a quadrupled demand for pet food in one decade threatening the human food supply, it cannot be overemphasized that finding cheaper alternative raw materials for pet and human food is a priority.

Considerable research for alternative foods for both humans and livestock is under way all over the world. It took fifteen years of testing for scientists in Israel to produce a crop of algae that not only purifies sewage but also feeds chickens and fish.[3]

After twenty years of research petroleum-derived proteins are being made for livestock feed, and for new animal food sources, scientists are experimenting with insects such as caterpillars. Recycled garbage is a potential food supply, as are some types of industrial wastes, such as that from the brewing industry and coal-slurry wastes which are fed to fish and shellfish. Kelp farming is under way off the California coast and cattle manure is being fed back to beef cattle. Technology from the American space program has produced fake fruit from seaweed, a product which will be readily available as a part of a normal diet for people in about twenty years.[4] Wood pulp used in bread baked by the largest bread manufacturer in the United States is now available in 70 per cent of the country's grocery stores.[5] Chicken feathers are used in making cookies (mothers all over America will be saying, "Eat your cookie, dear, before it flies away") and up to 3 per cent ground bone may now be added to American salami and wieners.[6]

As is apparent, new and unconventional resources are being tapped and these endeavours must continue if both the human and animal populations on earth are to be fed.

It is the responsibility of governments to compel the pet food industry to develop inexpensive foodstuffs for pets so that the millions of tons of conventional raw materials they use – e.g. grains – will be released back into the human food chain. The industry spends millions of dollars a year trying to determine if one product will outsell another. It is time that at least some of this vast expenditure of both money and talent be diverted to help mankind conquer the battle against a dwindling world food supply.

Small Dogs

The enormous tonnage required to feed pets would be substantially decreased if there were fewer large dogs. According to the Canine Caloric Requirements chart, published by Ralston Purina, a medium-sized dog – a German Shepherd weighing seventy pounds and categorized as a "house dog," as opposed to an "active" or "working" dog – requires 2,240 digestible calories per day. The dog could get this by eating seven to eight cups of dry food daily. A ten-pound Dachshund requires only 400 calories a day or 1.5 cups of dry food.[7] At this rate the German Shepherd would get 2,737.5 cups of food a year, compared to the Dachshund's 547.5 cups.

Notwithstanding the precarious world food situation, another compelling argument against large dogs is that the larger the dog, the larger the litter size. Chihuahuas and

Pekingese produce a mean litter of 3.19 puppies, Poodles average four, Beagles 5.79, and German Shepherds produce an average of 8.12 puppies per litter.[8] Thus, if the pet population comprised fewer large dogs the result would be a natural lessening of the growth rate through reduction of large litters.

Creating the desire for small dogs must be undertaken, just as has been done to shift the public away from buying gas-guzzling, eight-cylinder cars. This can be achieved through education messages and ads sponsored by pet food companies, through the animal welfare movement, and through the incentive of having to pay lower licence fees for small dogs.

Advertising

It is imperative that these important pet food commercial regulations be enforced without delay:

1. that all dogs be shown on leashes when out of the owner's house;
2. that dogs wear licence tags;
3. that all dogs be small breeds;
4. that every commercial devote 10 per cent of its time toward educating viewers about responsible pet ownership;
5. that commercials refrain from attaching human behaviour and voices to pets and from making pets' unacceptable behaviour endearing. For example, it must not be portrayed as funny or cute for a pet to run away or not come when called.

Due to the powerful influence of television, when dogs in commercials are not leashed, people deduce that the leash is unnecessary or at least unfashionable. Dogs leaping in open meadows, free as the wind, are more attractive than dogs on leashes. Licence tags are not worn, I suspect, because they are a distraction. When the camera moves in for a close-up of the dog at the food dish the eagerness with which the dog laps up the food is what the advertiser wants to convey and you will notice that nothing, not a licence tag, a collar, or hair ribbon distracts the viewer's attention from this magic moment.

Large breeds are repeatedly shown in advertising because they symbolize conspicuous consumption, status, power, and virility. People react to these stimuli, acquire a large dog, and then discover it eats them out of house and home and they cannot control it; in short order the dog ends up in the animal pound.

Toronto Humane Society operations manager, Arthur Allibone, spoke of the increasing number of large, purebred dogs taken in recently at the shelter, and said there were fifteen sheep dogs in 1975, "whereas two or three years ago we wouldn't have seen any." Among other large dogs were eight or nine Great Danes, five Newfoundlands, and numerous Doberman Pinschers and German Shepherds. Allibone laid the cause squarely on the media. "Television advertising seems to feature large dogs and they have a certain appeal to people." In the case of Afghans he claims young couples acquire them because they want to be "in style with a showy dog seen a lot in fashion magazines." However, in his experience, "the voguish dog isn't a life-long pet and the novelty wears off when the style changes. Then the dog becomes a dispensable commodity." Purebreds accounted for 8 to 10 per cent of the shelter population in 1976, one that was composed almost exclusively of mutts only a few years ago.[9]

A Vancouver SPCA official reported that in 1976, the size of animals destroyed in the city had increased from an average of 22.4 pounds to 51.8 pounds, an increase of 131 per cent in the past five years.[10] Multiply the situation by thousands and you have a day-by-day, city-by-city problem facing animal shelters. In England, the United States, and Canada, broadcast regulations protect the consumer from misleading or false advertising claims. Citing Canada as an example, beer advertising (where still permitted) is now subject to stringent regulations as to what may be claimed about the beer, what percentage of the message may "sell," what activities the actors in the commercials may be engaged in, and, recently, in Ontario even attitude has been legislated – commercials cannot imply that alcohol contributes to a good social time.

On a thirty-second pet food commercial, if only the message "Please leash your dog" or "Clean up after your dog" were transmitted, this could have an enormous impact. If television commercials alone can persuade whole nations to spray their armpits and wash their mouths out, surely they can get people to stoop and scoop. Commercials have great potential for helping to solve the dog crisis, and it is essential that advertisers, with the gigantic profits from their products, make their contribution.

Packaging

Society can no longer afford the millions of pet food cans being thrown out every day. Tons of steel are used by the pet food industry and in a time characterized by diminishing global resources this valuable material should be used to serve human needs. Worth about six cents, the can is obviously the most expensive item in canned pet food. To provide lower cost pet food while at the same time considering environmental and pollution issues, the industry must be forced to re-design its packaging. Bottle returns and paper re-cycling are environmental facts of life and ecological exceptions accorded the pet food industry are no longer acceptable. Bio-degradable packaging is a must. Or what about edible packages? This wouldn't take much, according to the food scientist who analyzed various human breakfast foods and concluded that people would be better off nutritionally if they threw out the cereal and ate the box.

For humans to pollute on a massive scale is bad enough; that millions of pets contribute, by causing millions of cans and packages of their food to be pollutants, is unjustifiable.

Non-renewable Resources

In the winter of 1976-77, one of the coldest on record in many states, U.S. President Jimmy Carter appealed to citizens to keep their thermostats turned down to 63°F, and lower, when they went to bed. People complied as they shivered, recognizing that a serious energy shortage demanded their co-operation and this slight sacrifice. The same citizens had already reduced their highway speed to fifty-five miles an hour to comply with a new law. Nevertheless, while individuals conserved energy factories extravagantly drained off billions of kilowatts of non-renewable energy to manufacture food for dogs and cats.

Legislation must be enacted that requires pet food companies to investigate ways of reducing the amount of energy consumed in processing pet food, a product of no benefit to humans. The human food industry, which uses an estimated 11 per cent of the country's total energy consumption processing food,[11] is looking into conservation methods, their spokesmen say, and supermarket chains have made effective reductions in energy expenditures in many areas, as have numerous other industries.

Indications are that we are heading toward a conserver society in the 1980s, a reversal of the present consumer society, and should this trend materialize the whole question of pet keeping will be under severe scrutiny.

Licensing

Municipalities that currently do not have licensing differentials fail to do their share in encouraging responsible pet ownership. The following, paid annually, are now necessary:

1. an increased licence fee for large dogs;
2. double the fee for the second owned dog, where two are permitted;
3. double the fee for a guard dog;
4. half the licence fee for spayed or neutered pets;
5. a kennel licence for over two dogs.

When owners of eight-cylinder automobiles pay higher licence fees then owners of four-cylinder cars, so ought owners of large dogs pay a higher licence fee.

A person should maintain the right to choose what kind of a dog to own. However, if a person chooses a dog that eats five times the amount of food of a smaller dog, that is acceptable providing the individual pays five times as much for a licence. While thirty-two countries in the world are threatened with starvation, anything less is a social aberration.

Easily half the dogs in any given municipality are unlicenced and it could be as many as 90 per cent. For this reason, municipalities would benefit by devoting more attention to collecting licence fees, thus adding to the public treasury, which would help pay for bylaw enforcement.

Identification

Even the best-mannered dogs are apt to run away when nobody is looking, and for this reason identification is important in order that the pet may be returned to its owner. The identity of the dog is essential in respect to its being a public nuisance, biting, and attacking people, spreading disease, etc. Local bylaws should be amended as follows:

1. All dogs must wear an identity tag attached to their collar. The tag should identify the owner by his or her social insurance number, or the dog by its licence number. Any system that unmistakably establishes ownership should be used. Perhaps Frederich, Prince of Wales, had the right idea with his dog's tag. It read:
   > I am his Highness's dog at Kew;
   > Pray tell me, sire, whose dog are you?
2. In addition to the tag, all dogs should be tattooed on the inside hind leg (until a better method is devised that doesn't wear out or fade) with the owner's social insurance or licence number.
3. Guard dogs must wear a special identification plaque of a size large enough to communicate to children, or to those who don't understand the language, that the dog is vicious and not to be petted.

Breeding Controls

To reduce breeding abuses and control overproduction of dogs, especially puppies bred by puppy mills, local municipalities would do well to endorse these measures:

1. Prohibit the sale in pet shops of puppies under eight weeks of age.
2. Ensure through inspection that puppies for sale in pet shops have been acquired from licensed breeders.
3. Impose and strictly enforce the bylaw that anyone owning more than three (or four) dogs must have a breeder's licence.
4. Any person who registers more than four litters per year from the same bitch is obliged to have a kennel licence.
5. Penalize breeding abuses, such as mating dogs with wolves or other wild animals, with heavy fines, along with suspension of breeding licence.
6. Persons buying puppies from pet shops must sign a spay and neuter or controlled breeding agreement at the time of purchase.
7. The municipality, animal welfare organizations or veterinary associations must provide printed material to pet shops and kennel operators on the responsibilities demanded of the new pet owner.

Kennel clubs or other purebred registration bodies must ensure that breeding abuses are curtailed by field inspections. For one, the American Kennel Club took in more than $7,000,000 in purebred registrations in 1975 and the question begs asking: is the AKC adequately sharing the responsibility of policing breeders, especially puppy mills, who fail to uphold breeding standards?

Obedience Training

Dogs have been trained to dance the can-can, go to the corner store for cigarettes, and toss hand grenades into enemy bunkers and yet in sheer versatility little can match the temple guard dogs of the Sicilian god Adranus that were well behaved with visitors during the daytime and at night were known to tear thieves apart. When guests imbibed too liberally the dogs escorted the incapacitated fellows right to their homes, at times displaying their contempt by rolling them in the mud.[12] In spite of the thousands of remarkable tasks dogs can be trained to perform, people still complain their dogs won't come when called. Since the uncontrolled behaviour of dogs causes so many social headaches, simple obedience training must be a mandatory condition of pet owning.

One must also be aware of the abuses perpetrated in the name of training. As quickly as individuals and businessmen acquire large dogs for protection against crime, the fast-buck operators move in, for example, dog trainers specializing in guard and attack training. The 1976 Yellow Pages of the Manhattan telephone directory carried thirty-two listings of companies in the business of obedience and guard training. They play directly into peoples' fears with quarter-page ads that picture German Shepherds and Doberman Pinschers, some in attitudes of fierce attack, and with bold typeface headlines such as "Don't live in fear!" and "Protect your family, your property," and "Stop Burglars! Muggers! Robbers! Rape!" A number of advertisers noted that their dogs are K-9- or army-trained.

The law is now recognizing that dogs can be trained to a dangerous level, as in the case of the Boston man who, allegedly during the course of an armed robbery, threatened the victim with his German Shepherd dog. The Massachusetts Court of Appeals ruled that his dog was a "dangerous weapon" in the crime, capable of inflicting bodily harm.[13]

If it can be said that art imitates life, fiction writers face tough competition from actual fact when it comes to contemporary horror stories about dogs. Consider a recent novel about a woman who trains her dog to kill her husband and compare this with the true case of dogs who were trained to torture political prisoners in Chile. In this instance, which came to light in 1975, a special panel appointed by the Commission on Human Rights expressed its "profound disgust" at having to report to the United Nations General Assembly on the political atrocities, among them: "Women are forced to lie naked on a cot, and trained dogs are made to run over their naked bodies, suck and bite their nipples, and in some cases rape them."[14]

With training producing aggression and breeding producing ferocity, guard dogs have become unsocialized. Because they cannot be trusted and are unsafe around children the City of New York requires that guard dogs, like all dangerous substances, must be clearly labelled.

The result is that New York guard dogs now wear a plastic disc around their necks bearing a caricature of a vicious dog, which, like the skull and crossbones, symbolizes *danger*.

Mandatory obedience training for dogs might be difficult to enforce, as would legislation that prohibits people from training dogs to commit crimes. But that should not foreclose discussion on the subject.

Animal Welfare Organizations

Britain's Royal Society for the Prevention of Cruelty to Animals, founded in 1824, is the oldest charitable organization in the English-speaking world and to this day the RSPCA, along with thousands of affiliates, remains dedicated to the welfare of animals. There are well over 1,000 animal protection organizations in North America, new entries in the field being private organizations with special ecological interests, concern for animals used in medical research, humane hunting and trapping, protection of endangered species, and the like. Their crusades tug at the hearts of people and inspire many a dotty little old lady to leave her million-dollar estate to her animal friends. Animal organizations are generously endowed with bequests and legacies and it is no exaggeration that massive fortunes are tucked away in animal funds all over the world. The Seeing Eye Inc., for one, ceased soliciting funds in 1959, due to the generosity of donors and has operated since then on the interest from its investments and legacies. Take the year 1974-75. With securities valued at $21,000,000, that earned just over a million dollars in income, and public donations of three-quarters of a million dollars, the company's annual expenses were met by these two sources alone. (In spite of such a healthy financial picture, the Seeing Eye gave a mere $20,000 in grants, the lowest amount since 1966.)[15] The concern is how the largesse of countless gilt-edged animal organizations may be more equitably distributed to the cause of animals as they relate to people.

For their work in helping to alleviate suffering and cruelty to animals, many animal welfare organizations are to be commended. Yet much more could be done. For example:

1. Rather than depending so heavily on government subsidies, fund-raising activities in the private sector should be stepped up.
2. Production of educational films, television programs, printed materials, and seminars should be undertaken, financed by private industry, particularly the pet industry.
3. To operate programs humane societies must collaborate with the private organizations which provide funding.
4. Private funding must be solicited to provide spay and neuter services. These should not be subsidized by tax dollars since pets do not benefit society as a whole.
5. A spay or neuter agreement must be mandatory in each animal shelter, and no mature dog or cat adopted without being sterilized.
6. The choice of small dogs for adoption must be encouraged.
7. Courses in obedience training should be offered on a non-profit basis.
8. Although admirable work is being done by many organizations, educational programs on responsible pet ownership must be expanded, particularly in the schools.
9. While many organizations attempt to find the most suitable families for pets, animal shelters should give more consideration to the other side – is the pet suitable for people? The pet cult espouses the notion that all pets are perfect, but like humans, there are canine misfits – the destructive ones, the killers, the ill behaved. These kinds of animals do not belong with people.
10. Public awareness of the existence of animal welfare organizations and the services they provide to the community should be accelerated by vigorous publicity campaigns.

The Veterinary Profession

Veterinarians must pledge their support to programs which help abate the overpopulation problem. Although no one can be legislated into benevolence, veterinarians who are not presently doing so might consider donating a small amount of service over a year's time to help disseminate the responsible pet owner's message and to periodically volunteer his or her services in a public clinic or animal shelter. A schoolroom talk or an evening's address now and then is surely not an imposition on a helping profession, particularly when its "patients" are in such dire need.

Governments

A problem confronting most municipalities is that animal control laws are shared by local, provincial or state, and national governments. The Province of Ontario typifies an existing complexity with ten provincial acts governing animals generally and an additional five acts relating specifically to animal control. Add to this local bylaws and various national animal acts and it is a wonder that controls of any kind are effected.

Clearly, revision of present animal legislation is necessary – and a priority. Dr. Harry Rowsell, the internationally acclaimed Canadian veterinarian, suggests that legislation ought to take into account the differences between rural and urban areas; he suggests urban legislation must ensure the rights of people, property, public health, and the environment, and that rural legislation must ensure the rights and safety of livestock, wildlife, people, and property.[16]

Expanding on these distinctions it is worth considering the consolidation of all animal legislation into one urban act and one rural act. A local Animal Control Office* would be an effective means of dealing with animal problems and the enforcement of the acts, with violations handled by a member

* The Animal Control Office could be a department of the local government or its function could be relegated to the existing animal control administration.

218

of the Animal Control Office and a policeman who would issue tickets on the spot. As is possible with traffic tickets the offender could appeal to the Animal Control Office and be heard by a Violations Arbitrator, a person especially trained in animal affairs and animal law, so as not to clog up courts with lengthy and costly hearings which would impede the processing of more urgent legal matters.

New rules of evidence may have to be established in order that complaints may be dealt with quickly and justly. In addition, enactment of a "hot pursuit" law would facilitate enforcement of the acts by allowing field personnel of the Animal Control Office to apprehend a loose animal, even if it has run onto someone's private property, without having to obtain a search warrant, which delays and in many cases aborts the apprehension.

Recognizing that revising legislation is complex, local, provincial or state and national governments should appoint qualified persons to form a task force to make meaningful recommendations within given jurisdictions. In the meantime, here are some ways in which governments, be they local, provincial, state, or federal, can help solve the animal problem:

1. If local dog licensing requirements are not being met, consideration might be given to licensing the owner rather than the dog. Just as a person is tested to prove he or she can drive a car responsibly before being issued a driver's licence, a pet owner ought to pass a responsibility test which indicates he or she is able to care for a pet.
2. More than two infractions of animal bylaws against a dog owner should result in licence suspension for a period of two years, after which the person would have to re-apply. Lifelong suspensions would be applicable in certain circumstances.
3. Eliminate forever the myth that every dog is entitled to one bite. Owners of vicious dogs must be held responsible for their dog's behaviour, and governments that fail to recognize such responsibility ignore a basic individual right of protection of life and limb.

4. Governments must stimulate, through grants and sponsorship, co-operation between veterinarians, animal welfare organizations, breeders and kennel clubs to combat the overpopulation problem and educate the public to be responsible pet owners.

5. Governments must offer tax incentives to corporations that fund animal education programs.

6. The victim-compensation concept for offenders may be applied. For instance, the owner who fails to clean up after his or her dog may contribute to a stoop-and-scoop program in a neighbourhood park.*

7. Grants must be made available to those engaged in contraceptive research as well as animal health research.

8. Governments must disseminate and/or fund public information and education campaigns to portray the seriousness of the pet problem, both to promote responsible pet ownership and to establish a climate that will ensure that elected representatives are not voted out of office for supporting tough laws.

9. Animal shelters subsidized by public funds must be required to launch or expedite, as the case may be, a three-way program of pet owner responsibility, public education, and spaying and neutering (which, when offered by the municipal animal shelter, must be privately funded – see item 10, below). No single program can be deemed effective without the other two.

10. No additional municipal funds should be allotted to surgical sterilizations; these must be the responsibility of the individual pet owner. When spaying and neutering is offered by a municipal animal shelter these services must be provided through fund-raising in the private sector.

11. Bylaw updating should have the input of concerned citizens' groups, the veterinary profession, and the department or organization which administers local animal control programs.

12. Designated public areas must be provided where dogs

*As in the precedent-setting case in September 1976 of a judge in Peterborough, Ontario who sentenced a boy convicted of cruelty to animals to thirty hours' work in an animal shelter.

may run and new building codes drawn up to accommodate "pets only" housing.

13. The keeping of exotic animals usually defined in bylaws as wild animals, e.g. lions, ocelots, monkeys, etc. as pets must be prohibited.
14. Puppies or kittens must not be given away as prizes.
15. Research into the utilization of carcasses of euthanized pets should be encouraged.
16. In areas where there are shortages of veterinarians governments should establish paramedical training in order to add to the personnel that is urgently required to sterilize pets.
17. Visceral larva migrans in humans (contracted from the dog worm, *Toxocara canis* – page 143) should be added to the list of diseases that physicians and hospitals must report. New York City (the first American city to do so) amended its health code in January 1977, to include visceral larva migrans as a reportable disease.

A sample animal bylaw, as proposed by the Humane Society of the United States, is reproduced in its entirety in Appendix D.

The Individual

Whether you are a dog owner or not, if you are concerned about dog problems you will be surprised to find you are not alone. Seek out people who share your concerns and voice them in some of these ways:

1. Let your local politician know about your feelings and demand action. Write or phone to make an appointment to see him or her. Don't accept No for an answer.
2. Draw up a series of changes you would like to see in the law, or present a copy of Appendix D as a sound, *conservative* bylaw proposal.
3. Organize. Take up a petition on your street if there are specific problems, such as excessive fouling, overturned garbage cans, a vicious dog. Present this to your elected

representative or make a deputation to the local council. Have your facts well organized, be brief, remain calm, and ask for action. Politically, dog owners are generally better organized than non-dog owners, hence politicians often hear only the dog owners' points of view.

4. Bring up the subject of responsible pet ownership and the undue humanizing of pets in children's literature at your local parent-teacher group or school board. Solicit the help of a local newspaper editor or writer to publicize your case.

5. Here are some approaches you might take on an individual problem with a neighbour's bothersome dog:

a) Let the person who allows his or her dog to run loose know that you find this behaviour anti-social and unacceptable.

b) If your neighbour's dog has a fondness for defecating on your lawn, ask the owner to come and clean it up. Or do as one annoyed gentleman did: scoop it up, place it in a plastic bag and deliver it to the owner, saying politely, "Your dog forgot something on my lawn."

c) Clip stoop-and-scoop news items and give them to your neighbour.

d) If the dog scatters your garbage, again, ask the owner to clean it up. And be certain garbage cans are tightly covered.

e) When a barking dog has you at your wits' end, and discussions with its owner have not resolved the problem, find out if the noise contravenes a local bylaw – it usually does – and charge the dog owner. If that doesn't work you might borrow a bugle and blow it when the dog barks, especially if you've been repeatedly awakened in the dead of night. This may elicit an ultimate resolve in the neighbourhood. Finally, you could get an electronic device that barks back at the dog. It is not heard by humans.

f) Should things get heated call the local authority and continue to do so until you get satisfaction. Have a back fence meeting and persuade other offended neighbours to take turns complaining.

g) Call an immediate "cease fire" when dog owners are seen to be making an attempt to correct the problem.

h) Join a citizens' group that shares your concern – the strength-in-numbers principle. Organize.

i) Run for office yourself or convince one of your group to do so. If you don't win, at least you will have done a good job publicizing your cause.

j) Never hesitate to call your local newspaper, radio or television station when real problems emerge. If the matter is legitimate news – and it's a slow day – your story might get told.

k) If you object to the fact that dogs in commercials are never leashed and never wear licence tags, that large dogs are shown, and that animal behaviour is humanized, write a letter outlining your objections in full and send it directly to the company involved. Companies that advertise their products take letters from consumers seriously.* They regard that one letter of complaint generally represents the views of 100 more offended persons who haven't written. In addition, send a copy of the letter to the television station that aired the commercial, and also a copy to the national agency that governs advertising. These are:

In Canada: Canadian Radio & Television Commission
Berger Building
100 Melcalfe Street
Ottawa, Ontario
K1A 0N2

In the U.K.: Independent Broadcasting Authority
70 Brompton Road,
London SW 3, England

In the U.S.: Federal Trade Commission
Pennsylvania Avenue
at 6th Street, N.W.
Washington, D.C. 20580

---

*One extreme example is the Canadian company that withdrew its television commercial for an antacid because of one letter from an outraged doctor.

The history of man and his relationship with animals is characterized by extremes. On the one hand is mutual companionship and dependence, while on the other is the exploitation and abuse of animals by man. Society's leaders will honour a dog who rescues a child from an overturned canoe one day and the next mount a horse and unleash a pack of hounds to kill a fox. To achieve historical perspective one must consider whether the animal-human combats in the Roman arenas are as barbarian as killing 15 million surplus pets a year.

Pet animals have been dealt with in this book primarily from the sociological point of view. There are many more contemporary issues that demand discussion and resolve, among them the philosophical issue of animals' rights, the slaughter of baby seals, whales and, for that matter, all animals killed by man under the various guises of sport or pleasure, the feeding of any one species to another, factory farming, the use of animal skins in expensive, fashionable coats, their various glands and secretions for the manufacture of cosmetics, the preservation of species threatened by extinction, the establishment of wildlife preserves, the humanity of zoos – although the subject matter is wide-ranging all issues return to man's humane treatment of animals.

Animals are magnificent creatures that deserve to be protected and respected by man, while at the same time, they, either by their habits or numbers, must not be permitted to jeopardize the quality of human life. An overhaul of the prevailing philosophies and attitudes is essential to eliminate the imbalances in order that both animal and man may live together in a state of grace.

Appendix A

100 Most Popular Dogs Registered With The American Kennel Club From 1964 to 1976

Listing the top 100 purebred dogs registered with the American Kennel Club (AKC) from 1964 to 1976 does not necessarily correspond to the general dog population with its millions of mutts and mixes. However, it is an indication of the kinds of breeds people choose to own. In 1976 a total of 1,048,648 purebred dogs were registered in 122 breeds (the last twenty-two have been omitted from this list), while in 1964 there were 648,267, an increase of 62% in twelve years.[1] The greatest increase in this period of a single breed is for Lhasa Apsos, which increased 3,436 per cent, followed by Old English Sheepdogs at 3,148 per cent. It is interesting to note the tremendous increases in large breed dogs – Doberman Pinschers at 1,423 per cent (leaping from twenty-second place in 1964 to third in 1976), Siberian Huskies at 1,365 per cent, Irish Setters at 1,268 per cent, Salukis at 1,017 per cent – which directly reflects the growing trend toward owning large dogs for protection and as a conspicuous fashion accessory.

It has been said that a 72 per cent increase within a breed means the breed is "holding its own," not in danger of being overpopulated. At a percentage rise of 360 and over the breed is in danger of, or already has been, exploited.[2] In this category there are twenty-five breeds out of the 100, exactly one-quarter.

Breed	AKC 1964 Ranking	Number Registered	AKC 1976 Ranking	Number Registered	Difference	
Poodles	1	178,401	1	126,799	29%	decrease
German Shepherds	2	63,163	2	74,723	18%	increase*
Doberman Pinschers	22	4,815	3	73,615	1423%	increase
Irish Setters	25	4,015	4	54,917	1268%	increase
Cocker Spaniels	8	15,632	5	46,862	200%	increase
Beagles	3	53,353	6	44,156	17%	decrease
Labrador Retrievers	13	10,340	7	39,939	286%	increase
Dachshunds	4	48,569	8	38,927	20%	decrease
Miniature Schnauzers	11	13,593	9	36,816	170%	increase
Golden Retrievers	26	3,993	10	27,612	592%	increase
Collies	7	18,424	11	25,161	37%	increase
Shetland Sheepdogs	16	7,533	12	23,950	218%	increase
Lhasa Apsos	54	598	13	21,145	3436%	increase
Siberian Huskies	40	1,406	14	20,598	1365%	increase
Pekingese	6	23,989	15	20,400	15%	decrease
Yorkshire Terriers	29	3,412	16	20,392	498%	increase
Brittany Spaniels	18	7,247	17	20,222	179%	increase

*In the early 1970s sharp increases, from 60 to 100 per cent were seen in German Shepherds. This low 1976 increase may be seen as lack of confidence in the breed, even though it remains highly ranked. It must be remembered that numbers do not necessarily reflect the true situation; huge numbers of mixed German Shepherds exist in most canine populations.

Great Danes	28	3,467	18	19,869	473% increase
St. Bernards	24	4,098	19	17,537	328% increase
English Springer Spaniels	21	5,181	20	16,842	225% increase
Chihuahuas	5	40,966	21	16,478	60% decrease
Old English Sheepdogs	57	473	22	15,364	3148% increase
Pomeranians	9	13,960	23	15,241	9% increase
Basset Hounds	10	13,716	24	14,997	9% increase
German Shorthaired Pointers	19	5,908	25	14,269	142% increase
Boxers	15	8,892	26	13,057	47% increase
Shih Tzu	43	2,811	27	12,562	347% increase
Boston Terriers	12	12,231	28	10,806	12% decrease
Samoyeds	32	2,106	29	10,147	382% increase
Afghan Hounds	43	1,242	30	10,045	709% increase
Alaskan Malamutes	50	772	31	8,324	978% increase
Norwegian Elkhounds	33	2,039	32	8,037	294% increase
Dalmatians	31	3,108	33	7,241	133% increase
Scottish Terriers	23	4,677	34	7,202	54% increase
Airedale Terriers	30	3,138	35	6,835	118% increase
Pugs	17	7,284	36	6,660	9% decrease
Bulldogs	27	3,597	37	6,554	82% increase
Cairn Terriers	34	1,899	38	6,432	239% increase
Weimaraners	20	5,398	39	6,243	42% increase
Chow Chows	47	924	40	6,211	572% increase
Maltese	37	1,531	41	6,183	304% increase

Breed	AKC 1964 Ranking	Number Registered	AKC 1976 Ranking	Number Registered	Difference	
West Highland White Terriers	39	1,409	42	6,072	331%	increase
Keeshonden	41	1,366	43	5,871	330%	increase
Fox Terriers	14	9,713	44	4,673	52%	decrease
Silky Terriers	53	667	45	2,829	324%	increase
Chesapeake Bay Retrievers	52	721	46	2,650	268%	increase
Newfoundlands	56	490	47	2,113	331%	increase
Welsh Corgis (Pembroke)	*		48	2,061		
Vizslas	49	799	49	1,807	134%	increase
English Setters	48	839	50	1,756	109%	increase
Basenjis	35	1,681	51	1,674	.4%	decrease
Borzois	63	330	52	1,658	402%	increase
Great Pyrenees	68	263	53	1,529	481%	increase
Bichons Frises	*		54	1,512		
Bloodhounds	62	391	55	1,445	270%	increase
Irish Wolfhounds	86	138	56	1,409	921%	increase
Rottweilers	80	178	57	1,405	690%	increase
Gordon Setters	65	317	58	1,383	336%	increase
Schipperkes	46	1,028	59	1,260	23%	increase
Akitas	*		60	1,213		

*Not ranked in 1964

Breed	1964	Rank	1964 Reg.	1994 Reg.	% Change	
Miniature Pinschers	36	61	1,571	1,126	28%	decrease
Bouviers Des Flandres	87	62	118	1,053	792%	increase
Whippets	61	63	429	1,050	148%	increase
German Wirehaired Pointers	79	64	180	1,021	467%	increase
Bearded Collies	*	65		998		
English Cocker Spaniels	60	66	442	942	113%	increase
Australian Terriers	66	67	312	939	201%	increase
Bull Terriers	72	68	219	929	324%	increase
Welsh Terriers	44	69	1,214	888	27%	decrease
Rhodesian Ridgebacks	71	70	252	846	238%	increase
Mastiffs	42	71	1,279	810	37%	decrease
Standard Schnauzers	58	72	465	785	69%	increase
Salukis	94	73	66	737	1017%	increase
American Staffordshire Terriers	85	74	143	732	412%	increase
Bullmastiffs	70	75	258	676	162%	increase
Kerry Blue Terriers	45	76	1,366	661	52%	decrease
Pulik	67	77	294	609	199%	increase
Giant Schnauzers	92	78	70	565	707%	increase
Belgian sheepdogs	73	79	211	552	162%	increase
Soft-Coated Wheaten Terriers	*	80		539		
Manchester Terriers	37	81	1,531	536	65%	decrease
Italian Greyhounds	55	82	536	506	6%	decrease

*Not ranked in 1964

Breed	AKC 1964 Ranking	Number Registered	AKC 1976 Ranking	Number Registered	Difference	
Papillons	96	48	83	490	921%	increase
Pointers	64	323	84	439	36%	increase
Belgian Tervuren	93	69	85	430	523%	increase
Bedlington Terriers	51	732	86	370	49%	decrease
Black and Tan Coonhounds	83	155	87	357	130%	increase
Japanese Spaniels	68	263	88	356	35%	increase
Welsh Corgis (Cardigan)	*		89	356		
American Water Spaniels	75	198	90	302	53%	increase
Bernese Mountain Dogs	109	11	91	292	2555%	increase
Staffordshire Bull Terriers	58	465	92	291	37%	decrease
Norwich Terriers	33	2,039	93	278	86%	decrease
Irish Terriers	25	4,015	94	273	93%	decrease
Tibetan Terriers	*		95	242		
Dandie Dinmont Terriers	82	167	96	235	41%	increase
Skye Terriers	78	185	97	226	22%	increase
Brussels Griffons	27	3,597	98	219	94%	decrease
Briards	98	45	99	216	380%	increase
French Bulldogs	72	91	100	208	129%	increase

*Not ranked in 1964

Appendix B

THINGS TO REMEMBER WHEN TRYING TO GET ZONING FOR A PET CEMETERY*

1. Mums the word. Don't say anything to any one until your zoning is cleared. All you need is one neighbor to object and it could cost you hundreds of dollars and a years time.

2. When facing the zoning board, use humility. It pays and doesn't hurt a bit. It also helps if you know someone on the board. "Brown nosing" could pay off richly.

3. Send a rough sketch of your planned cemetery and a brief story outline on it. Your Association in return will send a letter to "Whom It May Concern" saying your pet cemetery plans have been accepted and you are a recognized member of the National Association of Pet Cemeteries. That a progressive, expanding community should be commended for having the foresight to include the service of a pet cemetery to their public. They are among the 450 elite communities offering this public and unique service.

4. When looking for land for your pet cemetery if it is not properly zoned, buy it only "subject to correct zoning".

5. Make sure the land has good drainage. Try to see it in the rainy season.

6. Take a shovel along to make sure it is fairly easy to dig a grave.

7. Population

*Complete as supplied by the National Association of Pet Cemeteries, West Chicago, Illinois.

Appendix C

LAST WILL & TESTIMONY

I, _____ , being happy in my home with my family hereby request:

My family remember my mischievious moments such as the time I jumped into your bed with muddy, wet, cold feet and crawled under the covers. Master, that was the time you managed to laugh and show your teeth!

That you remember my bark, my way of welcoming you home, my way of always wanting to be with you even in the car. I enjoyed looking out the window and sniffing the air – you made me feel like I was really a member of the family.

I, _____ , also hereby request that when I die:

I will be buried in Paw Print Gardens Pet Cemetery and that a small, modest marker be placed at the head of my grave; when you put my name on it, also put my family name on it. I would love it that way.

I, also hereby request that Paw Print Gardens Pet Cemetery, in West Chicago, Illinois will handle all the arrangements as I know they will care for me as a loved member of your family.

I know I will get good care at Paw Print Gardens, but no sleep will be too deep to keep me from wagging my tail when you come walking down the path to pay me a visit.

No greater tribute could you pay me, than to miss me so much, that you replace me with a pet similar to me. Replace me in our home, but not in your heart, for memories cannot be replaced or erased.

This Last Will & Testimony was made after I heard Judy's family, next door, talk about the way Paw Print Gardens cared for _____ – and she was just a _____ !

Signed this day by your pet,

_____

Appendix D

A suggested ordinance for the humane control and regulation of animals and for other purposes.

Prepared and recommended by:

THE HUMANE SOCIETY OF THE UNITED STATES
2100 L Street, N.W.
Washington, D.C. 20037*

BE IT ORDAINED BY THE COUNCIL OF THE CITY OF
———————— :

SECTION 1. Definitions

As used in this ordinance the following terms mean:
Animal: Any live, vertebrate creature, domestic or wild;
Animal Shelter: Any facility operated by a humane society, or municipal agency, or its authorized agents for the purpose of impounding or caring for animals held under the authority of this ordinance or state law;
Auctions: Any place or facility where animals are regularly bought, sold, or traded, except for those facilities otherwise defined in this ordinance. This section does not apply to individual sales of animals by owners;
Circus: A commercial variety show featuring animal acts for public entertainment;
Commercial Animal Establishment: Any pet shop, grooming shop, auction, riding school or stable, zoological parks, circus, performing animal exhibition, or kennel;

---

*For copies of this proposed bylaw write to the Humane Society of the United States at the above address and enclose $1.50. In Canada, animal control bylaw inquiries may be directed to: Canadian Federation of Humane Societies, 101 Champagne Avenue, Ottawa, Ont., K1S 4P3.

Grooming Shop: A commercial establishment where animals are bathed, clipped, plucked, or otherwise groomed;

Humane Officer: Any person designated by the State of___, a municipal government, or a humane society as a law enforcement officer who is qualified to perform such duties under the laws of this State;

Kennel: Any premises wherein any person engages in the business of boarding, breeding, buying, letting for hire, training for a fee, or selling dogs or cats;

Owner: Any person, partnership, or corporation owning, keeping, or harboring one or more animals. An animal shall be deemed to be harbored if it is fed or sheltered for three consecutive days or more;

Performing Animal Exhibition: Any spectacle, display, act, or event other than circuses, in which performing animals are used;

Pet: Any animal kept for pleasure rather than utility;

Pet Shop: Any person, partnership, or corporation, whether operated separately or in connection with another business enterprise except for a licensed kennel, that buys, sells, or boards any species of animal;

Public Nuisance: Any animal or animals which:

1. molests passersby or passing vehicles
2. attacks other animals
3. trespasses on school grounds
4. is repeatedly at large
5. damages private or public property
6. barks, whines, or howls in an excessive, continuous, or untimely fashion;

Restraint: Any animal secured by a leash or lead, or under the control of a responsible person and obedient to that person's commands, or within the real property limits of its owner;

Riding School or Stable: Any place which has available for hire, boarding and/or riding instruction, any horse, pony, donkey, mule, or burro;

Veterinary Hospital: Any establishment maintained and operated by a licensed veterinarian for surgery, diagnosis and treatment of diseases and injuries of animals;

Vicious Animal: Any animal or animals that constitute a physical threat to human beings or other animals;

Wild Animal: Any live monkey (non-human primate), raccoon, skunk, fox, poisonous snake, leopard, panther, tiger, lion, lynx, or any other warmblooded animal which can normally be found in the wild state;

Zoological Park: Any facility, other than a pet shop or kennel, displaying or exhibiting one or more species of non-domesticated animals operated by a person, partnership, corporation, or government agency.

SECTION 2. Licensing

(a) Any person owning, keeping, harboring, or having custody of any animal over three months of age within this municipality must obtain a license as herein provided. This provision may not apply to the keeping of small cage birds, or aquatic and amphibian animals solely as pets.

(b) Written application for licenses shall be made to the Licensing Authority which shall include name and address of applicant, description of the animal, the appropriate fee, and rabies certificate issued by a licensed veterinarian or anti-rabies clinic.

(c) If not revoked, licenses for the keeping of dogs and cats shall be for a period of up to one year.

(d) Application for a license must be made within thirty days after obtaining a dog or cat over three months, except that this requirement will not apply to a non-resident keeping a dog or cat within the municipality for no longer than sixty days.

(e) License fees shall not be required for seeing eye dogs or governmental police dogs.

(f) Upon acceptance of the license application and fee, the Licensing Authority shall issue a durable tag or identification collar, stamped with an identifying number and the year of issuance. Tags should be designed so that they may be conveniently fastened or riveted to the animal's collar or harness.

(g) Dogs and cats must wear identification tags or collars at all times when off the premises of the owners.

(h) The Licensing Authority shall maintain a record of the identifying numbers of all tags issued and shall make this record available to the public.

(i)   The licensing period shall begin with the fiscal year and shall run for one year. Application for license may be made thirty days prior to, and up to sixty days after the start of the fiscal year. Persons applying for a license during the licensing year shall be required to pay 50% of the fee stipulated in this section.

(j)   Persons who fail to obtain a license as required within the time period specified in this section will be subjected to a fine of $10.

(k)   A license shall be issued after payment of the applicable fee:

		1 year
1.	for each unneutered male dog	$10
2.	for each unneutered male cat	5
3.	for each unspayed female dog	10
4.	for each unspayed female cat	5
5.	for each neutered male dog	2
6.	for each neutered male cat	2
7.	for each spayed female dog	2
8.	for each spayed female cat	2

(l)   A duplicate license may be obtained upon payment of a $2 replacement fee.

(m)   No person may use any license for any animal other than the animal for which it was issued.

SECTION 3.   Permits

(a)   No person, partnership or corporation shall operate a commercial animal establishment or animal shelter without *first* obtaining a permit in compliance with this section.

(b)   The Licensing Authority shall promulgate regulations for the issuance of permits and shall include requirements for humane care of all animals and for compliance with the provisions of this ordinance and other applicable laws. The Licensing Authority may amend such regulations from time to time as deemed desirable for public health and welfare and for the protection of animals.

(c)   Upon a showing by an applicant for a permit that he is

236

willing and able to comply with the regulations promulgated by the Licensing Authority, a permit shall be issued upon payment of the applicable fee.

(d) The permit period shall begin with the fiscal year and shall run for one year. Renewal applications for permits shall be made thirty days prior to, and up to sixty days after, the start of the fiscal year. Application for permit to establish a new commercial animal establishment under the provisions of this ordinance may be made at any time.

(e) If there is a change in ownership of a commercial animal establishment, the new owner may have the current permit transferred to his name upon payment of a $10 transfer fee.

(f) Annual permits shall be issued upon payment of the applicable fee:

1. for each kennel authorized to house less than 10 dogs or cats $25
2. for each kennel authorized to house 10 or more but less than 50 50
3. for each kennel authorized to house 50 or more dogs or cats 100
4. for each pet shop 75
5. for each riding stable 75
6. for each auction 50
7. for each zoological park 100
8. for each circus 25
9. for each performing animal exhibition 50
10. for each grooming shop 50

(g) Every facility regulated by this ordinance shall be considered a separate enterprise and requires an individual permit.

(h) Persons operating kennels for the breeding of dogs or cats may elect to license such animals individually.

(i) No fee may be required of any veterinary hospital, animal shelter, or government-operated zoological park.

(j) Failure to obtain a permit before opening any facility covered in this section shall result in a fine of $200.

(k) Any person who has a change in the category under which a permit was issued shall be subject to reclassification and appropriate adjustment of the permit fee shall be made.

SECTION 4. License and Permit Issuance and Revocation

(a) The Licensing Authority may revoke any permit or license if the person holding the permit or license refuses or fails to comply with this ordinance, the regulations promulgated by the Licensing Authority, or any law governing the protection and keeping of animals.

(b) Any person whose permit or license is revoked shall, within ten days thereafter, humanely dispose of all animals owned, kept, or harbored by such person and no part of the permit or license fee shall be refunded.

(c) It shall be a condition of the issuance of any permit or license that the Licensing Authority shall be permitted to inspect all animals and the premises where animals are kept at any time and shall, if permission for such inspections is refused, revoke the permit or license of the refusing owner.

(d) If the applicant has withheld or falsified any information on the application, the Licensing Authority shall refuse to issue a permit or license.

(e) No person who has been convicted of cruelty to animals shall be issued a permit or license to operate a commercial animal establishment.

(f) Any person having been denied a license or permit may not reapply for a period of thirty days. Each reapplication shall be accompanied by a $10 fee.

SECTION 5. Restraint

(a) All dogs shall be kept under restraint.

(b) No owner shall fail to exercise proper care and control of his animals to prevent them from becoming a public nuisance.

(c) Every female dog or cat in heat shall be confined in a building or secure enclosure in such a manner that such female dog or cat cannot come into contact with another animal except for planned breeding.

(d) Every vicious animal, as determined by the Licensing Authority, shall be confined by the owner within a building or secure enclosure and shall be securely muzzled or caged whenever off the premises of its owner.

238

SECTION 6. Impoundment and Violation Notice

(a) Unrestrained dogs and nuisance animals shall be taken by the police, animal control officers, or humane officers and impounded in an animal shelter and there confined in a humane manner.

(b) Impounded dogs and cats shall be kept for not less than five working days.

(c) If by a license tag or other means, the owner of an impounded animal can be identified, the animal control officer shall immediately upon impoundment notify the owner by telephone or mail.

(d) An owner reclaiming an impounded cat shall pay a fee of $5, plus $1 for each day the animal has been impounded.

(e) An owner reclaiming an impounded dog shall pay a fee of $10, plus $2 for each day the animal has been impounded.

(f) Any animal not reclaimed by its owner within five working days shall become the property of the local government authority, or humane society, and shall be placed for adoption in a suitable home or humanely euthanized.

(g) In addition to, or in lieu of, impounding an animal found at large, the animal control officer, humane officer, or police officer may issue to the known owner of such animal a notice of ordinance violation. Such notice shall impose upon the owner a penalty of $10 which may, at the discretion of the animal owner, be paid to any agency designated by the Licensing Authority within seventy-two hours in full satisfaction of the assessed penalty. In the event that such penalty is not paid within the time period prescribed, a criminal warrant shall be initiated before a magistrate and upon conviction of a violation of this ordinance, the owner shall be punished as provided in Section 13 of this ordinance.

(h) The owner of an impounded animal may also be proceeded against for violation of this ordinance.

(i) The Licensing Authority shall review automatically all licenses issued to animal owners against whom three or more ordinance violations have been assessed in a twelve month period.

SECTION 7. Animal Care

(a) No owner shall fail to provide his animals with sufficient good and wholesome food and water, proper shelter and protection from the weather, veterinary care when needed to prevent suffering, and with humane care and treatment.

(b) No person shall beat, cruelly ill treat, torment, overload, overwork, or otherwise abuse an animal, or cause, instigate, or permit any dogfight, cockfight, bullfight, or other combat between animals or between animals and humans.

(c) No owner of an animal shall abandon such animal.

(d) No person shall crop a dog's ears, except when a licensed veterinarian issues a signed certificate that the operation is necessary for the dog's health and comfort, and in no event shall any person except a licensed veterinarian perform such an operation.

(e) Chickens or ducklings younger than eight weeks of age may not be sold in quantities of less than twenty-five to a single purchaser.

(f) No person shall give away any live animal, fish, reptile, or bird as a prize for, or as an inducement to enter, any contest, game, or other competition, or as an inducement to enter a place of amusement; or offer such vertebrate as an incentive to enter into any business agreement whereby the offer was for the purpose of attracting trade.

(g) Any person who, as the operator of a motor vehicle, strikes a domestic animal shall stop at once and render such assistance as may be possible and shall immediately report such injury or death to the animal's owner; in the event the owner cannot be ascertained and located such operator shall at once report the accident to the appropriate law enforcement agency or to the local humane society.

(h) No person shall expose any known poisonous substance, whether mixed with food or not, so that the same shall be liable to be eaten by any animal, provided that it shall not be unlawful for a person to expose on his own property common rat poison mixed only with vegetable substances.

SECTION 8. Keeping of Wild Animals

(a) No person shall keep or permit to be kept on his premises any wild or vicious animal for display or for exhibition purposes, whether gratuitously or for a fee. This section shall not be construed to apply to zoological parks, performing animal exhibitions, or circuses.

(b) No person shall keep or permit to be kept any wild animal as a pet.

(c) The Licensing Authority may issue a temporary permit for the keeping, care, and protection of an infant animal native to this area which has been deemed to be homeless.

(d) The Licensing Authority shall have the power to release or order the release of any infant wild animal kept under temporary permit which is deemed capable of survival.

SECTION 9. Performing Animal Exhibitions

(a) No performing animal exhibition or circus shall be permitted in which animals are induced or encouraged to perform through the use of chemical, mechanical, electrical, or manual devices in a manner which will cause, or is likely to cause, physical injury or suffering.

(b) All equipment used on a performing animal shall fit properly and be in good working condition.

SECTION 10. Animal Waste

The owner of every animal shall be responsible for the removal of any excreta deposited by his animal(s) on public walks, recreation areas, or private property.

SECTION 11. Sterilization

No unclaimed dog or cat shall be released for adoption without being sterilized, or without a written agreement from the adopter guaranteeing that such animal will be sterilized.

SECTION 12. Enforcement

The civil and criminal provisions of this ordinance shall be enforced by those persons or agencies designated by municipal authority. It shall be a violation of this ordinance to interfere with a humane officer in the performance of his duties.

SECTION 13. Penalties

Any person violating any provision of this ordinance shall be deemed guilty of a misdemeanor and shall be punished by a fine of not less than $25 nor more than $500. If any violation be continuing, each day's violation shall be deemed a separate violation. If any person be found guilty by a court of violating Section 8, his permit to own, keep, harbor, or have custody of animals shall be deemed automatically revoked and no new permit may be issued.

SECTION 14. Conflicting Ordinances

All other ordinances of the City of_____that are in conflict with this ordinance are hereby repealed to the extent of such conflict.

SECTION 15. Severability Clause

If any part of this ordinance shall be held invalid, such part shall be deemed severable and the invalidity thereof shall not affect the remaining parts of this ordinance.

References

Chapter 1

1 Dembeck, H., *Animals and Men*, New York: Natural History Press, 1965.

2 Lewinsohn, R., *Animals, Men and Myths*, New York: Harper and Brothers, 1954.

3 Zeuner, F.E., *A History of Domestic Animals*, London: Hutchinson, 1963.

4 Dembeck, *op. cit.*

5 Dempewolff, R.F., *Animal Reveille*, Garden City, N.Y.: Doubleday Doron, 1943.

6 *ibid.*

7 Gaddis, V. and M., *The Strange World of Animals and Pets*, New York: Cowles, 1970.

8 Gannon, R., "Canine Cops . . . Can They Put Teeth in the Law?" *Popular Science*, January 1963.

9 Personal communication with Brian Lee, Public Information Division, U.S. Department of Customs. Also *Customs Today*, Fall 1976, and *Challenge and Change, 1789 – 1974*, published by the U.S. Department of Customs.

10 Stowe, L., "How K-9s Catch Crooks," *Nation's Cities*, October 1974.

11 Levinson, B., *Pet-Oriented Child Psychotherapy*, Springfield, Illinois: Charles C. Thomas, 1969.

12 Corson, S.A., E. O'L. Corson and P.H. Gwynne, "Pet-facilitated Psychotherapy," in *Pet Animals & Society*, ed. R.S. Anderson. Published for the British Small Animal Veterinary Association by Bailliere Tindall, London, 1975.

13 Sauer, C.O., *Agriculture Origins and Dispersals*, 2nd ed., Cambridge, Mass.: The M.I.T. Press.

14 Lum, P., *Fabulous Beasts*, New York: Pantheon, 1951.

15 Fernand, M., *The Life, History and Magic of the Cat*, (translated by Emma Street), New York: Grosset & Dunlap, 1968.

16 Friendly, A., "Ancient Animal Worship on the Nile," *Smithsonian Institution Magazine*, August 1973.

17 Dembeck, *op. cit.*

18 Sloan, A. and A. Farquhar, *Dog and Man – The Story of a Friendship,* New York: George H. Doran Company, 1925.

19 Darmesteter, J., ed., *Sacred Books of the East*, Vol. IV, The Zend Avesta, Part 1, Fargard XIII.

20 Hyde, W.W., "The Prosecution and Punishment of Animals and Lifeless Things in the Middle Ages and Modern Times," *University of Pennsylvania Law Review*, 64:696-730.

21 Szasz, K., *Petishism*, New York: Holt, Rinehart & Winston, 1969.

22 Hyde, *op. cit.*

23 O'Connell, J., "Holy Cats and Sacred Cows," *Science Digest*, May 1970.

24 Dembeck, *op. cit.*

25 Sloan and Farquhar, *op. cit.*

26 Fernand, *op. cit.*

27 *Chambers Encyclopedia*, George Newnes, 1950, p. 264.

28 Lechy, W.E.H., *History of European Morals from Augustus to Charlemagne*, Longmans Green, 1911.

29 Léhane, B., *The Compleat Flea*, London: John Murray Ltd., 1969.

30 Whelton, C., "Scooping the Poop," *Village Voice*, August 19, 1971.

31 Sauer, *op. cit.*

32 Veblen, T., *The Theory of the Leisure Class*, London: George Allen & Unwin, 1949.

33 Bell, Q., *Of Human Finery*, 2nd ed., London: Hogarth Press, 1976.

34 Phineas, C., "Household Pets and Urban Alienation," *Journal of Society History*, Vol. 7, 1973-74.

Chapter 2

1 Ryder, R., *Pets Are Good For People*, a booklet published by the Pet Food Manufacturers' Association, London. This is a shortened version of an address, "Pets in Man's Search for Sanity," given to the annual congress of the British Small Animals Veterinary Association, April 1973.

2 Brossard, J.H.S., "The Mental Hygiene of Owning a Dog," *Mental Hygiene*, 1944, 28:403-413.

3 Szasz, K., *Petishism*, New York: Holt, Rinehart and Winston, 1969.

4 Levinson, B., *Pet-Oriented Child Psychotherapy*, Springfield, Illinois: Charles C. Thomas, 1969.

5 Personal communication (by research assistant Patricia

Pattinson) with Dr. Quentin Rae-Grant, Psychiatrist-in-
Chief, Hospital for Sick Children, Toronto, Ontario.

6 Newsletter of the Ontario Humane Society, *Animal Voice*,
Winter 1975. Also, Ontario Humane Society brief for
increased funding submitted to the Government of Ontario,
November 1976.

7 Information folder of the Ontario Humane Society, *News*,
June 1975.

8 "More Dogs Being Left at Pounds in Recession," *New York
Times* (UPI), August 10, 1975.

9 "A Psychiatrist Talks About Children and Cruelty to
Animals," *Family Circle*, May 1976.

10 From "What Can You Do About 50,000,000 Stray Cats and
Dogs?" by Clark Whelton, which first appeared in *Esquire*
(March 1973). Excerpted by permission of *Esquire*
Magazine; copyright © 1973 by Esquire, Inc.

11 Hellman, D.S. and N. Blackman, "Enuresis, Firesetting and
Cruelty to Animals: a Triad Predictive of Adult Crime,"
American Journal of Psychiatry, June 1966.

12 Turner, E.S., *All Heaven in a Rage*, London: Michael Joseph,
1964.

13 Personal communication with Dr. Jim Evans, veterinary
surgeon and developer of Ovaban, London.

14 Mugford, R.A. and J.G. M'Comisky, "Some Recent Work on
the Psychotherapeutic Value of Cage Birds with Old
People," in *Pet Animals & Society*, ed. R.S. Anderson,
published for the British Small Animal Veterinary
Association by Bailliere Tindall, London, 1975.

15 Personal communication with Dr. Roger Mugford, London.

16 King, W., "Texas a Major U.S. Centre for Illegal Dogfighting
and Gambling," *New York Times*, September 16, 1974.
Information for this segment was supplied by numerous
articles in the *New York Times, Harper's, Nation*, various
humane society publications and by Duncan Wright, former
Executive Director of the ASPCA, interviewed in New York
by research assistant Stacey Mizl.

17 Meadows, E., "An American Pastime," *Harper's*, March 1976.

18 King, *op. cit.*

19 Sloan, A. and A. Farquhar, *Dog and Man – The Story of a
Friendship*, New York: George H. Doran Company, 1925.

20 Lynch, D.T., *The Wild Seventies*, New York: 1941.

21 Turner, *op. cit.*

22 Morse, M., *Ordeal of the Animals*, Englewood Cliffs, N.J.:
Prentice-Hall, 1968.

23 King, *op. cit.*
24 Menninger, K.A., "Totemic Aspects of Contemporary Attitudes Toward Animals," in *Psychoanalysis and Culture*, eds., G.B. Wilbur and W. Muensterberger, New York: 1951.
25 *ibid.*
26 Michaels, M., *A Dog in My Bed*, San Diego, California: Late-hour Library, Phoenix Publishers, 1969.
27 Hollander, X., *The Happy Hooker*, New York: Ballantine Books, 1971.
28 Savage, J., ed., *The History of New England from 1630-1649*, from the journals of John Winthrop, Boston: Little, Brown, 1853.
29 "Bestiality Found of Little Appeal, Jury Acquits Wholesaler," *New York Times*, December 18, 1977.

Chapter 3

1 Regan, T. and P. Singer, eds., *Animal Rights and Human Obligations*, Englewood Cliffs, N.J.: Prentice-Hall, 1976.
2 *Society for Animal Rights Newsletter*, June 1976.
3 This figure, commonly cited, originated with the Humane Society of the United States, which estimates that 12 per cent of the pet population is killed each year, and that 75 per cent of all animals handled in animal shelters are destroyed annually.
4 Personal communication with the Georgia Fulton County SPCA.
5 Schneider, R., "Observations on Overpopulation of Dogs and Cats," *Journal of the American Veterinary Medical Association*, Vol. 167, No. 4.
6 These figures are from three sources: for Canada – *The Chatelaine Pet Food Study*, conducted by the Chatelaine Consumer Council, prepared by the Maclean Hunter Research Bureau in September 1975, Toronto. For the U.S. – a survey, *Pets, Pet Ownership, and Animal Control: Social and Psychological Attitudes*, 1975, conducted by the Pet Food Institute. For the U.K. – a survey by a pet food manufacturer who wishes to remain anonymous. This 50 per cent figure is cited by many others.
7 Carding, A.H., "The Growth of Pet Population in Western Europe and the Implications for Dog Control in Great Britain," in *Pet Animals & Society*, ed. R.S. Anderson.

Published for the British Small Animal Veterinary
Association by Bailliere Tindall, London, 1975.

8 Djerassi, C., A. Isreal, and W. Jochle, "Planned Parenthood
for Pets?" *Bulletin of the Atomic Scientists*, January 1973.

9 *ibid.*

10 Carding, *op. cit.*

11 Information from this survey was supplied by an executive of
the British pet food company that undertook the study, who
wishes his company to remain anonymous.

12 Personal communication with Marshall Turner, Assistant Chief
of Demographic Staff, United States Census Bureau.

13 Report of the Joint Advisory Committee on Pets in Society
(JACOPIS), *Dogs in the United Kingdom*, July 1975.

14 Personal communication with Guy R. Hodge, Director,
Research and Data Services, The Humane Society of the
United States.

15 "Stray Dogs and Cats Top Urban Complaint," *New York
Times*, (AP), August 28, 1977.

16 Hummer, R.L., "Pets in Today's Society," *American Journal of
Public Health*, October 1975.

17 Berman, C., "A Member of the Family," *New York Times
Magazine*, October 7, 1973.

18 Department of the Environment (DOE), *Report of the Working
Party on Dogs*, Her Majesty's Stationery Office, 1976. This
figure was estimated in 1974.

19 *Christian Science Monitor*, December 10, 1973.

20 *Philadelphia Enquirer*, July 14, 1976.

21 Tuohy, W., "Vacationers in Italy Abandon 1 Million Pets,"
Los Angeles Times, August 3, 1972.

22 "Stray Dogs and Cats Top Urban Complaint," *op. cit.*

23 "Stray Dogs Peril Jersey City Area," *New York Times*, July 27,
1975.

24 Beck, A.M., *The Ecology of Stray Dogs*, Baltimore: York Press,
1973.

25 Department of the Environment Report, *op. cit.*

26 Annual Report 1976 of the New York ASPCA.

27 Annual statistical reports for 1974, 1975, and 1976, furnished
by the Toronto Humane Society.

28 "Health Hazard Seen When Pets Run Loose," *Toronto Star*,
May 31, 1976.

29 *New York Times*, March 1, 1974.

30 Personal communication (by researcher Patricia Pattinson)
with Col. Réal Comptois, Executive Director, and Barry

Tyler, Vice-President of Finance, Canadian SPCA.
31 Newsletter of the Toronto Humane Society, *Humane Viewpoint*, Vol. 3, No. 1, Winter 1977.

Chapter 4

1 Personal communication with *Pets/Supplies/Marketing*, Susan Kolberg, secretary to the editor.
2 Benning, L.E., *The Pet Profiteers*, New York: Quadrangle, The New York Times Book Company, 1976.
3 Djerassi, C., A. Isreal, W. Jochle, "Planned Parenthood for Pets." *Bulletin of the Atomic Scientists*, January 1973.
4 Benning, *op. cit.*
5 *Humane Information Services Newsletter*, June 1976.
6 *Dogs*, a booklet printed by the American Kennel Club.
7 Personal communication with Daniel Z. Henkin, Vice President, Public Relations, Air Transport Association of America, New York.
8 "Some Dog's Life," *Globe and Mail*, October 8, 1976.
9 Humane Information Services, *Report to Humanitarians*, No. 26, December 1973.
10 Benning, *op. cit.*

Chapter 5

1 Unless otherwise noted, advertising, market share and sales figures are furnished by courtesy of Leading National Advertisers Inc., New York, a company which estimates advertising expenditures in six media – billboards, newspaper supplements, magazines, network radio, spot and network television. (For further information on company and brand advertising expenditures, contact Leading National Advertisers, 345 Madison Ave. New York, N.Y. 10017.) And by *Advertising Age*, an advertising trade publication, which regularly publishes estimated statistics supplied by a number of industry sources. Reprinted with permission from Leading National Advertisers, Inc., and from the April and August 1977 issues of *Advertising Age*. Copyright 1977 by Crain Communications Inc.
2 This quote is from a Ralston Purina publication, *Special*

Report 1974. Background information and other company data, unless otherwise noted, were obtained from a number of Ralston Purina sources, namely company magazines, brochures and booklets made available to the author at the company's head office in St. Louis, Missouri.

3 *World Bank Annual Report 1976.*
4 This figure was arrived at based on figures supplied by an executive of a Canadian railway.
5 *Advertising Age, op. cit.*
6 Rhodes, H.E., "Overview of United States Pet Food Industry," *Cereal Foods World*, Volume 20, No. 1 Courtesy American Association of Cereal Chemists.
7 "Trading Down Can't Stop a Winner," *Progressive Grocer*, February 1976.
8 Fears, R., "Pet Food and Human Nutrition," *New Scientist*, March 18, 1976.
9 Szasz, K., *Petishism*, New York: Holt, Rinehart & Winston, 1969.
10 Carson, G., *Men, Beasts and Gods: A History of Cruelty and Kindness to Animals*, New York: Scribner's, 1972.
11 Rhodes, *op. cit.*
12 Tracy, E.J., "Lush Times for the Pet Food Producers," *Fortune*, December 1971.
13 Rhodes, *op. cit.*
14 Whiteside, T., "Din-din," *New Yorker*, November 1, 1976. Reprinted by permission.
15 *ibid.*
16 Town, H., *Albert Franck: Keeper of the Lanes*, Toronto: McClelland and Stewart, 1974.
17 *The Chatelaine Pet Food Study*, conducted by the Chatelaine Consumer Council, prepared by the Maclean Hunter Research Bureau in September 1975, Toronto.
18 Personal communication with Dr. S.N. Ward, Co-ordinator, Animal Care Program, Sheridan College of Applied Arts and Technology, Toronto.
19 Rhodes, *op. cit.*
20 Personal communication with Bob Mohrman, Senior Manager, Pet Nutrition and Care Research, Ralston Purina, St. Louis, Missouri, and material from a Ralston Purina booklet: "The Purina Pet Care Center – Its Role in Purina Research."
21 "The Tender Vittles Tale," *RP Magazine*, March/April 1972.
22 Rhodes, *op. cit.*
23 Personal communication with Bob Mohrman, *op. cit.*

24 "Dog Food Ads 'Misleading,'" *Toronto Star* (UPI), December 16, 1975.

25 Personal communication with Joel N. Brewer, Staff Attorney, Division of Food and Drug Advertising, Federal Trade Commission. Mr. Brewer forwarded a copy of the complaint: General Foods Corporation, 84 F.T.C. 1572 (Consent Order, 1974) dated December 3, 1974, and advised that a "consent order does not constitute an admission of wrongdoing on the part of the respondent."

26 "Some Questions and Answers About the Pet Food Industry," a brochure published by the Pet Food Institute, Washington, D.C.

27 Fears, *op. cit.*

28 Personal communication with the Director, The Garbage Project, Department of Anthropology, University of Arizona, Tucson, who supplied the following material: W.L. Rathje, W.W. Hughes, G.G. Harrison, and S.L. Jernigan, "Food Loss at the Household Level: a Perspective from Household Residuals Analysis," a paper prepared for the National Science Foundation, July 30, 1976; M. Mitchell, "Tucson's Telltale Garbage," in *Tucson Magazine*, n.d.; G.G. Harrison, W.L. Rathje, W.H. Wilson, "Food Waste Behavior in an Urban Population," in *Journal of Nutrition Education*, Jan-Mar. 1975.

29 Sloan, A., and A. Farquhar, *Dog and Man: The Story of a Friendship*, New York: George H. Doran Co., 1925.

30 Personal communication with Bob Mohrman, *op. cit.*

31 Hunt, J., *A World Full of Animals*, New York: David McKay Co., 1969.

32 Fears, *op. cit.*

33 Rhodes, *op. cit.*

34 "Pet Food Purchases Help Sustain Healthy Markets for Agricultural Products, By-products," press release issued by the Pet Food Institute, July 1, 1975.

35 Personal communication with the Director, Grain Marketing Office, Department of Industry, Trade and Commerce, Government of Canada.

36 "Pet Food Purchases," *op. cit.*

37 "Domestic Production of Soybeans" from *Statistical Abstracts of the United States, 1976*, U.S. Department of Commerce, Bureau of the Census, citing U.S. Department of Agriculture, Statistical Reporting services.

38 Personal communication with Dr. Roger Mugford, Animal

Studies Centre, Pedigree Petfoods Ltd., Leicestershire, England.

39 Ehrlich, P., "Paying the Piper," *New Scientist*, 1967, 36:652-657.

40 Lappé, F.M., *Diet for a Small Planet*, New York: Ballantine Books, 1971.

41 World Health Organization Technical Report, Series No. 522, *Energy and Protein Requirements*, Report of a Joint FAO/WHO Ad Hoc Expert Committee, Geneva, 1973.

42 Fears, *op. cit.*

43 Rhodes, *op. cit.*

44 British Small Animal Veterinary Association Minimum Nutritional Standards for Canned Dog and Cat Foods, *Journal of Small Animal Practises* (1970) 11, 271-275.

Chapter 6

1 *The Chatelaine Pet Food Study*, a survey conducted by the Chatelaine Consumer Council, prepared by the Maclean Hunter Research Bureau in September 1975, Toronto.

2 Personal communication (by research assistant Patricia Pattinson), with Col. Réal Comptois, Executive Director, and Barry Tyler, Vice-President Finance, Canadian SPCA.

3 "Shove Off, Kitty, Dogs Are Tops on Pet Parade," Toronto Star (UPI London), August 4, 1977.

4 "Pets Are the Most Expensive Hobby that Americans Pursue," *Philadelphia Inquirer*, June 15, 1975.

5 *Supermarketing Magazine*, September 1976.

6 "Pets Are the Most Expensive Hobby," *op. cit.* Hobby figures are according to *Mass Merchandiser Magazine*.

7 Most of these prices were obtained in a phone survey conducted by the author in Toronto in 1977, in addition to figures quoted in veterinary journals and information supplied by Toronto veterinarian, Dr. Wally Stonehouse.

8 Personal communication with Dr. Wally Stonehouse, Toronto.

9 Most of this information was supplied by Dr. Wally Stonehouse.

10 Company history on Sergeant's provided through personal communication with Richard Thrope, Brand Manager, Pet Care Products, Miller-Morton Company, Richmond, Virginia.

11 Keeger, T., "A Look Back at The Pet Food Industry in

America," *Pet/Supplies/Marketing*, July 1976.

12   Tracy, E.J., "Lush Times for the Pet Food Producers," *Fortune Magazine*, December 1971. Background information on the company was requested of Hartz in Harrison, New Jersey, and a reply was received from Claud W. Kissin, Vice President, which thanked me for my letter and continued, "We very much appreciate your interest in our company and wish you every success with the writing of your new dog and cat book. We do not have available a history of the company and we do not seek publicity but, nevertheless, we would like to thank you again for your interest."

13   Personal communication with *Pets/Supplies/Marketing*, Susan Kolberg, secretary to the editor.

14   "Trading Down Can't Stop a Winner," *Progressive Grocer*, February 1976.

15   "Highly Profitable Line Straining at the Leash to Reach Full Potential," *Progressive Grocer*, July 1975.

16   "Trading Down," *op. cit.*

17   "Lush Times," *op. cit.*

18   Personal communication with Gerry Finkelstein, manager, Gimbel's pet shop department, New York.

19   "The Great American Animal Farm" [cover story], *Time Magazine*, December 23, 1974.

20   "Wraparound," *Harper's Magazine*, March 1976.

21   Taylor, A., "Hotel Goes to Dogs (Cats, Too)," *New York Times*, November 13, 1975.

22   "This Hotel has Really Gone to the Dogs," *Toronto Star*, December 18, 1976.

23   "The Essential Holiday Guilt Chasers," *Globe and Mail*, Toronto, May 11, 1977.

24   "America's 600 Million Pets – Centre of Growing Controversy," *U.S. News and World Report*, August 26, 1974.

25   *ibid.*

26   "Decadence for Dogs" [editorial], *Globe and Mail*, Toronto, April 13, 1976.

27   Survey conducted by the Canadian magazine, *Dogs in Canada*, published in the fall of 1974.

28   Personal communication with Aldstate Animal Crematory in Brooklyn, New York.

29   Promotional brochure of the Bide-A-Wee Pet Cemetery in Long Island, New York.

30   Personal communication with Patricia Blosser, founder and

Executive Director of the National Pet Cemeteries
Association, who supplied printed material about the
association and the pet cemetery she and her husband
operate.

31 Promotional mailer of Angel Rest Caskets and Vaults, United
    General Company, Lannon, Wisconsin.
32 *Cherub by Wilbert*, promotional brochure, Wilbert Inc. Forest
    Park, Illinois.
33 Patricia Blosser, *op. cit.*
34 Engelhardt, T., "Dog Death Afternoons," *Harper's Magazine*,
    December 1976.
35 "Philanthropy: Going to the Dogs," *Newsweek*, February 4,
    1974.
36 Newsletter of the National Association of Pet Cemeteries,
    News and Views, July and September 1976 issues, which
    reprinted an article by Barbara W. Schwartz dealing with
    estate planning for pets that originally appeared in *Trusts
    and Estates Magazine*.
37 Gaddis, V. and M., *The Strange World of Animals and Pets*,
    New York: Cowles Books, 1970.
38 Newsletter of the National Association of Pet Cemeteries, *op.
    cit.*
39 "Psych 'em Fido," *Time Magazine*, July 7, 1967.
40 *ibid.*
41 Fletcher, W.R., "House Calls for Problem Dogs," *New York
    Times*, November 7, 1976.
42 Fletcher, W.R. "Guard-Dog Trainers Set High Standards,"
    New York Times, May 30, 1976.
43 Brodie, I., "In California Acupuncture is for the Dogs as Well
    as for Humans," *Globe and Mail*, Toronto (Los Angeles
    Bureau), May 16, 1977.

Chapter 7

1 Personal communication (by research assistant Patricia
   Pattinson) with Col. Réal Comptois, Executive Director and
   Barry Tyler, Vice-President Finance, Canadian SPCA.
2 Personal communication with Guy R. Hodge, Director,
   Research and Data Services, The Humane Society of the
   United States. Mr. Hodge's estimated number of animal
   facilities operated by animal welfare agencies formed a
   directory which appeared in the 1974 book, *Underdog*.

3   "America's 600 Million Pets – Centre of Growing
     Controversy," *U.S. News and World Report*, August 26,
     1974.
4   Brody, J.E., "The Problem of Dog Bites Reaching Frightening
     Proportions in U.S.," *New York Times*, July 14, 1977.
5   *Toronto Star*, September 13, 1977.
6   Homes, J., "Operation Tattoo – Low Cost Spay and Neuter
     Clinic," a paper presented to the 1976 Annual General
     Meeting of the Canadian Federation of Humane Societies.
7   "Summary of Survey re Livestock Losses Caused by Dogs,"
     conducted in 1973 by the Ontario Ministry of Agriculture
     and Food, Live Stock Branch.
8   Personal communication with sheep farmer Robert C. Walker,
     Ontario Sheep and Livestock Farmers.
9   Department of the Environment (DOE), *Report of the Working
     Party on Dogs*, Her Majesty's Stationery Office, London,
     1976.
10 Sears, P.B., "Reply to a Critical Dog," *Science*, May 23, 1975.
11 Personal communication with William P. Lunnie, Assistant
     District Agriculturalist, Department of Agriculture and
     Rural Development, New Brunswick.
12 Personal communication with Michael Dorrance, Zoology
     Section, Department of Agriculture, Alberta.
13 Shuttlesworth, D., ed., *Animals that Frighten People: Fact vs
     Myth* [juvenile], New York: E.P. Dutton, 1973.
14 Walker, R.C., "Rural and Agricultural Problems," in
     Proceedings of the First Canadian Symposium on Pets and
     Society, An Emerging Municipal Issue, June 23-25, 1976,
     Toronto.
15 Personal communication with Dr. Murray Smith, deer
     biologist, Ontario Ministry of Natural Resources.
16 *ibid.*
17 Department of the Environment. Report, *op. cit.*
18 "America's 600 Million Pets," *op. cit.*
19 Djerassi, C., A. Isreal, and W. Jochle, "Planned Parenthood
     for Pets," *Bulletin of the Atomic Scientists*, January 1973.
20 Carding, A.H., "The Growth of Pet Population in Western
     Europe and the Implications for Dog Control in Great
     Britain," in *Pet Animals & Society*, ed. R.S. Anderson.
     Published for the British Small Animal Veterinary
     Association by Bailliere Tindall, London, 1975.
21 Andresen, J., letter to the editor, *Science*, November 1974.
22 Lappé, F.M., *Diet for A Small Planet*, New York: Ballantine
     Books, 1971.

23 Committee for Humane Legislation, *Annual Report 1975.*
24 Crawford, L., "Dognapping," *New Dawn*, June 1976.
25 "Blind Woman's Dog Returns: 'I'm so happy,'" *Toronto Star*,
   March 21, 1978.
26 Crawford, L., *op. cit.*
27 Personal communication with Bob Frank, founder of the
   Society of St. Francis, Chicago.
28 Senn, C.L. and J.D. Lewin, "Barking Dogs as an
   Environmental Problem," *Journal of the American
   Veterinary Association*, June 1, 1975.
29 Lewin, J., "Barking Dog Noise in Veterinary Hospitals,"
   Journal of the American Animal Hospital Association,
   March/April 1974.

Chapter 8

1 Personal communication with Fran Lee, New York.
2 "Society Better Geared to Look After Pets," *Globe and Mail*,
   Toronto, April 7, 1977.
3 Medical sources used in this chapter are cited after reference
   25 in Selected Medical Bibliography.
4 Personal communication with Dr. B.H. Kean, author of
   toxoplasmosis papers (see Selected Medical Bibliography)
   and professor of tropical medicine and parasitology at
   Cornell University Medical Centre in New York City.
5 Personal communication with Dr. J.P. Lautenslager, Veterinary
   Services Branch, Ontario Ministry of Agriculture and Food,
   Guelph, Ontario.
6 *ibid.* Experiments conducted by him in 1966 regarding
   development and survival of *T. canis* eggs.
7 Heron, I., *When Trees Were Green*, London: Michael Joseph
   Ltd., 1978.
8 Steele, J.H., "Dog Parasite Contamination of the Environment
   in Houston," in *Proceedings of the National Conference on
   Dog and Cat Control*, held in Denver, Colorado, February
   3-5, 1976.
9 Seah, S.K.K., G. Hucal, and C. Law, "Dogs and Intestinal
   Parasites: a Public Health Problem," *Canadian Medical
   Association Journal*, May 17, 1975.
10 Personal communication with Dr. J.P. Lautenslager *op. cit.*
   From 1972-73 data accumulated by the diagnostic
   parasitology laboratories of the Ontario Veterinary College

and the Veterinary Services Branch, Ontario Ministry of Agriculture and Food.

11 Fowler, N.G., "Pets and Pollution." Presented to symposium Ecology and the Veterinary Surgeon, 16th BSAVA Congress, London, 1973. In *Journal of Small Animal Practises*, 14, (1973) 677-685.

12 "Britain mounts massive campaign against rabies," *Medical World News*, July 12, 1976.

13 Léhane, B., *The Compleat Flea*, London: John Murray Ltd., 1969.

14 Hoeppli, R., *Parasites and Parasitic Infections in Early Medicine and Science*, Singapore: University of Malaya Press, 1959.

15 Personal communication with Dr. Alan Beck.

16 "Cause of Big Increase in Spotted Fever Unknown," *News American* (AP) Baltimore, April 5, 1978.

17 Chan, W., "Multiple Sclerosis and Dogs," *The Lancet*, February 26, 1977.
    Cook, S. D. and P.C. Dowling, "A Possible Association Between House Pets and Multiple Sclerosis," *The Lancet*, May 7, 1977.
    Jotkowitz, S., "Multiple Sclerosis and Exposure to House Pets," *Journal of the American Medical Association*, August 22, 1977.

18 Personal communication with Dr. Alan Beck.

19 Beck, A., and R. Lockwood, "Dog Bites Among Letter Carriers in St. Louis," Public Health Reports, May-June (1975).
    Beck, A., H. Loring, and R. Lockwood, "The Ecology of Dog Bite Injury in St. Louis, Missouri," Public Health Reports,
    Beck, A., H. Loring, and R. Lockwood, "The Ecology of Dog Bite Injury in St. Louis, Missouri," Public Health Reports, May-June, 1975.

20 Winkler, W.G., "Human Deaths Induced by Dog Bites, United States 1974-75," *Public Health Reports*, September-October 1977.

21 Personal communication with Duane K. Enger, Assistant Chief, Safety Division, United States Department of the Interior, National Park Service. Mr. Enger reports that from 1967 to 1975 there were no fatalities in the National Parks System attributed to bears. In 1976 two campers were killed by bears, one in Montana, the other in Alaska.

22 Brody, J.E., "The Problem of Dog Bites Reaching Frightening

Proportions in U.S.," *New York Times*, July 14, 1977.

23 Harris, D., P.J. Imperato and B. Oken. "Dog Bites – an Unrecognized Epidemic," *Bulletin of the New York Academy of Medicine*, October 1974.

24 "Woman mauled to death by own dog team," *Globe and Mail*, March 29, 1978.

25 Burden, J., "How to Protect Yourself from an Aggressive Dog," *Woman's Day*, November 1976, citing *Behaviour Problems in Dogs* by E. Campbell.

The following medical sources were used for this chapter:

Selected Medical Bibliography

Askew, R.R. *Parasitic Insects*. London: Heinemann Education Books.

Baker, J.R. *Parasitic Protozoa*. Hutchinson University Library, 1969.

Beaver, P.C., C.H. Snyder, G.M. Carrera, J.H. Dent, and J.W. Lafferty, "Chronic Eosiniphilia Due to Visceral Larva Migrans." *Pediatrics*, 9:7-19, 1952.

Beaver, P. C. "The Nature of Visceral Larva Migrans." *Journal of Parisitology*, 55:3-12, 1969.

Benenson, A.S., ed. *Control of Communicable Diseases in Man*, 12th ed. American Public Health Association, 1975.

Bisseru, B. *Diseases of Man Acquired From His Pets*. Philadelphia: Lippincott, 1967.

Brown D.H. "Ocular Toxocara canis." *Journal of Pediatric Opthalamology*, August 1970.

Chamberlain, K.W., guest editor. *The Veterinary Clinics of North America: Symposium on Allergy in Small Animal Practise*, February, 1974.

Chandler, A.C. and C.P. Read. *Introduction to Parisitology*, 10th ed. Wiley and Sons, 1969.

Dawes, B., ed. *Advances in Parasitology*, Vol. II. London and New York, Academic Press, 1973.

Dubey, J.P. "Feline Toxoplasmosis and Coccidiosis: a Survey of Domiciled and Stray Cats." *Journal of the American Veterinary Medical Association*, May 15, 1973.

Dubey, J.P., N. Miller, and J.K. Frenkel, "The Toxoplasma Gondii Oocysts From Cat Feces." *Journal of Experimental Medicine*, 132:636-662.

Emus, W.H. and W.R. Jeffrey. *Parasites in Man in Nuigini*. The Jacaranda Press.

Faust, E., P.C. Beaver and R.C. Jung. *Animal Agents and Vectors of Human Disease*, 3rd. ed. Philadelphia: Lea & Febiger, 1968.

Frenkel, J.K. "Breaking the Transmission Chain of Toxoplasma: a Program for the Prevention of Human Toxoplasmosis." *Bulletin of the New York Academy of Medicine*, February 1974.

Frenkel, J.K. "Toxoplasmosis: Parasite Life Cycle, Pathology and Immunology," in *The Coccidia*. Hammond and Long, eds. Baltimore: University Park Press.

Harris, M.C. and N. Shure. *All About Allergies*. Englewood Cliffs, N.J.: Prentice-Hall Inc., 1969.

Hoeppli, R. *Parasites and Parasitic Infections in Early Medicine and Science*. Singapore: University of Malaya Press, 1959.

Hubbard, C.A. *Fleas of Western North America, Their Relation to Public Health*. New York: Hafner Publishing, 1968.

Hubbert, W.T., W.F. McCulloch and P.R. Schnurrenberg, eds. *Diseases Transmitted From Animal to Man*, 6th ed. Springfield, Illinois: Charles C. Thomas, 1974.

Hutchison, W.H. "The Nematode Transmission of Toxoplasma Gondii," *Transactions of the Royal Society of Tropical Medicine and Hygiene*, Vol. 61, No. 1, 1967.

Jacobs, L. "New Knowledge of Toxoplasma and Toxoplasmosis," in *Advances in Parasitology*, Vol. 5 (*op. cit.*).

Jacobs, L. "Toxoplasmosis: Epidemiology and Medical Importance." *Journal of Wildlife Diseases*, Vol. 6, October 1970.

Johnston, D.H. and M. Beauregard. "Rabies Epidemiology in Ontario," *Bulletin of Wildlife Disease Association*, July 1969.

Kean, B.H., "Clinical Toxoplasmosis – 50 years." *Transactions of the Royal Society of Tropical Medicine and Hygiene*, Vol. 66, No. 4:549-571, 1972.

Kimball, A.C., B.H. Kean, F. Fuchs. "The Role of Toxoplasmosis in Abortion." *American Journal of Obstetrics and Gynecology*, September 15, 1971.

Lapage, G. *Animals Parasitic in Man*, Rev. Ed. Dover Publications, 1963.

Léhane, B., *The Compleat Flea*. London: John Murray Ltd., 1969.

Marr, J.S. and A.M. Beck. "Rabies in New York City, with New Guidelines for Prophylaxis," *Bulletin of the New York Academy of Medicine*, June 1976.

Noble, E.R. and G.A. Noble. *Parisitology*, 4th ed. Philadelphia: Lea & Febiger, 1976.

Ontario Ministry of Agriculture and Food Factsheet No. 71-125: Toxoplasmosis, by W.S. Bulmer, Veterinary Services Branch, November 1971.

"Questions and Answers About Toxoplasmosis," a professional
service bulletin from the American Veterinary Medical
Association.

Remington, J.S., "Toxoplasmosis and Mental Retardation."
Presented at the 18th Annual Colloquium of the Lt. Joseph P.
Kennedy Jr. Foundation Palo Alto, California, April 1, 1965.

Tabel, H., A.H. Corner, W.A. Webster and C.A. Casey. "History
and Epizootiology of Rabies in Canada," *Canadian Veterinary
Journal*, October 1974.

Tuft, L. and H.L. Mueller. *Allergy in Children*. Philadelphia: W.B.
Saunders Co., 1970.

van Leeuwen, W. and Storm. *Allergic Diseases*. Philadelphia: J.B.
Lippincott, 1925.

West, G. *Rabies in Animals and Man*. New York: Arco Publishing,
1973.

Wilder, H.C. "Nematode Endophthalmitis." *Transactions of the
American Academy of Ophthalamology Otolar*, 55:99-109, 1950.

Wilder, H.C. "Toxoplasma Choriorentinitis in Adults." *Archives of
Ophthalmology* (Chicago), 48: 127-137.

WHO Expert Committee on Rabies. *Sixth Report*. World Health
Organization, Technical Report Series No. 523, Geneva, 1973.

Zinsser, H. *Rats, Lice and History*. Boston: Little, Brown & Co.,
1963.

Chapter 9

1   "SPCA is Indicted in Animal Deaths," *New York Times*, April
    6, 1975.

2   "SPCA May Sue Town Council Over Dog Pound," *Globe and
    Mail*, Toronto, May 3, 1977.

3   Development of the Euthanair Method of "High Altitude"
    Euthanasia, printed specifications of Model LU and Model
    SU.

4   World Federation for the Protection of Animals, Memo
    760301, "Euthanasia of Dogs and Cats: an Analysis of
    Experience and Current Knowledge with Recommendation
    for Research," Chief Consultant, WFPA Secretariat, Zurich,
    Switzerland, March 1976.

5   Duffy, J., *History of Public Health in the City of New York*,
    New York: Russell Sage Foundation, 1968.

6   Unless Otherwise cited, data regarding the Los Angeles spay
    program has been provided by James McNamara, Public

Relations Representative of the Department of Animal Regulation, City of Los Angeles. Material furnished: *Status Report, Spay and Neuter Clinic Program*, April 1974, prepared by the Department of Animal Regulation; *Annual Report*, Department of Animal Regulation, fiscal year ending June 30, 1975; and a press release dated January 9, 1978.

7 "Spay Clinics: Boon or Boondoggle?" *Modern Veterinary Practise*, March 1973.

8 Allen, S.D., "Controlling the Number of Unwanted Pets," paper presented to Animal Protection Institute's Forum '73.

9 Personal communication with James McNamara, *op. cit.*

10 "Spay Clinics: Boon or Boondoggle?" *op. cit.*

11 Katz, B.J., "Every Litter Hurts a Bit, Dogs, Cats Suffer as Pet Population Soars," *National Observer*, March 31, 1973.

12 "Spay Clinics: the Other Side of the Story," *Modern Veterinary Practise*, April 1973.

13 "Spay Clinics: Boon or Boondoggle?" *op. cit.*

14 Personal communication with Friends of Animals, New York, President Alice Herrington.

15 Official Position of the American Veterinary Medical Association on "Animal Population Control and Ovariohysterectomy ('Spay') Clinics," adopted by the House of Delegates on July 15, 1973, published in *Business Sessions of the 110th Annual Meeting*, July 16-19, 1973.

16 Sokolowski, J.H., "Androgens as Contraceptives for Pet Animals with Specific Reference to the Use of Mibolerone [Cheque] in the Bitch," in *Pharmacology in the Animal Health Sector*, L.E. Davis and L.C. Faulkner, eds., Colorado State University Press, 1976. Additional background material: Sokolowski, J.H., "Pharmacologic Control of Fertility in Small Domestic Animals," in *Friskies Research Digest*, published by Friskies Pet Food Division of Carnation Co. Also, personal communication with Graham Lute, Vice-President, Marketing, Carnation Co. (Canada).

17 Personal communication with Dr. Sokolowski, Kalamazoo, Michigan.

18 Personal communication with Dr. James Evans, Veterinary Advisor to Glaxco Co., London.

19 Faulkner, L.C., "Alternative to Ovariohysterectomy," Proceedings of the National Conference on Dog and Cat Control, held February 3-5, 1976, in Denver, Colorado.

Chapter 10

1   These figures have been calculated as follows: renovating 17,000 houses at $30,000 each would be $510,000,000; one kidney dialysis machine and full-time treatment for a year is approximately $50,000 – 10,000 would be $500,000,000.

2   *New York Times*, September 25, 1975.

3   "Yachtsman is Charged with Letting 2 Drown While Saving Dog's Life," *Globe and Mail*, (AP), Toronto May 21, 1975.

4   "'We Can't Leave Them in the Water,' Sailor Cried as Dog Lived, Mates Died," *Toronto Star* (AP-UPI), May 7, 1976.

5   "Sister, 19, Tells of Sharing Room with Girl Locked in for 4 Years," *Globe and Mail*, Toronto (AP), June 21, 1976.

6   Harpur, T., "Babies Barred from Font unless Parents are Religious," *Toronto Star*, February 21, 1976. Also, Pastoral Letter, which was published in *Guidelines for Baptismal Discipline*, by the Anglican Church of Canada, Diocese of Toronto, Doctrine and Worship Committee, Toronto Anglican Book Centre, 1976.

7   *Annual Report 1973*, American Society for the Prevention of Cruelty to Animals.

8   Szasz, K., *Petishism*, New York: Holt, Rinehart & Winston, 1969.

9   "Municipal Government Today: Problems and Complaints," *Nation's Cities*, April 1974. Citing the survey "America's Mayors and Councilmen," conducted by the National League of Cities, 1974.

10 A random survey of City of Toronto aldermen by the author, compiled by research assistant Joan Coleman, April 1978.

11 Carding, A.H., "The Growth of Pet Population in Western Europe and the Implications for Dog Control in Great Britain," in *Pet Animals & Society*, ed. R.S. Anderson. Published for the British Small Animal Veterinary Association by Bailliere Tindall, London, 1975.

12 Report of the Joint Advisory Committee on Pets in Society (JACOPIS), *Dogs in the United Kingdom*, July 1975.

13 A survey conducted by the author, compiled by research assistant Joan Coleman, in 1977.

Chapter 11

1   *Pet Food Industry*, July/August, 1976.

2   Borgstrom, G., *The Hungry Planet—The Modern World at the Edge of Famine*, New York: Macmillan, 1965.

3   Klein, K., "Israeli Experiment, Water Purifer Feeds the Chickens," *Globe and Mail* (AP), Toronto, December 23, 1976.

4   "Fake Fruit Made from Seaweed, Sugar, Gelatin, Pectin and Vitamins," *Globe and Mail*, Toronto, January 27, 1977.

5   Nystrom, L., "Maintain Ban on Bread Made from Wood Pulp," *Globe and Mail*, Toronto, January 26, 1977.

6   "U.S. Hot Dogs May Get Some Extras," *Globe and Mail* (AP), October 6, 1977.

7   "Canine Caloric Requirements," chart published by Ralston Purina.

8   Djerassi, C., A. Israel, and W. Jochie, "Planned Parenthood for Pets," *Bulletin of the Atomic Scientists*, January 1973.

9   Grant, D., "Trend to Purebreds at the Pound," *Globe and Mail*, June 17, 1976.

10 Homes, J., "Operation Tattoo—Low Cost Spay and Neuter Clinic," a paper presented to the 1976 Annual General Meeting of the Canadian Federation of Humane Societies.

11 "Fault Found in President's Plan," *New York Times*, January 25, 1975.

12 Halliday, W.R., "Animal Pets in Ancient Greece," *Discovery*, Vol. 3: 151-154, 1922, citing AElian, Nat. An. vii 38.

13 "Dog Considered a Weapon in Massachusetts Robbery," *New York Times*, August 4, 1974.

14 "Dogs Raped Chilean Prisoners, UN Report Says," *Toronto Star* (Reuter), October 15, 1975.

15 The Seeing Eye Inc., *Annual Report 1974-75*.

16 Rowsell, H.C., "Principles of Animal Control," in Proceedings of the First Canadian Symposium on Pets and Society, an Emerging Municipal Issue, held in Toronto June 23-25, 1976.

Appendix A

1. All percentages in Appendix A are derived from figures supplied by the American Kennel Club.

2. *The Pet Profiteers* (New York: Quadrangle, The New York Times Book Company, 1976), p. 201.

Selected Bibliography

Anderson, R.S., ed. *Pet Animals and Society*, published for the British Small Animal Veterinary Association, London: Bailliere Tindall, 1975.

Bates, M. *Animal Worlds*. New York: Random House, 1963.

Beadle, M. *The Cat, History, Biology and Behavior*. New York: Simon & Schuster, 1977.

Beck, A.M. *The Ecology of Stray Dogs*. Baltimore: York Press, 1973.

Bell, Q. *On Human Finery*. 2nd ed., London: Hogarth Press, 1976.

Benning, L.E. *The Pet Profiteers*. New York: Quadrangle, New York Times Book Company, 1976.

Borgstrom, G. *The Hungry Planet – The Modern World at the Edge of Famine*. New York: Macmillan Company, 1965.

Bowen, I. "Fourteen Million Homeless Dogs and Cats – How Man Can Be Their Best Friend," Committee for Humane Legislation, *Special Bulletin*, Summer 1975.

Breland, O. *Animal Life and Lore*. New York: Harper & Row, 1948.

Bridger, H. "The Changing Role of Pets in Society," *Journal of Small Animal Practises*, 17, 1-8, 1976.

Budge, Sir E.A.W. *Egyptian Religion*. London: Routledge & Kegan Paul Ltd., 1972.

Budge, Sir E.A. *The Gods of the Egyptians*. London: Methuen & Co., 1904.

Carson, G. *Men, Beasts and Gods: A History of Cruelty and Kindness to Animals*. New York: Scribner's, 1972.

Clark, Sir K.M. *Animals and Men*. Toronto: McClelland and Stewart, 1977.

Dembeck, H. *Animals and Men* (translated by Richard Winston & Clara Winston), the Natural History Press, published for the American Museum of Natural History, 1965.

Dempewolff, R. *Animal Reveille*. Garden City, N.Y.: Doubleday Doran, 1943.

Department of the Environment. *Report of the Working Party on Dogs*, Her Majesty's Stationery Office, 1976.

Djerassi, C.A. Isreal A. and W. Jochle. "Planned Parenthood for Pets," *Bulletin of the Atomic Scientists*, January 1973.

Duffy, J. *The History of Public Health in New York City*. New York: Russell Sage Foundation, 1968.

Fairholme, E.G. and W. Pain. *A Century of Work for Animals: The History of the RSCPA 1824-1924* London: John Murray, 1924.

Faulkner, L.C. "Dimensions of the Pet Population Problem," *Journal of the American Veterinary Medical Association*, March 1, 1975.

Fernand, M. *The Life, History and Magic of the Cat* (translated by Emma Street). New York: Madison Square Press, 1968.

Fernand, M. *The Life, History and Magic of the Dog*, New York: Grosset & Dunlap, 1970.

Fiennes, R. and A. *The Natural History of Dogs*. New York: Bonanza Books, 1968.

Fowler, N.G. "Pets and Pollution," *Journal of Small Animal Practises*, 14, 677-685, 1973.

Fox, M., ed. *Abnormal Behavior in Animals*. Philadelphia: Saunders, 1968.

Frazer, Sir J.G. *The Golden Bough*. New York: S.G. Phillips, 1968.

Froman, R. *The Nerve of Some Animals*. Philadelphia: Lippincott, 1961.

Gaddis, V. and M. *The Strange World of Animals and Pets*. New York: Cowles Books, 1970.

Glyn, Sir R. *Champion Dogs of the World*. London: Harrap, 1967.

Godlovitch, S. and R. *Animals, Men and Morals*. London: Gollancz, 1971.

"Great American Animal Farm, The," *Time Magazine*, December 23, 1974.

Harrison, R. *Animal Machines*. New York: Ballantine Books, 1966.

Herriot, J. *All Creatures Great and Small*. London: Michael Joseph Ltd., 1975.

Hunt, J. *A World Full of Animals*. New York: David McKay Co., 1969.

Joint Advisory Committee on Pets in Society (JACOPIS). *Dogs in the United Kingdom*. London, 1975.

Kinney, J.R. *How to Raise a Dog in the City and in the Suburbs*. New York: Simon & Schuster, 1938.

La Barré, W. *The Human Animal*. Chicago: University of Chicago Press, 1954.

Lappé, F.M. *Diet For a Small Planet*. New York: Ballantine Books, 1971.

Leach, M. *God Had a Dog*. New Brunswick, N.J.: Rutgers University Press, 1961.

Lechy, W.E.H. *History of European Morals from Augustus to Charlemagne*. Longmans, Green, 1911.

Levinson, B. *Pet-Oriented Child Psychotherapy*. Springfield, Illinois: Charles C. Thomas, 1969.

Lewinsohn, R. *Animals, Men and Myths*. New York: Harper & Bros., 1954.

Linzey, A. *Animal Rights*. London: SCM Press, 1977.

Lorenz, K. *Man Meets Dog* (translated by Marjorie Kerr Wilson). Baltimore: Penguin, 1953.

Lorenz, K. *On Aggression*. New York: Harcourt, Brace & World, 1966.

Milne, L. and M. *The Nature of Animals*. Philadelphia: Lippincott, 1969.

Milne, L. and F. Russell. *The Secret Life of Animals*. New York: E.P. Dutton, 1975.

Morris, D. *The Naked Ape*. London: Jonathan Cape, 1967.

Morris, D. *The Human Zoo*. New York: McGraw-Hill, 1969.

Morse, M. *Ordeal of the Animals*. Englewood Cliffs, N.J.: Prentice-Hall, 1968.

Packard, V. *The Human Side of Animals*. New York: Pocket Books, 1951.

Pappworth, M.H. *Human Guinea Pigs*. London: Penguin, 1970.

Pirie, N.W. *Food Resources – Conventional and Novel*. London: Penguin, 1969.

Police Dogs, Training and Care, Home Office, Her Majesty's Stationery Office, London, 1973.

Proceedings of First Canadian Symposium on Pets and Society, An Emerging Municipal Issue, June 23-25, 1976, Toronto.

Proceedings of National Conference on Dog and Cat Control, February 3-5, 1976, Denver.

Proceedings of National Conference on the Ecology of the Surplus Dog and Cat Problem, May 21-23, 1974, Chicago.

Proceedings of National Conference, A Policy for Dogs in Society, British Small Animal Veterinary Association, October 21, 1976.

Report of the Technical Commission to Enquire into the Welfare of Animals kept under Intensive Livestock Husbandry Systems. Command Paper 2836, Her Majesty's Stationery Office, London, 1965.

Schaller, G.B. *The Marvels of Animal Behavior – The Social Kingdom*. National Geographic Society, 1972.

Schickel, R. *The Disney Version*. New York: Simon & Schuster, 1968.

Scott, N. *A Ladybird Book About Dogs*. Ladybird Book Series 682 [juvenile]. London: Wills & Hepworth, 1968.

Shuttleworth, D.E. *Animals That Frighten People: Fact vs. Myth*, [juvenile], New York: E.P. Dutton, 1973.

Singer, P. *Animal Liberation, a New Ethics for our Treatment of Animals*. New York: 1975. New York Review of Books.

Singer, P. and T. Regan, eds. *Animal Rights and Human Obligation*. Englewood Cliffs, N.J.: Prentice-Hall, 1976.

Sloan, A., and A. Farquhuar. *Dog and Man: The Story of a Friendship*. New York: George H. Doran, 1925.

Smith, A. *The Human Pedigree*. London: George Allen & Unwin, 1975.

Smith, M.C. *Famous Dogs of Famous People*. New York: Dodd, Mead Co., 1944.

Speck, R.V. "Mental Health Problems Involving the Family, the Pet and the Veterinarian," *Journal of the American Veterinary Medical Association*, July 15, 1964.

Szasz, K. *Petishism*. New York: Holt, Rinehart & Winston, 1969.

Thrope, W.H. *Animal Nature and Human Nature*. New York: Anchor Press, 1974.

Turner, E.S. *All Heaven in a Rage*. London: Michael Joseph, 1964.

van Vechten, C. *The Tiger in the House*. New York: Knopf, 1968.

Veblen, T. *The Theory of the Leisure Class*. London: George Allen & Unwin, 1949.

"World Food Situation and Prospects to 1985," the U.S. Department of Agriculture, Economic Report No. 98, 1974.

Zeuner, F.E. *A History of Domesticated Animals*. London: Hutchinson, 1963.

Index

Accidents and dogs, 44, 127, 240
Acupuncture for dogs, 119-120
Advertising, 14-15, 16, 59, 69, 70, 71, 72, 78-84, 89, 209-211; suggested regulations for, 209
Allergies, 168
American Humane Association, 41, 181
American Kennel Club (AKC), 50, 51, 52, 76, 214, 225
American Society for the Prevention of Cruelty to Animals (ASPCA), 27, 36, 41, 122
American Veterinary Medical Association, 39, 186
Ancylostoma caninum, 148, 151, 152, 153
Animal control bylaw, recommended, 233-242
Animal control programs, 82, 122, 196, 197, 199, 202, 206, 218, 219. *See also* Animal shelters; Killing of animals; Licensing
Animal shelters, 21, 35, 44, 45, 122, 180, 204, 217, 220
Animal welfare organizations, 15, 216-217. *See also* Society for the Prevention of Cruelty to Animals; Society for the Protection of Animals
Animal worship, 8-15
Anthropomorphization, 10-11, 13, 18, 59, 66-67, 84, 87, 94, 201, 204
Attitudes towards animals: conditioned by media, 13-15, 47-48, 201-202, 209; and pet foods, 68-72. *See also* Animal worship; Anthropomorphization; Cruelty to animals; Psychology of pet keeping; Rights

Barking, 131-133, 222
Beck, Dr. Alan, xiv-xviii, 43, 44, 166, 169-172
Bites, 122, 169-175, 219
Boarding and kennelling, 108-110
Breeding, 4, 47, 48-52, 54, 171, 184, 199; controls necessary, 213-214; 100 most popular breeds, 225-230. *See also* Population problem
Bubonic plague, 164
Burial of pets, 111-114, 115
Bylaws: recommended for animal control, 233-242. *See also* Legislation
Canadian Veterinary Medical Association (CVMA), 73
Canicola fever, *see* Leptospirosis
Carcasses, disposal of, 45, 122, 123
Cat scratch fever, 168
Children: attitudes towards animals, 13-14; pets as surrogate, 17; emotional need for pets, 17; dogs as providers of learning experiences for, 20-25; reactions to death of pets, 22-23; and risk of infection by dog worms, 144, 146, 205; and risk of dog bites, 169-173
Class system, and pets, 17
Conspicuous consumption, 16, 210
Cost: of dog owning, 98-120; social costs of pets, 121-133
Contraceptives for pets, 67, 187-190
Creeping eruption, *see* Cutaneous larva migrans
Cruelty to animals, 23-25. *See*

also Fighting dogs, Party dogs

Cryptococcosis, 168

Cutaneous larva migrans, 147-148

Death of pets: children's reaction to, 22-23; burial, 111-114, 115; and pet population problem, *see* Killing of animals

Deer: destruction by dogs, 125-127

Dipylidium caninum, 149-150, 152, 153, 165

Diseases, 43, 50, 53, 75, 128, 133, 134-169, 174-175, 205

Disney, Walt, 13-14, 201-202, 204

Dognapping, 129-131

Drug traffic: use of dogs to combat, 6, 7

Ecological effects of dogs, 127-129

Education for pet ownership, 181, 200, 201, 202, 203-205, 217, 220

Emotional need for pets, 19-20

Environmental problems and pets, 127-129, 198-199, 211

Eosinophilia, 145, 147

Estate planning for pets, 115-116

Evans, Dr. Jim, 26, 188-189

Excrement, 43, 123, 127-128, 195, 200-201, 205, 222, 241; transmission of disease by, 54, 128, 138, 140, 143-150

Facts of life: and pet keeping, 21-22

Family size: and pet keeping, 17

Faulkner, Dr. Lloyd C., 189

Federal Trade Commission (FTC), 74, 83, 106

Feral dogs, 36, 39-42, 44, 124-126

Fighting dogs, 27-29

Fleas, 163-166

Food for pets: advertising of, 14-15, 59, 69-72, 78-84; purchasers of, 36, 66-67, 68-72; size and development of industry providing, 59-66; future products as, 67-68; ingredients of, 72-75; research on, 76-78; packaging of, 79-80, 211; scraps as, 84-86; human consumption of, 86-91; and world food shortages, 91-95, 197; guidelines for, 95-96; minimum standards for canned, 96-97; cost of, 98-101; alternatives as, 207-208; energy consumed in processing, 212

Garbage: and dogs, 43, 123, Tucson Garbage Project, 86

Giardia lamblia, 168

Governments: and animal control, 51, 218-221

Grooming parlours, 110

Guard dogs, 4, 5, 6, 171, 215, 216

History of dogs, 1, 2, 3-7, 8-13, 15-16, 28-29, 32, 86, 214

Hookworm, *see Ancylostoma caninum*

Humane Society of the United States (HSUS), 23, 36, 41, 45, 48, 122, 178, 184-185; animal control bylaw as recommended by, 233-242

Hunting, 3, 4, 5, 15

Hydatid disease, 149

Identification tags, 213

Impoundment: section of recommended animal control bylaw, 239. *See also* Animal shelters

Joint Advisory Committee on Pets in Society (JACOPIS), 39-40

Kennels, 108-110; suggested bylaw covering permits for, 236-237, 238

Killing of animals, 21, 34-35, 36, 44-47, 122, 176-179, 180, 199, 224

Kindness: and pet keeping, 23-25
Large breeds: as status symbol, 16, 210; and increasing incidence of dog bites, 171, 172; need for running space, 206; calorie requirements of, 208; and pet population problem, 208-209; featured in advertising, 210
Lautenslager, Dr. J.P., 141, 148
Learning experiences: dogs as providers of, 20-25
Lee, Fran, 134, 198
Legislation, 51, 55, 82, 199, 202, 206, 214, 218-221; recommended animal control bylaw, 233-242. See also Animal control programs; Licensing
Leptospirosis, 156-158
Levinson, Boris, 8, 21-22
Licensing, 100, 101, 103-104, 181, 183, 199, 212-213, 219, 239; section of recommended animal control bylaw, 235-236, 238
Listening-ear dogs, 7
Livestock: destruction by stray dogs, 44, 124-125
Mange, see Scabies
Media: attitudes towards animals conditioned by, 13-14, 15, 47-48, 201-202, 209. See also Advertising
Medical research, 7, 45, 46
Merchandising of pets, see Pet shops
Mites, 167
Mugford, Dr. Roger, 26, 91
Multiple sclerosis, 168-169
Myths, 8, 9, 10, 13, 29
Newspapers, see Media
Old people: dogs as companions for, 25-26
Ontario Humane Society, 23

Packaging of pet foods, 79-80, 211
Packs of dogs, 3, 43
Parasites, 135, 136, 137. See also Ancylostoma caninum; Cutaneous larva migrans; Dipylidium caninum; Hydatid disease; Toxocara canis; Toxoplasmosis
Party dogs, 29
Performing animals, 241
Pet food, see Food for pets
Pet Food Institute (PFI), 62, 68, 85, 88, 89, 91
Pet keeping: origin of, 15-16; as "conspicuous consumption," 16, 210; and class system, 17; psychology of, 17, 18-26; "underground" uses for, 26-32
Pet shops, 47, 50, 53, 54, 55, 105
Police dogs, 6
Politicians and pet problems, 195-197
Population problem, 32-33, 34-39, 47, 55, 59, 193, 196, 197, 208-209, 220; ecological effects of, 127-129. See also Contraceptives for pets; Killing of animals; Spaying and neutering
Psittacosis, 169
Psychiatric services for dogs, 116-118
Psychology of pet keeping, 17, 18-26, 68-72
Psychotherapy, use of dogs in, 7, 8
Puppy mills, 48-52, 55, 213, 214
Rabies, 41, 135-136, 158-162, 173
Railway dogs, 5
Registration papers, 50-52
Religion and animals, see Animal worship
Responsibilities of pet ownership, 20-21, 199, 200-201, 202, 203-204, 205, 215, 219, 220

Rights: of dogs against rights of people, 191-202
Ringworm, 162-163
Rocky Mountain spotted fever, 166-167
Roundworm, *see Toxocara canis*
Royal Society for the Prevention of Cruelty to Animals, 216. *See also* Society for the Prevention of Cruelty to Animals
Sabin-Feldman dye test, 142
Scabies, 167
Seeing-eye dogs, 7
Seeing Eye Inc., 216
Sex: observation of animal as learning experience, 21-22; human-animal relationships, 29-32
Shows and trials, 111
Social benefits of pets, 7, 8, 19-20, 21-22, 24, 192
Social costs of pets, 121-133, 192-193, 196, 200
Society for the Prevention of Cruelty to Animals, 28, 194, 195. *See also* Royal Society for the Prevention of Cruelty to Animals
Society for the Protection of Animals (SPA), 42
Sokolowski, Dr. James, 187-188
Spaying and neutering, 102, 104, 179-187, 196, 199, 201, 217
Status: dogs as a symbol of, 16-17, 210
Stray dogs, 36, 37, 38, 39-46, 170; abandoned dogs (permanent strays), 38, 40-44; uncontrolled dogs (temporary strays), 40, 82
Supplies and accessories for pets, 104-108

Surrogates, pets as human, 17, 18, 83, 193
Tapeworm, *see Dipylidium caninum*; Hydatid disease
Taxes: and amateur breeders, 49; for animal control, 122; and spay clinics, 180, 186, 199, 217; on pet industry, suggested, 206-207
Television, *see* Advertising; Media
Ticks, 166
Toronto Humane Society, 46
Totemism, 10
Toxocara canis, 54, 135, 143-147, 151, 152, 153-155, 156, 174, 205
Toxocara cati, 144, 147
Toxoplasmosis, 135, 137-143, 156
Training: by primitive man, 3, 4; in ancient Greece and Rome, 5, 214; in modern times, 5, 6, 7, 118-119; obedience, 214-216. *See also* Guard dogs
Transportation of pets, 52-53
Urine, 43, 123, 127, 128; transmission of disease by, 156, 157
Veterinarians, 53, 218; costs of veterinary care, 100, 101-102; finding a good veterinarian, 102-103; opposition to spay clinics, 181-182, 186-187
Visceral larva migrans, 144, 145, 146, 221
War, dogs in, 5, 6
Wild animals: keeping of, 240-241
World Health Organization, 157, 160
Worms, 54, 136, 143-147, 148-155
Zoonoses: defined, 134-135. *See also* Diseases